Marketing Knowledge Management

Marketing Knowledge Management

Managing Knowledge in Market Oriented Companies

Gabriele Troilo

*Professor of Marketing, Università L. Bocconi
and SDA Bocconi School of Management, Milan, Italy*

Edward Elgar
Cheltenham, UK • Northampton, MA, USA

Published by
Edward Elgar Publishing Limited
Glensanda House
Montpellier Parade
Cheltenham
Glos GL50 1UA
UK

Edward Elgar Publishing, Inc.
William Pratt House
9 Dewey Court
Northampton
Massachusetts 01060
USA

A catalogue record for this book
is available from the British Library

Library of Congress Cataloguing in Publication Data

Troilo, Gabriele.
  Marketing knowledge management : managing knowledge in market oriented companies / Gabriele Troilo.
      p. cm.
  Includes bibliographical references and index.
1. Marketing–Management. 2. Knowledge management. 3. Marketing. I. Title.
  HF5415.13.T734 2006
  658.8'02–dc22

                                        2006014937

ISBN-13: 978 1 84542 907 2
ISBN-10: 1 84542 907 9

Printed and bound in Great Britain by MPG Books Ltd, Bodmin, Cornwall

Contents

Figures

Tables

Acknowledgements

As theorized in this book, a portion of every individual's knowledge is situated in the interactions with other individuals. As such, my knowledge about marketing knowledge management has been developed interacting with some colleagues of the Marketing Department at Università L. Bocconi, with whom I have been working in many research projects in the last few years. Among them, I am particularly grateful to Salvio Vicari, Paola Cillo, Luigi De Luca and Paolo Guenzi. Salvio Vicari has also reviewed the first edition of this book, and I benefited a lot from his thoughtful suggestions.

The whole Marketing Department of Università L. Bocconi has always been a stimulating environment for me to challenge prior convictions and beliefs and develop new knowledge. I am very grateful to all my colleagues for the time spent in discussing, agreeing and especially disagreeing on the ideas presented in this volume.

I am also grateful to Anna Grandori and Graham Hooley for their helpful suggestions to improve the international edition of the book.

I worked on the final revision of the volume during my stay as visiting professor at the Universidad Autònoma de Barcelona, where I could experience the friendly and stimulating environment of the Departament d'Economia de l'Empresa. To Joan Llonch, Josep Rialp, Jordi López, Rossano Eusebio, Pilar López and all other colleagues go my special thanks.

Finally I wish to express my gratitude to Jill Connelly who translated the book with passion and patience, and helped me in reducing the complexity of some of its parts. I owe a great deal to her.

Introduction

THIS IS A BOOK ON MARKETING

From glancing at the table of contents, or randomly thumbing through a few pages, one may be surprised to find no mention of classic strategic marketing decisions, nor marketing mix tools, nor other decision-making domains typical of this area of management. In fact, the basic premise of this book is that marketing, as a specific realm of management, is called to take on a new role: that of actively managing a part of organizational knowledge.

The importance of this role stems from the recognition that companies which successfully attain sustainable competitive advantage are those that effectively manage their knowledge repository, and consider satisfying the needs of their customers in the long term as their primary goal. In other words, these companies are *knowledge based* and *market oriented.* Till now, both marketing scholars and practitioners have shared the assumption that taking marketing decisions in a proper way will ensure customer satisfaction and competitive advantage. The basic assumption of this book, instead, is that all this is not enough. On the contrary, it is the effective management of marketing knowledge that allows companies to achieve these objectives.

THIS IS ALSO A BOOK ON MANAGEMENT

The managerial tools described in various chapters, in fact, refer to the broadest area of management, that is, the different ways managerial knowledge and competences can be used to reach company goals. Often, both in the specialized literature and in business practice, marketing managers are reproached for being too sensitive to the wide variety of customer needs, and not attentive enough to the company's requirements of efficiency, profitability and competitiveness. The purpose of this book is to contribute to making marketing more closely connected to management, while preserving the specific decision-making domain and specialization of the former. The foundation on which this dialogue has been constructed is knowledge management. To attain this objective, the book attempts to provide answers to the following questions:

WHY SHOULD A COMPANY BE MARKET ORIENTED AND WHAT EXACTLY DOES THIS MEAN?

In the first chapter, ample space is dedicated to the debate which has most markedly characterized the last 15 years of marketing studies: the meaning of market orientation. Though there has been a multitude of opinions on this question, recently a certain consensus has been reached on the statement that what distinguishes a market oriented company is the ability to efficiently and effectively manage specific managerial processes, in particular those pertaining to the management of marketing information.

However, the theory put forth in Chapter 1 is that market orientation does not always, nor does it necessarily, contribute to achieving superior organizational performance. To guarantee the attainment of this goal, the company must correctly manage the organizational antecedents that favour the effective adoption of this orientation. Moreover, managers must be aware of the fact that market orientation does not directly influence organizational performance; rather it enhances organizational innovativeness and learning capacity, outcomes which contribute to improving financial and competitive performance.

WHAT IS MARKETING KNOWLEDGE?

The concept of knowledge has long fascinated scholars in many disciplines. This has contributed to making the issue extremely complex. In fact, different perspectives have placed emphasis on specific aspects related to knowledge. These perspectives have given rise to the development of different methodologies by which knowledge can be studied, and have often lead researchers to recommend very different ways for analysing, interpreting and managing knowledge. Given this, a clarification of the basic epistemological assumptions behind a definition of knowledge is necessary, otherwise no argument will stand on solid ground. Also for those who are interested specifically in managerial knowledge, an exploration of fields which are apparently more abstract and less linked to the business practice proves to be fundamental in order to design appropriate managerial processes and mechanisms.

Chapter 2, then, provides a wide-angle view of various research streams on organizational knowledge, with quite a high theoretical flavour, but with an equally concrete goal: to arrive at the definition of a descriptive model of organizational marketing knowledge. These research streams are categorized on the basis of two different paradigms: cognitivist and constructionist. For each, the differences in basic assumptions, hypotheses and conclusions are highlighted, so as to unveil the ruggedness of the field of study, and the traps inherent to the process of managing marketing knowledge.

An analysis of these two major paradigms will clarify the perspective adopted in designing the descriptive model of marketing knowledge presented in Chapter 3. The purpose of the model is to shed light on the components of an organization's marketing knowledge, with the belief that an effective management process must necessarily start with the identification of these components. In fact, to design and implement marketing knowledge management processes without a clear definition of what knowledge should be managed sets up the conditions for wasting effort. The conclusion of the third chapter is dedicated to the presentation of a model for managing marketing knowledge, which is discussed in detail in successive chapters.

HOW DOES A COMPANY MANAGE MARKETING KNOWLEDGE?

Managing marketing knowledge requires designing and implementing an ad hoc process, which must take into account the specificities of this area of organizational knowledge. In order to plan and execute such a process effectively and efficiently, it should be broken down into a number of phases, and for each phase key problems should be identified, as well as managerial tools most suitable for solving them. Project leaders, and managers either from Marketing or other organizational departments, can make use of specific organizational and technological tools to reach their objective, which are described in Chapters 4, 5 and 6 of the book, each focusing on a phase of the management process.

HOW DOES THE COMPANY FIND OUT WHAT IT KNOWS ABOUT MARKETING?

This question would seem at best ambiguous, at worst, trite. There is an implicit belief in most research on the topic and in business practice: that organizational marketing knowledge is always available for use in making decisions and implementing marketing activities. But this belief is rooted in a three-fold assumption regarding marketing knowledge: that it can be communicated, that it can be de-contextualized, and that people are conscious of it.

In Chapter 4, attention is focused on the challenge that companies must overcome in order to make marketing knowledge available for decision-making and implementation of activities. The takeoff point for every process of managing marketing knowledge is the awareness of potentially available knowledge. This awareness can be achieved when the company is capable of using specific methodologies in order to let marketing knowledge emerge. In fact, there are various types of knowledge: some is readily expressed and communicated, some does not emerge easily because it is embedded in interactions between individuals, other knowledge is utilized unconsciously because it was acquired unconsciously, and yet other knowledge is simply forgotten by the company that possesses it. What seems to be generally apparent is that companies know more than they are able to communicate, and marketing knowledge is not unaffected by this problem. Most of Chapter 4, therefore, is dedicated to an analytical description of a number of methodologies which prove to be helpful in making the different components of marketing knowledge emerge.

HOW CAN A COMPANY GENERATE NEW MARKETING KNOWLEDGE?

A company that is willing to achieve sustainable competitive advantage in highly dynamic markets, must have a repository of marketing knowledge to be systematically replenished with new components. Knowledge is usually considered the outcome of mental activity, of an exclusively cognitive process. The choice of the epistemological field made in the second chapter brings me to argue, in Chapter 5, that action is central to generating new marketing knowledge. Companies, taken as socio-cognitive systems (that is, systems that produce knowledge in order to reach their objectives) naturally tend toward inertia – that is, they confirm knowledge that has worked up till that moment. The creation of new knowledge implicates effort, intent – that is, action – the final aim of which is to reach something that is different from pre-existing knowledge. Only this way will a company defeat inertia and integrate new elements in its marketing knowledge repository.

Chapter 5 provides an analytical examination of the generation of new marketing knowledge. The phases that make up this process and the relationships between them are detailed. Moreover, since marketing knowledge also concerns market actors, specific attention is given to the description of the contribution that customers make in enriching the marketing knowledge repository of a company. First, knowledge and competence of customers are outlined. Second, specific methodologies are highlighted which are suitable to this purpose, so as to emphasize once again that various types of knowledge require different methodologies in order to emerge.

HOW IS MARKETING KNOWLEDGE SHARED AND USED WITHIN A COMPANY?

Today quite a widespread belief is that sustainable competitive advantage does not depend as much on the availability of knowledge, but on its actual use in decision-making and behaviours. This conviction alone would justify sharing and utilizing marketing knowledge among the various organizational units of a market oriented company. Surprisingly enough, however, some companies with a rich, detailed repository of marketing knowledge do not make this knowledge available to the personnel who need it. Similarly, but in a certain sense conversely, these same people may have marketing knowledge, but do not consider it useful.

Chapter 6 centres on a discussion of typical barriers to sharing and utilizing organizational marketing knowledge. These are generally associated with particular organizational conditions or features of communication processes which do not favour sharing and use of knowledge. Once single barriers are identified, the most suitable management tools for overcoming these obstacles are presented. An analysis of such tools is provided in the second half of the chapter, with fitting emphasis on which are most appropriate with respect to every specific barrier.

1. Market Orientation and Organizational Knowledge

1.1 THE MARKETING CONCEPT: DEFINITION AND LIMITATIONS

In the 1950s and 1960s, when marketing was moving from the world of mere techniques to the broader field of management, many scholars called attention to the fact that companies had to adopt a management philosophy by which customer satisfaction was the ultimate aim of all organizational activities. This management philosophy has traditionally been associated with the term *marketing concept*.

Some memorable quotations illustrate this desire for a new way to do business. For example, Drucker (1954: 37) asserts: 'There is only one valid definition of business purpose: to create a satisfied customer.' Felton (1959: 55) instead defines the marketing concept as: 'a corporate state of mind that insists on the integration and coordination of all of the marketing functions which, in turn, are melded with other corporate functions, for the basic objective of producing maximum long-range corporate profits.'

The consensus generated around the new management philosophy (Keith, 1960; Levitt, 1960; Kotler, 1967; McNamara, 1972) has played an important role in the evolution of marketing thought. In fact, this broad acceptance served both to affirm the relevance of marketing as a scientific discipline and to enable scholars to identify and recommend a set of decisions and behaviours consistent with the new management philosophy. As a matter of fact, the assertion that companies must recognize that customer satisfaction is the primary generator of their profitability, in turn leads us to recognize the criticality of marketing as a discipline, as it involves analysing exchange relationships with customers, and theorizing on the most effective and efficient ways to manage them.

The original definition of the marketing concept was necessarily broad and generic, though it is precisely these characteristics which have given rise to ample *ambiguity*, both in theoretical and normative terms. This ambiguity has persisted over time, as the marketing concept has fossilized in a definition that has remained unchanged for nearly forty years. The theoretical consequences of this definition were derived in a very ideological way, one lacking in rigorous methodology. What this means specifically is that some propositions associated with the definition of the marketing concept, which should have undergone empirical testing and investigation, were raised to the status of *axioms* and taken together like a 'profession of faith' that formed the basis for successive elaboration up to very recent times.

The first of these axioms is that *adopting the marketing concept is necessary for the company's success.* Marketing scholars, in fact, maintained that adopting the marketing philosophy improved a company's market and financial performance. But, until the 1990s this alleged relationship had never been tested empirically. Indeed, market orientation (the operational translation of the marketing concept) was always presented in evolutionary terms, as the final destination in a journey of enrichment for the organization's managerial capabilities (Keith, 1960; Levitt, 1960); as such it was implicitly associated with positive connotations.

This axiom, in a sense, represents marketing's 'original sin'. Though it may have found justification at the inception of the discipline, with the evolution of studies and the dissemination of marketing in business practices, it has constituted an easy target for critics from related managerial fields. Moreover, certain *corollaries* deriving from the preceding axiom have provoked even more numerous critical comments.

The first corollary is that *adopting the marketing concept is valid for any external environment the company has to face.*

Marketing experts, in other words, agreed that the marketing concept was a useful, even necessary philosophy in whatever type of industry, regardless of its structure, the intensity of competition, and the type of competitors. The justification was built by linking the need of the marketing concept to the complexification of markets, due to increasing demand uncertainty, intensified competitive rivalry, growing power of intermediaries, and technological turbulence (Webster, 1988). If markets are becoming more complex, satisfying needs expressed by customers would guarantee the company a better chance of attaining increased sales and superior profitability.

Over the years, this mindset has led to an extension of the theoretical *corpus* of the discipline. Initially proposed for marketing of mass market consumer goods, it was later extended to industrial and services marketing, to businesses operating in non-market economies, and to non-profit organizations (for a review see Rodriguez Cano et al., 2004; Kirca et al., 2005).

Proceeding along this path, the marketing concept is necessarily a context-independent management philosophy. In prescriptive terms, on the contrary, it would be more useful to point out some specific criteria for determining to what extent the marketing concept is a profitable management philosophy.

The second corollary is that *adopting the marketing concept is valid for any organizational environment.*

Just as with the preceding corollary, here too scholars did not give enough consideration to the organizational factors involved in adopting the marketing concept, especially those that could facilitate or hinder this particularly complex process. The belief was that the company, once it had accepted this change of philosophies, was consequently aware of the need of modifying its behaviours. In other words, the relationship between recognizing the need to take customer satisfaction as a goal to direct company activities, and implementing consistent behaviours was not seen as problematic. Instead, more attention should have been dedicated to different organizational factors – like organizational design and managerial systems – that may influence the adoption of the marketing concept.[1] But in this case also experts suggested extending the theoretical and normative *corpus* which was valid for marketing departments in major US corporations, quite indiscriminately to smaller businesses, to companies operating in countries with different managerial cultures, and to companies with fuzzy organizational structures and processes.

Hence, for the second corollary too this theoretical approach confirmed that the marketing concept was independent from context, and made the endorsement of this philosophy the incontestable vehicle for company profitability and success.

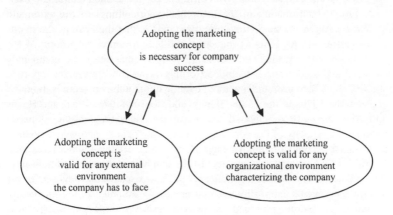

Figure 1.1   The marketing concept theory as a system of self-reinforcing axioms

In conclusion, the above description highlights how one of the cornerstones of modern marketing thought – the marketing concept – is theorized as a system of self-reinforcing axioms (Figure 1.1). The need to adopt this management philosophy is reinforced by the characteristics of modern economic and market environments and is not hindered by possible organizational barriers.

The core concept of the entire discipline, having been proposed in such broad, generic terms, and founded on an axiomatic system which had not been subject to testing, provoked a series of criticisms by scholars from marketing-related fields. This censure resurfaced regularly over the years, but noticeably fostered the evolution of the discipline, and of the marketing concept theory in particular.

Criticism has been voiced most strongly when the economy in industrialized countries, especially in the US, showed signs of crisis and recession. This coincidence is proof of two main original features of marketing. The first is that it is a discipline (and consequently a system of practices) which deals with development and growth strategies of companies. Hence, the absence of development can in some way be attributed to it. Secondly, it originated in the US, and so the more intense stimuli in the academic debate come from the same geographic/cultural area. Consequently, most of the contributions offered in response to the critics come from observation, analysis and interpretation of phenomena which characterize the same geographical/cultural sphere. This amplifies the difficulties in extending the proposals that arise to areas with different economic and cultural contexts.

A further confirmation of the theoretical shortcomings of the axiomatic system on which the marketing concept stands is that the crux of the major controversies always remains the same: the lack of empirical testing of the proposition that adopting the marketing concept guarantees the company's financial and market success. Indeed, critics of the concept found support in studies which demonstrated, over and over again, that the opposite is true.

From the 1970s to the 1980s, Bennet and Cooper (1979, 1981) and Hayes and Abernathy (1980) claimed that excessive focus on consumers' needs reduced the capacity of US companies to generate radical innovations leading to sustainable competitive advantage. Hence, these companies were less able to build solid barriers to defend against the toughest competitors of their day: the Japanese. The marketing concept, in fact, excessively deviates effort toward incremental innovations which are easily imitated, based on readily available indications provided by market research. This philosophy also encourages companies to focus on competitive tools such as advertising and promotions which are more easily countered by the competition as compared to product strategies that provide superior value to the customer. Here are some comments that clearly exemplify the harsh tone of the critics: 'The marketing concept has helped contribute to the death of true product innovation in North America' (Bennett and Cooper, 1979: 77). 'We have decided that it is easier to *talk about* our new products than actually to develop them' (Bennett and Cooper, 1981: 54).

Other authors (Wind and Robertson, 1983; Day and Wensley, 1983), instead, objected to the excessive focus on the short term encouraged by the marketing concept. This contributed to shifting attention away from competitors, who became more and more aggressive and sophisticated, toward customers, who do not necessarily provide stimuli useful for designing development and growth strategies.

Following the same line of reasoning a decade later, Christensen and Bower (1996) opened the debate once again[2] with a longitudinal study on the disk drive industry, in which they showed how leading companies in the technology that dominated the industry at a certain point in time systematically lost their leadership when new technology substituted their own. This happened, as the authors demonstrated, because too much emphasis was placed on customers' expressed needs in allocating investments in new product development processes. On the contrary, winning companies took risks, investing resources and energy in innovative projects that did not seem to have great market potential (according to insights gained from the biggest clients at the time); those proved to be products that later dominated the market.

Summing up, then, critics of the marketing concept, even from very different periods of time, all share the same view: it is not true that putting customers at the centre (that is, utilizing information on their motivations, preferences, behavioural intentions) is always rewarded. Therefore, more generally speaking, it is not true that adopting the marketing concept guarantees superior financial and competitive performance. Instead, when a company's external and internal environments have certain characteristics, adopting the marketing concept can bring about negative results. So once again, it is the axiomatic system on which the marketing concept stands which is subject to censure.

Through the years, the responses of marketing researchers have varied both in nature and effectiveness. In the 1960s, 1970s and 1980s their answers were formulated for the most part in order to cope with every single criticism raised. Therefore, they were not successful in building a theory able to provide the discipline with a solid and unifying foundation. This occurred only in the 1990s with the proposal of the market orientation construct. The debate that marked that decade is discussed in the following section.

1.2 FROM THE MARKETING CONCEPT TO MARKET ORIENTATION

The 1990s[3] was a decade characterized by a lively debate on the marketing concept which resulted in a transformation of the axiomatic system at its base into a set of propositions to be tested empirically. This transformation took the form of a two-step sequence. First the marketing concept was more clearly specified and the market orientation construct was defined; second, a theoretical framework of the antecedents and consequences of market orientation was built and their relationships empirically tested.

1.2.1 The Specification of the Marketing Concept and the Definition of Market Orientation

The first key step in renewing the marketing concept theory was to anchor it to the core of the research domain of the discipline: exchange processes.

Vital work in this regard is Houston's (1986), who proposes a reinterpretation of the marketing concept which laid the groundwork for the studies of later authors. He begins with three fundamental assumptions. First, in order to reach its objectives (whatever they may be) the company performs market exchanges. Second, it pursues specific goals other than customer satisfaction (for example, profit, market share). Lastly, a set of managerial approaches is available to the company beyond the marketing concept (for example, production or sales orientation).

Given these assumptions, the author claims that the marketing concept is a management philosophy that allows the company to reach its goals more efficiently than others *through an understanding of the motivations that lead potential partners to participate in an exchange.* The marketing concept should be adopted only if it proves more profitable than other alternative philosophies, on the basis of an analysis of the value of additional information on potential partners. Houston hypothesizes four environmental conditions, both internal and external, which make this additional information valuable:

- the presence of potential partners whose needs are not satisfied;
- the possibility/freedom to generate an adequate set of products/services;
- value of additional information on potential partners that is higher than the cost of acquiring it;
- the absence of limitations to modify products/services offered – should the need arise.

In other words, the author's hypothesis is that adopting the marketing concept is more profitable than other philosophies *if the company is able to acquire data on potential exchange partners in an efficient way, and to make products consistent with these data.* Houston, therefore, places key emphasis on what distinguishes the marketing concept from other management philosophies: the high information content. A major step is taken through Houston's proposition: the marketing concept becomes a refutable hypothesis. Moreover, Houston highlights the need to take one step further in order to test his hypothesis, that is, the articulation of the 'marketing concept' construct.

In the years that followed, this is done by breaking the marketing concept down into the set of processes a company needs to implement in order to ensure customer satisfaction. This is given the name *market orientation.*

The definition of the market orientation construct, therefore, plays two important roles: a heuristic one, as it becomes the core construct for testing propositions regarding the marketing concept; and a prescriptive one, highlighting the fact that adopting the marketing concept means implementing consistent behaviours. The relevance of market orientation is clearly demonstrated by the fact that this construct totally supersedes that of the marketing concept in the academic debate of the 1990s, and provides a means of escape from the 'axiomatic trap' of previous years.

Various definitions of market orientation have been suggested. Shapiro (1989) concentrates on certain characteristics of *organizational processes.* First of all, market information (regarding all variables that influence customer buying behaviours) has to permeate the entire organization. This means that the Marketing Department can not be the sole depository of market information, but that every department (Research & Development, Manufacturing, and so on) must have access to it so that these data make product development and product management processes more effective. Secondly, both strategic and tactical decisions have to be made through inter-departmental and inter-divisional coordination. In other words, it is not enough for information to be transmitted and disseminated; it is essential that information is also utilized by all organizational departments in decision-making processes. Lastly, there must be a broad-based commitment to market orientation. Everyone in the company must be motivated by the fact that his or her actions are determinant in satisfying customers, and that these actions must be oriented toward this common goal. However, Shapiro does not delve into his proposition to the point of coming up with a measure of market orientation.

Kohli and Jaworski (1990), instead, move in this direction. These authors, perhaps more than any others, influenced the academic debate of the time. Through an analysis of previous literature and a series of interviews with marketing and non-marketing managers, Kohli and Jaworski define the construct of market orientation as follows: 'The organizationwide *generation* of market intelligence pertaining to current and future customer needs, *dissemination* of the intelligence across departments, and organizationwide *responsiveness* to it' (1990: 6).

This definition delineates the domain of the construct in an extremely precise way. Contrary to Shapiro, who focuses on generic organizational processes of communication, coordination and commitment, Kohli and Jaworski describe market orientation on the basis of specific activities. In doing so, they stress once again that effectively implementing the marketing concept is what can influence organizational performance, and not simply claiming this orientation.

In addition, consistent with the description of the marketing concept proposed by Houston, the authors point out the considerable *information content* that denotes market orientation. A company can consider itself more or less market oriented depending on the degree of market information it succeeds in generating and disseminating, and its ability to implement activities in response to this information.

Instead, Narver and Slater (1990) propose a definition constructed on three elements they define as *behavioral components*: customer orientation, competitor orientation, and inter-departmental coordination.[4] As regards the first two, the authors simply focus on aspects of market information content proposed by Kohli and Jaworski. In doing so they reiterate the importance of understanding the customers' value chain and competitors' capabilities and strategies. The third component recalls process coordination proposed by Shapiro, and is actually not dissimilar to the concepts of *dissemination* and *responsiveness* underscored by Kohli and Jaworski. With respect to these two scholars, Narver and Slater place greater emphasis on the fact that it is fundamental to generate information not only on customers but also on competitors, broadening the traditional viewpoint, which sees current or potential customers as primary reference points for marketing activities.

Deshpandé et al. (1993) concentrate on the cultural dimension of market orientation, realigning this construct with the original marketing concept construct.[5] This, in fact, is defined as 'the set of beliefs that puts the customer's interest first, while not excluding those of all other stakeholders such as owners, managers, and employees, in order to develop a long-term profitable enterprise' (1993: 27). So, these authors stress that a company can call itself market oriented only if its behaviours (Narver and Slater's behavioural components) are slotted into a set of values centred on the primary interest which must be served: that of the customer.[6] The idea suggested by these authors is to consider market orientation a multi-dimensional construct regarding both organizational culture (cf. Deshpandé and Webster, 1989), and, at a more operational level, organizational processes and activities.

An additional proposal is that put forth by Greenley (1995). This author, utilizing Narver and Slater's behavioural components, and conducting research on a sample of British companies, demonstrates that various forms of market orientation can be identified, depending on which of its components a company emphasizes more. The distinctive contribution of Greenley, more than in this specification, lies in the evidence (which emerges from empirical research) of the presence of another characteristic process implemented by market oriented companies: *monitoring market performance*. For this reason, such companies are characterized not only by systematic generation and dissemination of information regarding customers and competitors, and by the ability to respond to it, but also by the attention placed on assessing the effectiveness and efficiency of their responsiveness.

Lastly, mention should be made of Gatignon and Xuereb (1997) who, in their study on new product performance, suggest broadening the concept of market orientation toward *strategic orientation*. The construct proposed by these authors contains an additional component with respect to customers and competitors in Narver and Slater's construct: technological orientation. The justification for including this type of orientation is that the contribution of technology in creating value for customers is more and more relevant in many markets. Hence, in innovation processes, a company would be penalized if it were simply market oriented. Furthermore, the authors do not consider inter-departmental coordination a component like all the others, but rather a necessary element which ensures that integration among the three components takes place. Compared to the preceding studies, then, Gatignon and Xuereb place greater emphasis on the need for market orientation to be a fundamental component of a company's strategic orientation, and on the relevance of coordination processes to achieve this integration.[7]

Therefore, a certain amount of agreement emerges among authors who have studied the market orientation construct. *Market orientation is an organizational cultural trait that assigns primary importance to satisfying the interests of a category of stakeholders – customers. This is accomplished through a number of processes shaped by the market information the company can generate.*

These critical processes allow a company to create superior customer value by transforming market information into consistent market behaviours (Homburg and Pflesser, 2000):

- inter-functional communication, to disseminate market information throughout the organization;
- inter-departmental integration (both in decision-making and

implementation), to align goals and activities of various organizational departments;

- assessment of market performance, to check for any deviation from planned objectives.

Hence, adopting a market orientation philosophy means acknowledging the principle that 'creating value for customers is much more than a marketing function' (Narver and Slater, 1990: 22). Market orientation consists of a set of activities which goes beyond those carried out by the Marketing Department. It is the implementation of a management philosophy – the marketing concept – which can prove to be profitable if the entire company moves in harmony with it.

1.2.2 The Theoretical Framework of Antecedents and Consequences of Market Orientation

The quest to define the market orientation construct has set in motion a voluminous series of studies which in a decade's time have transformed the axiomatic system at the basis of the marketing concept into a set of models. The relationships between these models have been subjected to empirical testing; this has played a part in eliminating the ideological accent in the argumentation supporting the adoption of the marketing concept.

The first relationship to be tested is the one which gave rise to the marketing concept and may be thought to have sparked the whole debate that followed: *the positive relationship between market orientation and business performance, measured at financial, market and employee level.*

As for financial performance, various indicators were utilized: some authors focused on the ROA in the preceding year (Narver and Slater, 1990; Slater and Narver, 1994), others on the ROA in the past five years (Ruekert, 1992), still others on ROI and net profit in the prior year (Valdani et al., 1994; Greenley, 1995).[8]

All previous research shows *a positive relationship between market orientation and financial performance*, with one exception worth noting which comes up in a Narver and Slater study (1990). Comparing various small business units in the same company, the authors highlight a positive linear correlation for SBUs that produce non-commodities, yet they find a U correlation for commodity producers.

This result is extremely interesting,[9] since together with previous research findings it substantially confirms the hypothesis that adopting the marketing concept provokes positive financial performance. At the same time it highlights how market orientation is not a discrete, bi-dimensional variable (yes/no type) but instead a continuous variable. This seems to suggest that *adopting the marketing concept is profitable if a high level of market orientation can be attained; otherwise other types of orientation are preferable.*

A second type of analysis involves testing the relationship between market orientation and market performance. In this case, indicators utilized are market share (Jaworski and Kohli, 1993; Valdani et al., 1994), customers' evaluations of the market orientation of their suppliers (Deshpandé et al., 1993), increase in turnover and new product success (Slater and Narver, 1994, Greenley, 1995; Gatignon and Xuereb, 1997). Once more, results show *a positive relationship between market orientation and market performance,*[10] but again with intriguing exceptions. For example, Jaworski and Kohli (1993) demonstrate that there is a difference in the relationship when subjective perceptions are used to measure performance (positive relationship) and when market share is used (insignificant relationship). This demonstrates that market orientation, more than influencing actual results, impacts cognitive representations of these results, with effects similar to self-fulfilling prophecies (Weick, 1977).

This result ties into the third test on the relationship between market orientation and organizational performance. Various authors, in fact, verify the *positive relationship (with no relevant exceptions) between market orientation and employees' attitudes,* regarding their job satisfaction, commitment to the organization, trust in managers, team spirit, and role stress (Ruekert, 1992; Jaworski and Kohli, 1993; Siguaw et al., 1994). This brings to light a sort of ethical motivation for one's work connected to the perception that the company is playing a 'social' role by satisfying the requests of its customers. In addition, in terms of motivation, it seems much easier to link one's work with the results of market orientation than with the financial performance of the company.

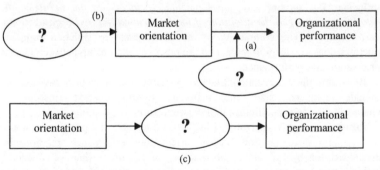

Figure 1.2   An analysis of the relationship between market orientation and organizational performance

This first series of empirical tests (even with the exceptions described) gives a response to the questions raised by the traditional – and much too ideological – view of the marketing concept. The adoption of market orientation is, in fact, assessable and justifiable in terms of financial, market and employees' performance. Doubts remain, though, concerning the effects of context (both external and internal) on the adoption of market orientation. This translates into further investigation regarding environmental variables that can moderate the link between market orientation and performance (Figure 1.2 – a), organizational factors that can make the adoption of market orientation more effective (Figure 1.2 – b) and finally variables that can mediate the link between market orientation and performance (Figure 1.2 – c).

(a) The influence of the environmental and organizational context on the relationships between market orientation and company performance

As mentioned in the first section, one of the corollaries on which the marketing concept was founded is that the relationship between market orientation and company success is not influenced by environmental factors. This would, in fact, justify the need for market orientation as a necessary consequence of the growing complexity of competitive arenas.

So, different authors set out to demonstrate this influence, concentrating in particular on the moderating effect that some environmental variables have on the market orientation/organizational performance relationship. Such variables included market turbulence, competitive intensity, technological turbulence, market growth and economic development (Jaworski and Kohli, 1993; Slater and Narver, 1994).

In keeping with expectations, but contrary to the explanation normally used to support this assertion, results consistently show there is no such influence. Put another way, *environmental variables do not influence the relationship between the adoption of market orientation and organizational performance.*[11] The complexity of the environment in which a company operates does not seem to impact on the positive relationship between market orientation and performance.

Regarding the organizational factors, variables that have been investigated include company size, the national cultural context, institutional characteristics and specificities of the organization's operations.

Results are highly intriguing. Liu (1995) highlights the positive influence of company size on the market orientation–performance relationship, accounted for by the greater availability of resources (human, financial, technological) of large companies. Justifications for not adopting market orientation given by managers in small and medium sized companies are also extremely interesting. The most common reasons given were lack of time (interpreted by the author as excessive focus on the short-term), difficulty in modifying technology to make processes more customer oriented, the belief that meagre financial returns would result from adopting this orientation, and lastly, the challenge of inter-departmental coordination needed to do so.

On the contrary, in a study on the relationships between market orientation and performance on a sample of German companies, Fritz (1996) shows how in national contexts where organizational culture is marked by considerable emphasis given to technical competences and to consensus around decisions to be taken, market orientation is considered secondary (with respect to production orientation, cost orientation or employee satisfaction) in reaching financial and market outcomes.[12]

Lastly, the study on a sample of US theatres by Voss and Voss (2000) regarding the relationship between market orientation and performance offers intriguing revelations. The most interesting is evidence of a negative relationship between customer orientation and performance: in a non-profit institution, where operations are marked by considerable creativity, being customer oriented proves to be penalizing in terms of organizational performance. The authors give a three-fold explanation for this: a) information on consumers' desires is highly biased by what they know about the creative potential of the actors in question; b) though there may be sufficient market information, rarely is it integrated into creative processes, which are highly intangible; c) even when creative processes take market information into account, the chance to customize a theatrical 'product' to respond to the demands of diverse audiences is very limited.

Summing up, then, contrary to the expectations of supporters of the traditional view of the marketing concept, those studies confirm that *organizational variables moderate the relationship between the adoption of market orientation and company performance* (Figure 1.3a).

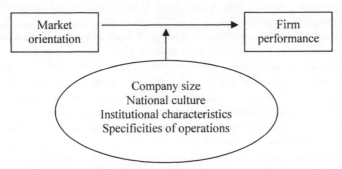

Figure 1.3a   Variables moderating the relationship between market orientation and organizational performance

(b) The relationships between organizational antecedents and market orientation

Beginning with the definition of the market orientation construct, a number of investigations have been conducted with the aim of verifying the existence of organizational antecedents to market orientation, and in particular to the generation, dissemination and utilization of market information at an inter-departmental level.

Specifically, the propositions put forth regard three categories of organizational variables: values and attitudes; structural variables; and managerial systems.

As regards the first category, Kohli and Jaworski (1990) maintain that adopting market orientation requires both appropriate attitudes and behaviours by top managers, as well as consistent attitudes throughout all departments. If the objective is to promote consistency between market information and company market behaviours, top managers have to tolerate the uncertainty that stems from the adjustment of behaviours to continuous market change (low aversion to risk, positive attitude toward change) and show a commitment to market orientation (no contrast between indications given at lower hierarchical levels and behaviours). In addition, marketing managers must be able to win the trust of other departments, so as to promote collaboration and acceptance of the market information provided. These other departments, in turn, must be open to inter-departmental contacts, accept ideas from elsewhere in the organization, and pursue common goals rather than department-specific ones.

Tests mostly confirm these hypotheses (Jaworski and Kohli, 1993). Interestingly enough, however, findings do not corroborate the relationship between market information dissemination and risk aversion of top management, and partially negate a relationship between the former and inter-departmental contacts. This demonstrates that the relationships hypothesized are excessively generic.

Concerning structural variables, again Kohli and Jaworski (1990) theorize that generation, transmission and utilization of market information are hindered by the presence of a high number of departments, and by excessive decisional formalization and centralization. In successive testing (Jaworski and Kohli, 1993), only for decisional centralization do the authors succeed in demonstrating the existence of a relationship with market orientation; instead, the number of departments and formalized decision-making do not negatively influence a company's market orientation.

Last of all, the authors focused their attention on managerial systems for personnel recruitment, training and reward systems (Payne, 1988; Kohli and Jaworski, 1990; Ruekert, 1992), indicating that:

- to stimulate market orientation, individuals must be selected who have skills supporting customer orientation;
- employees must be adequately trained in order to enhance their sensitivity to customer needs;
- rewards systems must be designed that include metrics which effectively measure the contribution of employee actions to customer satisfaction.

In conclusion, *the values and attitudes of company personnel, types of organizational structure and managerial systems impact on the effectiveness of market orientation adoption* (Figure 1.3b).

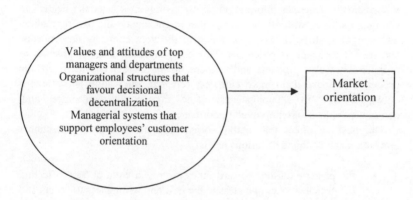

Figure 1.3b   Organizational variables that impact on the effectiveness of market orientation adoption

(c) Variables mediating the relationship between market orientation and organizational performance

The studies described to this point contribute quite effectively to moving the marketing discipline and some of its fundamental constructs back into a more methodologically rigorous framework. But on closer examination, some grey areas come to light.

Specifically, if it is true that the positive contribution of market orientation to organizational performance can be demonstrated, it is also true that this outcome (especially when measured in terms of indicators such as ROA, sales growth or market share) is determined by numerous factors beyond the company's strategic orientation. We can reasonably assume, in other words, that market orientation cannot be directly linked to performance even if the construct is broken down into its constituent processes that make adopting this orientation effective.

What is basically missing is a theoretical explanation for empirical evidence. Put another way, market orientation models proposed up until the mid-1990s do not explain why a company that systematically generates market information, disseminates it within the organization, and plans its processes so that they conform to this information, is able to attain better performance with respect to another organization that does not undertake such activities. Since performance is indicative of sustainable competitive advantage, the question is: in what way can adopting market orientation enable a company to attain sustainable competitive advantage?

The answer lies in *greater innovation.* Consider a company that systematically generates information on the evolution of customer needs and competitors along with all the factors that might impact the two (especially technology), distributes this information to different company departments, and uses it to adapt its processes. This company is in a better position to propose innovative products and services on the market and to modify its processes to make them more customer oriented. Innovation is, without a doubt, a key to attaining sustainable competitive advantage and, consequently, to ensure improved performance.

The positive effect that market orientation has on an organization's innovation can be found at various levels:

- the positive attitude toward innovation as a cultural trait, affecting the organizational openness to the new and willingness to accept and develop original ideas (Hurley and Hult, 1998);
- the skills needed to implement innovative processes, hence ability to design and run projects and processes which produce innovative results (Hurley and Hult, 1998; Hult and Ketchen, 2001);
- the ability to take advantage of opportunities which arise from the emergence of new needs (Li and Calantone, 1998);
- various types of innovation that the organization succeeds in implementing, not only technical (traditionally new product/service development) but also organizational (regarding managerial processes in general) (Han et al., 1998);
- the success of new products, measured by objective indicators (number of new products) and subjective ones (manager's perceptions) (Atuahene-Gima, 1995; 1996; Gatignon and Xuereb, 1997; Han et al., 1998; Lukas and Ferrel, 2000; Im and Workman, 2004);

- the innovativeness of new products, as determined by their novel features (Moorman, 1995; Gatignon and Xuereb, 1997; Li and Calantone, 1998; Im and Workman, 2004).[13]

Summing up, the results of these studies show consensus on the *positive relationship between market orientation and innovativeness, and between innovativeness and organizational performance.*

The contribution of market orientation to performance, which is a distinctive one compared to other factors, can therefore be identified in the solid link that exists between this orientation and the innovative ability of the organization.

To innovate for an organization, in any case, means to learn – to explore new territories, experiment with different technical and managerial practices, internalize ways of thinking and acting that are different with respect to the past (Hedberg, 1981; Senge, 1990; Van de Ven and Polley, 1992; Hamel and Prahalad, 1994; Vicari and Troilo, 1998). And so, extending the findings described above, we can easily assert that a market oriented company is more committed to organizational learning. In other words, a market oriented company has distinctive characteristics which are similar to those of a *learning company.*

Many studies have been dedicated to analysing the relationships between market orientation and a company's learning orientation, arriving at convergent yet distinct conclusions. Some authors maintain that market orientation is a cultural trait which is typical and distinctive of learning companies.[14] Slater and Narver (1995) theorize that market orientation, together with entrepreneurship, distinguishes the culture of companies that learn from those which do not. In fact, the accent on generating market information and its use in decisional processes stimulates the company to absorb the dynamism of competitive environments, and therefore to learn. Morgan et al. (1998), instead, demonstrate that highly market oriented companies also show learning skills with the following components: a) the personnel ability to face change, b) the capability to plan and implement activities that actually create change, and c) the presence of a participative leadership style.

Other authors, instead, focus more on distinctive capabilities of companies that are able to learn systematically from the market, suggesting a classification of these capabilities (Day, 1994a; 1994b; Valdani, 1994; Vorhies et al., 1999; Day and Van den Bulte, 2003; Weerawardena, 2003). This, in any case, refers back to the ability to generate, disseminate and utilize market information in decision-making processes (Sinkula, 1994).

Figure 1.3c   Variables mediating the relationship between market orientation and organizational performance

The research stream on organizational learning enriches the modelling of the relationship between market orientation and performance. In fact, assuming that the learning capacity of an organization influences its chances to attain sustainable competitive advantage, and considering market orientation as a factor which qualifies learning ability, the clear link between market orientation and organizational performance is reinforced (Figure 1.3c).

Summing up this section, it is clear that efforts have been made in the field to re-examine some of the basic premises of the marketing concept, and to transform the axiomatic system on which it is founded into a series of propositions and hypotheses subject to empirical testing. All this has brought to light results which are undoubtedly valuable.

The marketing concept is not a dogma, but rather a decision. Like all decisions, it must be made according to expected profitability, market performance and organizational sustainability. In fact, research findings show, in synthesis, that *market orientation allows a company to attain positive results only if the company achieves two general aims. First it must adopt cultural traits supporting market orientation. Second, it must develop resources, capabilities, organizational design and systems capable of translating the philosophy of the marketing concept into a consistent set of processes, activities and behaviours.*

However, there is no doubt that over the years the debate has not changed the conviction shared among marketing scholars: market orientation implies that the company must see itself in a new way, so that customers' interests are put before all others.

1.3   MARKET ORIENTATION AND KNOWLEDGE MANAGEMENT

What is clear from this interpretation of the ongoing debate is that at this point the issue of market orientation is anchored to certain cornerstones.

The first is most certainly *using the organization as the reference point* in assessing the adoption and implementation of the marketing concept. External environmental variables have very little impact on the relationship between market orientation and organizational performance, while those relating to organizational context are significant. These observations lead researchers to focus their studies on organizational resources and capabilities. We can assess the utility, adoptability and sustainability of the marketing concept with respect to other management philosophies only by considering two factors:

- how efficiently single companies gather market information with respect to the value that can be had from it;
- how effectively this information is transformed into knowledge which is widely circulated and utilized in generating customer value.

This also means that market orientation cannot be considered the sole organizational purpose, but rather one of the objectives to be achieved in pursuing the final goals of survival and development.

Focusing on the company, and moving the market to the background, two more decisive conclusions in the debate emerge: the *criticality of organizational factors*, and the *relevance of inter-departmental integration*.

Regarding the former, literature shows that a company cannot attempt to implement market orientation without intervening on its culture, organizational structure and managerial systems. While for the last of these, research confirms a strong relationship with the effectiveness of market orientation, for organizational structure conclusive findings are still lacking. As far as organizational culture is concerned, though it is easy to imagine that adopting the marketing concept is a cultural change of considerable magnitude, few studies have examined in any great detail the methods with which such change is implemented (for one exception, see Norman Kennedy et al., 2003). As we have seen in the preceding sections, in fact, most results are more descriptive than prescriptive, leaving further research options open.

Inter-departmental integration is indispensable for market orientation to be a characteristic of the whole organization and not only of the Marketing Department. Indeed, market orientation can be effectively adopted only if the company acts as a coordinated system, focused on the creation of value for its exchange partners. In order for this to happen, organizational conditions must exist which are favourable to coordination, integration, and sharing (Kahn, 1996; 2001; Dewsnap and Jobber, 2000; Maltz and Kohli, 2000; Leenders and Wierenga, 2002; Rouziès et al. 2005).

Reinforcing the idea that organizational factors are critical, there is evidence of the relationship between market orientation and organizational performance measured through employee indicators (dedication to one's job, satisfaction, team spirit, and so on). This shows how market orientation, if implemented effectively, is a catalyst for individual and collective efforts within the organization, which are then able to feed on one another.

An additional milestone in the market orientation debate is the relevance of the role of market information. Indeed, we can say that *the theory of market orientation is nothing more than a theory on market information processes.* From the outset scholars have emphasized the importance of processes involving generating, disseminating and utilizing market information. This conviction is further supported by evidence that in order for orientation to translate into superior performance, companies must develop the ability to innovate and to learn. All this demonstrates that *a market oriented company is one that effectively manages marketing knowledge.*

In this sense, though, the debate on market orientation highlights the limits of the theory developed till now. First of all, a traditional view of knowledge management (for example information processing) still predominates in the field of marketing. This view draws no distinctions between differing levels of information, quite often utilizing the terms 'data', 'information' and 'knowledge' as synonyms. Instead, different theories show that the three concepts represent different phenomena (though they all have a common origin) and so, managing these three levels requires differentiated approaches. For example, a company may have a rich repository of data but lack the competences needed to interpret them. Or in a company where these data are disseminated across departments, there may not be a common interpretation of market phenomena.

Secondly, the stimulating debate on how innovation and learning mediate the relationship between market orientation and performance only partly taps into the wealth of contributions on the impact of organizational knowledge on a company's financial and market performance.

Thirdly, consequent to the previous point, the debate on market orientation gives us a glimpse of the underlying theory of the firm commonly shared by marketing scholars. Still today the marketing discipline shares many assumptions of the neoclassical theory of the firm and the consumer (Webster, 1992; Troilo, 1993). Some innovative ideas on the topic have emerged in the last decade (cf. Dickson, 1992; Hunt and Morgan, 1995; Vargo and Lusch, 2004) which bring it closer to theories on the firm widely adopted in related disciplines, but the link is still weak.

In the course of this book, an attempt is made to fill these gaps. The initial assumptions are:

- a company is market oriented if it can generate marketing knowledge and transfer and utilize market information in its decision-making and value-generating processes;

- this orientation is justified by the fact that companies which effectively manage their knowledge attain superior financial and market performance.

The object of the remainder of this work is two-fold. First, a descriptive model of marketing knowledge is proposed that takes into account the complex, multi-faceted nature of such knowledge. Secondly, a three-phase normative model for marketing knowledge management – incorporated in the knowledge-based theory of the firm – is offered, with recommendations of methodologies and managerial tools suitable for each phase.

NOTES

1. This does not mean that no research has been done on organizational aspects of marketing, but rather that these studies have concentrated on the organization of marketing activities more than the organizational implications of adopting the marketing concept (in the timeframe discussed up to this point).
2. Christensen and Bower's article gave rise to a series of comments in the *Strategic Management Journal* (Slater and Narver, 1998; Connor, 1999; Slater and Narver, 1999) which contributed to articulate different positions in the debate on the effects of market orientation. By the same token, it helped broaden the debate beyond the sphere of marketing journals (and therefore marketing scholars). Ideas similar to those put forth by Christensen and Bower can also be found in Macdonald (1995), Frosch (1996) and Berthon et al. (1999).
3. We should note that some pioneering studies had already been published in the second half of the 1980s, but it was in the following decade that the debate developed in a systematic way. Among these studies, beyond Houston's (1986) which will be discussed shortly, see Payne (1988), Webster (1988), and Shapiro (1989).
4. In the definition the two authors initially included two other components as decisional criteria: *long term focus* and *profitability*. The reliability test showed that these two are not appropriate, and so they were eliminated.
5. A similar approach is also followed by Lichtenthal and Wilson (1992). In focusing on the adoption of the marketing concept, they indicate an interpretation of this process as a cultural change which can be brought about through the modification of the shared system of practices. A critical contribution to the conception and modelling of market orientation as organizational culture can be found in Harris and Ogbonna (1999).
6. Distinguishing themselves from Narver and Slater (1990), and consistent with Kohli and Jaworski (1990), Deshpandé, Farley and Webster claim market orientation and customer orientation are one and the same, limiting the

importance of competitor orientation. In fact, they maintain that 'a competitor orientation can be almost antithetical to a customer orientation when the focus is exclusively on the strengths of a competitor rather on the unmet needs of the customer' (1993: 27). Stated as such, though, in my view this assertion does not seem very plausible, as it is based on an obvious distortion of logic: no one has ever claimed (if this were possible) that the competitive dimension of market orientation consists in *exclusively* focusing on a competitor's strengths. And clearly, I would say tautologically, when considering an organization that focuses solely on competitors, the definitions provided by other authors would exclude the possibility that this organization could be called market oriented. Another comment prompted by this article is that, though market orientation is described as an organizational cultural trait, Deshpandé, Farley and Webster operationalize the construct with a variation of the scales proposed by Kohli and Jaworski and Narver and Slater, highlighting once again that the crux of the debate is centred on the actual activities of the market oriented company more than on elements of its organizational culture. An attempt to synthesize the three measures is provided by Deshpandé and Farley (1998).

7. Following this, a number of studies have explored the relationship between market orientation and other forms of strategic orientations. Among them: Baker and Sinkula (1999), Atuahene-Gima and Ko (2001), Matzuno et al. (2002) and Noble et al. (2002).

8. The two meta-analyses conducted by Rodriguez Cano et al. (2004) and Kirca et al. (2005) also confirm those results in studies of the following decade.

9. Gatignon and Xuereb (1997) find the same, which they associate with less demand uncertainty in commodities markets.

10. Rodriguez Cano et al. (2004) and Kirca et al. (2005) also confirm those findings in successive studies.

11. Also in this case the two meta-analyses conducted by Rodriguez Cano et al. (2004) and Kirca et al. (2005) confirm those results.

12. A confirmation of these findings can also be found in a more recent study by Nakata and Sivakumar (2001).

13. In the last few years some scholars have suggested that two different components can be detected within the market orientation construct – reactive market orientation and proactive market orientation – having a differential impact on incremental versus radical innovation (see Cillo et al., 2001; Narver et al., 2004; Atuahene-Gima et al., 2005).

14. Among these we can also include Hurley and Hult (1998), though their study is more focused on innovativeness.

2. Organizational Knowledge and Marketing Knowledge

2.1 THE KNOWLEDGE-BASED FIRM

As stated in the conclusion of the previous chapter, the marketing knowledge management model that will be proposed is founded on the principles of the resource-based theory of the firm, which has become a consolidated paradigm in management and strategy research. The central tenet of this theory is that the differential performance among competitors in an industry (or in a strategic group) can be traced back to diverse resource endowments of these firms. This concept markedly distinguishes the resource-based theory of the firm from the more traditional structure–conduct–performance theory, which instead associates the profit differentials of rivals with structural characteristics of the competitive environment.[1]

The purpose of this work is not to provide a critical examination of the evolution of the resource-based theory.[2] However, to better clarify how marketing knowledge can contribute to the generation of sustainable competitive advantage, some principles of the theory are delineated below, in particular with regard to:

- attributes that resources must possess in order to contribute to the generation of sustainable competitive advantage;
- types of resources that are most characterized by these attributes.

Regarding the first point, several authors (Barney, 1986; 1991; Dierickx and Cool, 1989; Amit and Schoemaker 1993; Peteraf, 1993) have underscored that resources must possess the following attributes (Figure 2.1).

- *Resources must be scarce.* In contrast to the neoclassical theories of the firm and competition, the resource-based theory begins with the assumption that there is no homogeneous distribution of resources among competitors (Barney, 1991). Heterogeneity can be caused both by imperfections in functioning mechanisms of the markets in which these resources are exchanged (Barney, 1986) and by firm-specific accumulation mechanisms (Dierickx and Cool, 1989). Beyond heterogeneous availability, resources must be distinctive (Prahalad and Hamel, 1990), that is, rare. If they are available to a large number of current or potential competitors, value generation strategies derived from these resources will not be differential and thus will not enable a company to realize extra profits. Such returns are guaranteed, instead, when resources are scarce.

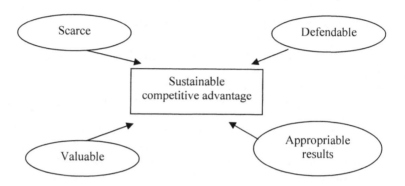

Figure 2.1   Resource attributes that determine sustainable competitive advantage

- *Resources must be defendable*. Scarcity makes resources good candidates for generating competitive advantage, but in order to sustain such an advantage, the firm must protect these resources from competitors. Generally, two factors are considered effective barriers against competition: difficulty of imitation and difficulty of substitution. Causes for such difficulties, which generate 'isolating mechanisms' of the firm (Rumelt, 1984), are typically ascribed (Barney, 1991) to:
  - the uniqueness of resources, as they are the consequence of the distinctive history of the company;
  - the presence of causal ambiguity (Lippman and Rumelt, 1992) which makes it hard for a competitor (indeed often for the firm itself) to understand which mechanisms link resources to performance;
  - the dimension of social complexity and tacitness that characterizes resources.

- *Resources must give rise to appropriable returns.* Though they may be scarce and defendable, resources lose most of their economic appeal if firms are not able to appropriate returns from competitive advantage. Appropriability derives from the imperfect mobility of resources, which prove to be idiosyncratic with respect to the firm that possesses them. Reasons for imperfect mobility may be excessive transaction, substitution, or sunk costs that limit the value of the exchange. In other words, the type of costs associated with the generation of resources reduces returns of potential buyers of the same resources. Where such costs exist, then, results become highly appropriable and the firm can reap the rewards that such resources are able to generate.

- *Resources must be valuable.* This attribute refers to whether resources can contribute to improving effectiveness and efficiency of the firm itself, that is their ability to generate value (Barney, 1991). In fact, even where there are scarce, defendable resources that generate appropriable economic returns, if the cost of acquiring and utilizing these resources proves too high, generating sustainable competitive advantage would not be profitable. Therefore, the attribute of being valuable is linked to both the ability of the firm to perceive the value of a given resource *ex ante*, and to the efficient utilization of that resource.

If the description of resource attributes that foster sustainable competitive advantage is a cornerstone of the resource-based theory of the firm, then the same is true for the classification of resources. The aim is to distinguish those which most probably possess these attributes from those which do not. By now, there is a consensus of opinion among researchers that these attributes are most commonly found in resources that are information-based, that is intangible resources.[3]

Clearly, tangible resources (plants, machinery, and so on) – which represent codified knowledge – can be imitated and substituted; moreover, they are not highly appropriable in terms of results. Therefore, efficient markets exist that guarantee access to a large number of competitors. On the contrary, characteristics of information-based resources, which tend to be idiosyncratic, flexible, and difficult to copy, make them particularly suited to generating sustainable competitive advantage.

Some authors (Prahalad and Hamel, 1990; Grant, 1991; 1996a; Leonard-Barton, 1992; Stalk et al., 1992; Teece et al., 1997)[4] emphasize how, more than resource endowment, it is the firm's ability to utilize resources in value-generating processes that potentially determines competitive advantage; this is what constitutes a firm's competences. In fact, it is the firm's competence in combining, integrating and coordinating its resource endowment and making it evolve which is scarce, defendable and a generator of appropriable returns. In conclusion, two levels within a firm's resource endowment can be identified: resources, which represent input for value-generating processes, and competences, which represent practices for managing these processes. At both levels, the firm can distinguish itself from competitors and in doing so acquire differential advantages which can in turn generate superior performance.

There is widespread agreement that it is information content which makes a resource or competence particularly suited to generating competitive advantage. This consequently underscores the fact that the knowledge repository a firm possesses makes it more or less able to achieve performance superior to its competitors (cf. Grant, 1996b; Probst et al., 1998).[5]

For the purposes of this book, then, it is important to stress that *a company's market orientation can contribute to competitive advantage, and consequently superior performance, by enriching the organizational knowledge repository through systematic, intentional and effective management of marketing knowledge.*

The aim of the following sections is to construct a model of marketing knowledge that can be used to assess the effectiveness of marketing knowledge management processes. Specifically, the construction of this model is founded on results from research on knowledge in several disciplines. However, diverse definitions of knowledge have been advanced, as do (more importantly) different interpretations of knowledge generating processes. Hence, I will begin with a critical analysis of the epistemological premises of two scientific paradigms in which knowledge research – and organizational knowledge studies in particular – can be rooted: the cognitivist paradigm and the constructivist paradigm. After illustrating the assumptions and hypotheses of each, I will propose a definition of knowledge which constitutes the foundation for a descriptive model of marketing knowledge, along with a set of rules regarding how it should be managed.

Before discussing the two paradigms, attention must be focused on approaches to the study of cognition and knowledge in numerous fields: from psychology to neuroscience, biology to sociology, economics to managerial sciences. Due to the particular nature of this topic, most research efforts have been undertaken in the field of psychology, providing an epistemological and methodological imprimatur which scholars from other sectors very often assimilated and transferred, *mutatis mutandis*, to their own fields. However, within these areas, researchers (in particular neurobiologists and sociologists) have experimented with new streams of research on cognition, applying methodologies typical of their own theoretical background and obtaining fascinating breakthrough results described in the upcoming sections.

2.2 THE COGNITIVIST PARADIGM: ORGANIZATIONAL KNOWLEDGE AS A REPOSITORY OF SHARED REPRESENTATIONS

The fundamental assumption of cognitivism is that 'actors make decisions beginning with a belief system through which they interpret the events of the world, and from which stem the actions considered most opportune in pursuing their aims' (Provasi, 1995: 258; my translation). Individuals are not seen as subjects 'at the mercy of environmental events' to which they can only react. They are, instead, thinking actors who perceive certain stimuli from the environment, apply their own belief systems, and, on the basis of these systems, decide what behaviour to adopt. Cognitivists, then, are interested in mental processes, like stimuli perception, categorization, causality attribution, decision-making, learning and so on.

In light of this basic assumption, the profile of an actor takes on very distinctive traits (Arcuri, 1985). The individual is a *consistency seeker*, attempting to maintain a stable consistency between her/his belief system and events, and between this belief system and consequent behaviours. Moreover, the individual is seen as a *naïve scientist*, attempting to attribute causes to various events he or she witnesses so as to justify their occurrence. Lastly, the individual is viewed as *economizer of cognitive resources*. In other words, individuals process information, though possessing limited rationality, by utilizing thinking strategies that allow them to deal with an environment that produces information overload.

By singling out the traits described above, we can make certain assumptions that are shared within the cognitivist tradition (Varela et al., 1991: Chapter 3).[6]

The first is that cognition is *intentional*, that is, directed toward a goal. Consequently, innate to cognition is a form of rationality (though limited) in relationships between means and ends. This does not necessarily mean that individuals are rational, but rather that they believe they decide/act in a rational way. In other words, from their own point of view there is always a certain logic connecting their own ends with the alleged appropriate means.

Cognition, moreover, is based on *mental representations*. The content of thought processes consists of symbols, and the mind of an individual basically computes symbolic representations of the world with which she or he interacts. As stated by Hastie and Dawes (2001: 7): 'The computational model of the mind is based on the assumption that the essence of thinking can be captured by describing what the brain does as manipulating symbols.'

Hence, processing information is essentially *computing symbols*. To understand cognition, the content of symbols is less important than their form. Processing information basically means giving form to raw data (symbols) by constructing relations between concepts (Doumas and Hummel, 2005). Thus, individuals need to recognize, codify and process raw data to give them meaning.

Lastly, representations regard *a world that is objective, real and external to the actor*. Cognition consists in perceiving and interpreting signals that come from the outside; the effectiveness of cognition lies in its ability to represent the real world adequately.

Though these are explicit assumptions in cognitive theories, careful analysis brings two more fundamental ones to light which prove to be more implicit:

- Cognition is a *mental activity* and it is separated both from the physical support with which it occurs – the brain – and by actions that derive from it: 'Thinking is the systematic transformation of mental representations of knowledge to characterize actual or possible states of the world, often in service of goals' (Holyoak and Morrison, 2005: 2). Both the former (the brain) and the latter (the action) play secondary roles: they make ordinary functioning of cognition possible, as well as attainment of goals in the pursuit of which cognition takes place. The brain is not an object of study for cognitive researchers, nor is its functioning considered influential for cognition to take place. Behaviour, on the other hand, is the output of cognition, hence it is necessarily separate from it. The fact that behaviour can manifest itself in one way or another has no effect on cognition.

- Cognition is an *individual phenomenon*. The mind, where cognition occurs, is an individual property. There is no such thing as a collective mind, or one that is distributed in an organization (cf. James et al., 1988). This does not mean that we cannot refer to collective cognition, but rather that we can do so only in a metaphorical sense,[7] or by considering this concept a composite form of individual cognitions (as we shall see shortly).

These epistemological premises significantly shape the more consolidated managerial decision-making models.[8] Decision-making is interpreted as a problem-solving process based on individual information processing. The innovation of these models with respect to neoclassical economics (which makes them implicitly cognitivist) lies in the principle that decision-makers have finite cognitive ability (bounded rationality) and do not have complete information on all possible alternatives. Therefore, subjects are forced to 'design' their own solutions by means of trial and error. This does not lead to an optimal solution, but instead to a satisfactory one. Clearly there are many references to the intentionality of the process, to computation, to the reality of the surrounding world as generator of data on which decisions are based.

From the discussion thus far, the concept of knowledge in the cognitivist paradigm is clearly defined: knowledge consists of an *evolutionary repository of symbolic representations.*

Analysis of knowledge and of the process of knowing, in the framework of this paradigm, essentially consists of examining the two fundamental components of knowledge: the repository of representations, and the evolutionary processes of this repository. The following sections focus on these aspects.

2.2.1 Knowledge Structures

The first step in examining the repository of representations is to understand how representations are organized and made consistent with one another. Knowledge structures can refer to various ways in which individuals organize environmental data in their minds. The fundamental concept in this regard is that of the *schema*, which can be defined as 'an organized set of cognitions about some concepts or stimulus' (Taylor et al., 2006: 78). Although schemas can take on numerous forms (as we will see further on), for our purposes it is useful to analyse some of their properties and their roles in cognition.

Schemas are made up of data and relationships among data which are representative of events, objects, people, actions, ideas, feelings, and so on. As such, schemas are complex structures of representations. The first element of complexity is *the organization on various vertical levels*, based on degree of abstraction. So, an 'aggressive competitor' schema may be associated with competitor behaviours such as 'react immediately to price manoeuvres', 'continually launch new products', and so on. Each of these behaviours is represented by a network of associations ('continually launch new products' is associated with 'systematically carry out market tests' and 'invest heavily in research and development'), to the point where concrete examples of single competitors are represented which coincide with those associations.

In addition, schemas are constituted both by *characteristics* which are *common* to all classified exemplars, and by others which typify only a few. For example, the schema 'typical consumer' can represent a certain age group of consumers with a number of common socio-demographic characteristics, though only a few of them have similar buying habits.

Schemas, then, are composed of both *defining elements* and *episodic elements*. The former, broadly speaking, define the characteristic properties of what they represent; the latter refer to episodes linked to experiences of the individual who possesses the schema. For instance, a 'collaborative distributor' has certain distinguishing features (defining elements). A manager, moreover, may have retained an experience with a specific distributor who, when a new product was launched, set up a special display in its stores to promote it (episodic element).

Lastly, *schemas build on other schemas* according to a network of relationships. Consequently, the reception of a signal can activate multiple schemas and produce a more or less intricate representation of an event. An example is a manager's 'market' schema, which might be made up of the schemas 'competitors', 'clients', 'government agencies', and so on. If a regulation is modified it works as a signal that activates both the schema 'government agencies', as the transmitter of the signal, and other schemas regarding for example competitors who can leverage on the new regulation, or customers who can get some price advantages.

In briefly describing these properties it is also crucial to contemplate the main *functions* of schemas (cf. Taylor and Crocker, 1981; Barr et al., 1992; Harris, 1994), which can be categorized as:

- recognition and selection of data;
- interpretation;
- guide to action.

Schemas allow individuals to *recognize the variety of stimuli flowing from the environment, and to select and codify them* according to some criteria. When the signal is perceived as being compatible with one's personal knowledge structures, *assimilation* occurs (Piaget, 1953). The 'recognizing' and 'selecting' functions performed by schemas satisfy the needs of the individual as economizer of cognitive resources, since rapid identification is made possible and re-codifying events each time they occur is not necessary.

Schemas also provide selection criteria so that, at least to a point, signals are assimilated by one schema or another.[9] This means that current schemas focus the actor's attention and perception, leading him/her (with greater probability) to notice stimuli that are very congruent or very incongruent with previously activated schemas (Arcuri, 1985: 30-35). In other words, people (as seekers of consistency) tend to look for signals in the environment that confirm their own schemas. At the same time, however, they selectively perceive those signals that are inconsistent with their schemas. This phenomenon generally brings about *accommodation* of current schemas (Piaget, 1953); that is, evolutionary change.

An example is in a belief commonly found in many markets, such as: 'In our industry competition is based on price'. This schema leads one to perceive competitors' manoeuvres in terms of price variation, and to be indifferent to actions taken on other competitive tools (for example large investments in advertising) to the point where such actions are not so incongruent with the schemas one possesses as to necessitate changing them.

The second function of cognitive schemas is *interpretative*. Schemas allow individuals to attribute meaning to stimuli. Schemas are constituted by organized data; hence they are elementary units of knowledge. They enable actors to understand why certain phenomena occur. The interpretative function places several data and schemas in relation to one another in the search for reasonable explanations for why things happen.

Moreover, interpretation makes it possible to fill information gaps. Since schemas are made up of data regarding events (objects, actions, and so on), when data emerge which are ambiguous but seem consistent with retained schemas, the individual utilizes default values of the schema to make data significant and to produce meaning. Schemas, therefore, are not passive data receptors; rather they actively produce supplementary information. For example, if a competitor from sector A moves into sector B by launching a new product, a manager from sector B can infer certain information on the newcomer by directly observing this company's behaviour and other information from the schema 'typical competitive strategies in sector A' (if such a schema exists).

Finally, schemas function as *guides to action*.[10] In cognitive theories behaviour is the fruit of an interpretation of events made possible by means of schemas. Schemas serve as strong mediators between the environment and the subject. Action takes shape consistently with knowledge structures behind it. It is the outcome of a complex information processing procedure and the one chosen is, actually, 'the best one' according to a means–end rationality. When the action does not bring about expected results there is a shift, a readjustment of schemas. That is learning.

2.2.2 Different Types of Schemas

Different forms of knowledge structures exist (cf. Lord and Foti, 1986; Sackmann, 1991). The following sections outline the characteristics of some of the most significant and widely used schemas in management research.

Categories, prototypes, taxonomies
Categories are schemas constituted by a *set of attributes which are considered typical of the object (event, action, and so on) represented* (Rosch, 1975; 1978). What allows assimilation in a category is the degree of

similarity of the object's attributes to those of the category. This process of assimilation is defined as categorization.

Within a category there are certain cases that are distinctive because they possess a high number of attributes shared by most components of the category. These are *prototypes*. In addition, categories have a hierarchical organization, hence each category can be considered part of other, super-imposed, categories. Such hierarchical systems are called *taxonomies*, and are characterized by different degrees of abstraction. The more abstract categories share few attributes while, on the contrary, less abstract categories show considerable overlap, since they have only a few distinguishing attributes.

Some events, therefore, could be classified in more than one category; they may be less prototypical than others. By means of inclusion relationships, the actor is able to represent how borderline cases link up with various categories. The definition of industry boundaries is a typical example of a taxonomic system; within this system single strategic groups represent categories.

Numerous articles underscore the importance of categorization processes in management practice.[11] Many highlight how the different categorization of events and environmental changes by executives result in different strategic choices and different actions. In particular, Dutton and Jackson (1987), Jackson and Dutton (1988) and White et al. (2003) analyse the effects of the categorization of environmental events as 'threats' or 'opportunities' on organizational responses. Labels such as 'opportunity' are related to an increase in the sense of control over events, the possibility for success, the search for and use of further information. Moreover, Dutton (1992) affirms that beyond these psychological effects, the category 'opportunity' takes on a noteworthy symbolic function within the organization, for example, stimulating the reinforcement of organizational values and commitment, signalling the beginning of a period of change, shifting focus toward the future.

Scripts

While categories are static representations, *scripts* are representations of *sequences of behaviours linked to a particular context* (Abelson, 1976; 1981; Schank and Abelson, 1977). Typical managerial scripts in the marketing field are, among others, procedures for market share analysis, assessment of salespeople, positioning analysis. In this sense, organizational routines can be considered scripts, even though scripts are much more detailed descriptions of specific behaviours or events. Scripts, in fact, are made up of vignettes linked together by a series of scenes. For example, the procedure for hiring new staff could be made up of the script of contacting candidates (that is, all actions to be performed, conventions to be respected, and so on), the script of the selection interview, that of communicating the final job offer.

In psychology literature, different forms of scripts are described (Abelson, 1981). *Tracks*, for example, are made up of details of a generic script (for example, a business negotiation script can have one track for the contact, one for the first sale, one for successive sales, and so on), and *script pointer + tag*, where tags represent episodes which are retained along with a generic script (a specific case of sales negotiation which took place in the past).

In management literature, the concept of script has been utilized mostly for interpreting organizational phenomena and suggesting the use of specific managerial systems. One example is Gioia and Poole's study (1984) about personnel assessment. Their findings demonstrate that the availability of certain scripts prompts the use of default values by evaluators: when a 'behaviour of a good team member' script is in place, for example, if a team member acts consistently with the script, even without complete information on his or her performance, the evaluator will tend to give a positive assessment.

Gioia and Manz (1985), instead, focus on the centrality of scripts in *vicarious learning* processes – that is, learning models without (or prior to) direct experience. The authors propose a path of progressive generalization by which a model initially provides an example which learners memorize and apply to their behaviour. Repeated application produces a more generic script, which can be utilized even for actions which are different from the original one. A managerial implication of this concept is, for example, for training new assistant marketing managers or salespeople, or for people who change their roles within the organization.

Cognitive Maps
Among the various forms that schemas take, cognitive maps[12] have received the most attention from management researchers. This is because of the dual utility of these maps: on one hand as possible forms of knowledge structures, on the other as analytical tools for eliciting and graphically representing these forms.[13] Maps are, in this second sense, representations of representations. So, we can refer both to maps of categories, and maps of sequences of events and concepts. As discussed further on, the success of maps as managerial tools is explained by the fact that they can be constructed and analysed immediately and easily with the help of software applications developed over the years (Eden, 1990b).

Considering cognitive maps as a type of representation that knowledge structures can take on, we must necessarily refer to a specific type: *causal maps*. These consist of concepts that are linked by a cause–effect relationship.

They can be thought of as sets of 'if … then' statements, and represent the perceptions of causal links between events.

Causal cognitive maps are utilized in management literature[14] for description, interpretation and prediction. In the first case, such maps have become quite common, particularly for describing managerial perceptions regarding links between environmental events. Secondly, these maps are often utilized to interpret the evolution of company strategies, or relationships between environmental events and strategic decisions. And in the final instance, which is less common, causal maps also prove useful for simulation purposes.

A pioneering study worthy of note for its influence in management research is the work edited by Axelrod (1976). In this book several authors analyse the composition, structure and evolution of causal maps at the basis of decisions taken or planned by politicians at various times in history. They verify that the number of concepts and relationships that constitute the basis of knowledge is very high, and their structure very complex. This demonstrates that decision-makers are both receptors who are sensitive to data from the environment, and sophisticated creators of meaning. In addition, Axelrod and his colleagues propose a series of indicators for analysing maps and a data-coding system which is very useful for constructing maps.

Hall (1984), through a longitudinal study, analyses the decline of the *Saturday Evening Post*, verifying that this was caused by the inability of top management to modify their perceptions of causal connections between specific environmental events which proved to be relevant to the future of the sector and of the companies that competed in it.

In a complementary study, Fahey and Narayanan (1989) examine the evolution over a twenty-year period of executive managers' causal maps in a company that produced television sets. This research showed a co-evolution of environmental events and maps, through the substitution of certain concepts and the modification of relationships between them.

2.2.3   Cognitive Processes: The Generation and Evolution of Individual Schemas

Having defined schemas as representations of events (objects, actions, and so on), it is clear that events must first take place in order for new schemas to come to be. Thus, *schemas are generated from the actor's experience of the real world*. However, the real world, or the environment, produces an enormous quantity of information. This means (keeping in mind the bounded rationality of the individual) there is always a difference between the complexity of information generated by the environment and the processing ability of the decision-maker.

How is it possible, then, that individuals are able to generate schemas while dealing with an environment that is, by definition, too complex for their thinking ability?

First of all, a schema emerges if an event is *recurring*. In such a case, the individual is stimulated to attribute meaning to this event. Individuals rarely expend energy on processing occasional, sporadic incidents or on slotting such phenomena into their personal cognitive repository. When faced with a situation that has never been experienced before, which then occurs a certain number of times, individuals create a schema which allows them to later recognize and interpret the event and which guides their behaviour.

Secondly, individuals utilize a series of thinking strategies, or mental shortcuts that allow them to filter information and conserve their cognitive resources. These strategies are defined *heuristics* (Tversky and Kahneman, 1974; 1982). Systematic distortions in inferential processes, called *biases*, work in the same way, diverting the course of information processing from the optimal path theorized in rational choice models.

Numerous studies have proven the existence of heuristics and biases in managerial decision making (Hogarth and Makridakis, 1981; Barnes, 1984; Schwenk, 1984). Given the critical nature of these elements in knowledge generation processes, here follows a description of those which have most captured the attention of scholars in managerial fields.

First and foremost is *representativeness* by which the decision-maker associates an event with a schema on the basis of non-probabilistic judgement of similarity. This association might not be adequate because, for example, if basic probabilities are not respected, certain attributes may be considered more significant than others, or small samples may be used to make inferences regarding the whole universe. Again taking up on the previous example, a competitor who launches a new product is associated with the 'aggressive competitor' schema without taking into account other potential motivations that may have led that company to take such action. Another example may be the widespread tendency among managers to predict the evolution of the market on the basis of actions of a small number of competitors that are considered prototypical.

Another typical heuristic is *availability*, by which the decision-maker calculates the probability that a given event will occur on the basis of how easy it is to recall details of the event. The underlying logic is that if it is easy to remember, the event must occur frequently. But, as we have seen before, since information is perceived if it is very consistent or very inconsistent with one's schemas, a very rare event (inconsistent with schemas) can be perceived and remembered more clearly and (based on the heuristic of availability) the individual believes that the event will very likely happen again. As an example, if some customers use a product in a creative way (inconsistency), this is considered the trend of the entire market. In the same way, information coming from actors deemed very credible increases the estimated probability that events connected with that information will come to pass.

Among the most common biases is the *illusion of control*, which leads subjects to overestimate their ability to control events. This bias leads individuals to sort through information so that whatever contradicts his or her personal hypotheses is not perceived, while that which confirms them is. This explains cognitive inertia common to managers in successful firms who tend to pay little attention to signals that conflict with the causes for success.

Another bias comes about in *attributing causes to events*; that is, a systematic tendency to attribute certain categories of events to specific types of causes. This is the case with managerial successes and failures: the former are credited to the company's or to the manager's own actions, abilities and efforts, while the latter are blamed on the situation or the external environment (economic recession, intensity of the competition, and so on).

Last of all, an often-found bias is *false consensus* – the tendency to consider one's own opinions shared by all and therefore expedient. This happens frequently with marketing managers who have to define marketing strategies on the basis of environmental factors. After having selected a strategy, they tend to think that everyone within the organization shares it.

Evidence of the existence of heuristics and biases, in my opinion, is fundamental to theorizing on organizational knowledge since thinking strategies produce *cognitive inertia*. Having defined organizational knowledge as a repository of evolutionary representations, the presence of inertia greatly influences the evolutionary process. In fact, attention to recurring events and strategies for simplifying complex information results in stable and self-preserving schemas. Once schemas are created, individuals will believe that events that are compatible with their schemas are more likely to occur, and they will seek out data which will not disprove their schemas.

How, then, can cognitive schemas evolve? How can knowledge evolve?

The evolutionary processes refer to one of the fundamental themes of cognitive science: learning. In keeping with initial assumptions, learning can be defined as the *evolution of an individual's knowledge*, or *a change in the repository of his/her schemas.* At first glance we may hypothesize that any *change* in one's set of schemas involves learning. However, on closer observation, it becomes clear that it is more useful to distinguish between different types of *changes*.

Referring back to remarks on cognitive inertia and on the stability of schemas, one can only conclude that learning is a *highly improbable phenomenon.* Such a provocative affirmation calls for more detailed explanation.

Learning takes place if *data are not assimilated in schemas.* In other words, these data penetrate the selective attention of the individual, and cannot 'find a place' in the current repository. In the traditional problem-solving model, this means that an action does not produce the expected results. Such a circumstance can lead to two strategies.[15]

The first, suggested by traditional models (Cyert and March, 1963; Newell and Simon, 1972), involves *adapting schemas* so that data become compatible. Schemas, in fact, have a complex structure that allows them to accept a variety of data. Therefore, in this case individuals may create sub-categories, a *track* or a *tag* in existing scripts that let them make sense of data. Hence, the knowledge structure will be readjusted: from a traditional problem-solving viewpoint, this will produce new behaviour until actual results coincide with expected results, and the individual's cognitive system finds new stability.

The second strategy occurs when the gap between expected events and actual information exceeds variety accepted within current schemas. At that point, new categories or taxonomic systems, new scripts and new causal maps have to be generated. In keeping with initial assumptions, we can say that the second strategy constitutes more authentic learning with respect to the first, which involves adapting present schemas. In this sense, one could argue that learning is an improbable phenomenon as it requires effort – a cognitive investment by the subject who tends, on the contrary, to act as an economizer of resources. Adaptation, instead, is innate to the ordinary functioning of cognition, and as such proceeds by means of quasi-automatic processes.

2.2.4 Cognitive Processes: The Generation and Evolution of Collective Cognitive Schemas

The transition from individual to collective or organizational knowledge is certainly one of the most hotly debated issues in knowledge management research. Among management scholars whose theories and models are rooted in the cognitivist paradigm, there is quite a variety of positions, which I will attempt to categorize in this section.

Differences are often ascribed to the lack of consensus on initial assumptions regarding what an organization is and what role individuals play within it. These differences correspond to a variety of views, most importantly on how to define organizational knowledge, and more specifically on the relationships between it and individual knowledge. Research on organizational knowledge shaped in a cognitivist mould may consider it as:

- knowledge developed by individuals within the organization;
- a different form of knowledge with respect to individual knowledge.

Authors who hold with the notion of *organizational knowledge as knowledge developed by individuals within an organization* focus prevalently on individual knowledge. In fact, they refer to organizational knowledge as that particular type of knowledge which individuals generate because they work in an organization, for example a company. The organization, however, is seen as a mere container, a stage where individual action is played out and individual knowledge is developed. A statement by Simon clarifies this position: 'All learning takes place inside individual human heads; an organization learns in only two ways: a) by the learning of its members, or b) by ingesting new members who have knowledge the organization didn't previously have' (1991: 125).

It is single individuals, therefore, who generate knowledge within an organization. When taken together, though, they are not capable of producing different forms of knowledge. This position derives once again from traditional managerial problem-solving models which, in focusing on individual managerial decisions, consider organizational knowledge and processes that generate it isomorphically with respect to individual processes. March and Olsen (1975) provide us with a good example. In describing the circular relationships between individual cognition, individual action, organizational action and environmental response, they position these elements in the sequence shown in Figure 2.2.

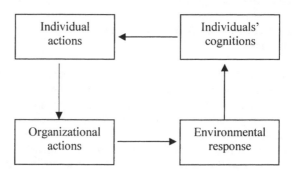

Source: March and Olsen (1975: 150).

Figure 2.2   The complete cycle of choice

Although the cycle of knowledge evolution can be interrupted at various stages, giving rise to different forms of learning,[16] the direction of the causal link is always from individual action to organizational action: it is only the individual who learns through environmental responses, and therefore it is only individual knowledge that can evolve.

Essentially, these authors make their observations *from the point of view of the individuals who constitute organizations*. Individuals, being actors who possess bounded rationality, create organizations so that joint decisions and actions allow them to reach objectives that they would not be able to attain on their own.

Clearly exemplifying this concept is the debate between Glick on one side and James, Joice and Slocum on the other regarding organizational climate.[17] The latter assert that organizational climate is an individual and not a collective construct because, 'attributing meaning to environmental stimuli is a product of cognitive information processing, and it is individuals, and not organizations, that cognize' (1988: 130). Glick, instead, states: 'Meaning creation may involve cognitions, but meaning is not limited to cognitions or other individual-level properties and processes' (1988: 134). This author proposes a distinction between *aggregate psychological climate*, which constitutes an individual but aggregate construct, and *organizational climate*, which is, instead, a collective construct.

These positions illustrate two different ways to interpret organizations, one which focuses on single individuals and the other on the entire organization. This shift in viewpoint, as we will see shortly, is one of the fundamental divergences in how relationships between individual knowledge and organizational knowledge are seen.

The second category is made up of studies that highlight how *individual knowledge and organizational knowledge are related, but diverse, entities*. Authors who share this thesis start from a sort of 'common sense' assumption. In fact, they maintain that if individuals inside an organization change frequently, if new members join and others leave, and the organization continues functioning and developing, this means that it possesses mechanisms beyond individual minds by which knowledge can be generated and stored (for example information systems, organizational routines and procedures, managerial systems) (Shrivastava, 1983; Walsh and Ungson, 1991).

In any case, all these authors agree on the relevance of individual knowledge for developing organizational knowledge. Hedberg (1981: 6), for example, asserts: 'Organizations have no other brains and senses than those of their members. [...] Although organizational learning occurs through individuals, it would be a mistake to conclude that organizational learning is nothing but the cumulative result of their members' learning. Organizations do not have brains, but they have cognitive systems and memories.' Similarly, Fiol and Lyles (1985: 804) state: 'Though individual learning is important to organizations, organizational learning is not simply the sum of each member's learning.'

From this, it can be deduced that organizational knowledge is not the sum of every individual's knowledge. This is, actually, the truly distinctive point that these scholars introduce to the debate. Organizational knowledge cannot solely be the collection of knowledge of the individuals who work in a company. It is something more: the organization, by means of its organizational systems and mechanisms, adds a further portion of knowledge to the aggregation of individuals' repositories. Therefore, these studies concur on the definition of organizational knowledge as *the set of theories, beliefs, points of view (that is representations) shared within the organization, the result of which exceeds the sum of individuals' knowledge.* However, this process is still in some way aggregative to individual knowledge (Walsh, 1995: 292).

Hence, the fundamental feature is *sharing* – the fact that the object of knowledge is common to members that make up the organization. The essential difference between individual and organizational knowledge is that the former derives from the experience of a single individual, while the latter arises out of a process of interaction, which necessarily requires more than one individual.

In addition, organizational knowledge, to be considered as such, must be legitimated, that is it must undergo *consensual validation* by organizational members. Only after this knowledge has been accepted by mutual consent does it become part of the set of shared representations. Lastly, shared, validated knowledge influences the actions of single individuals according to a circle of inverse causality with respect to that illustrated in Figure 2.2.

A great number of studies have empirically investigated knowledge sharing, having to operationalize and measure the construct. Generally, by analysing case studies, designing experiments, or through action research, these investigations single out knowledge sharing processes through the use of specific managerial tools. Most focus on cognitive maps for representing knowledge, and derive organizational knowledge from a *composition of individual cognitive maps* (Bougon et al., 1977; Ford and Hegarty, 1984; Langfield-Smith, 1992).[18]

Leveraging on the assumption that organizational knowledge is different from individual knowledge, despite there being a circular link between the two, organizational learning can be interpreted as the dissemination of individual knowledge within an organization by means of a validation process. Individual knowledge believed to be relevant and useful with respect to organizational goals becomes a part of the shared repository and can potentially modify organizational behaviours.

This position is clearly expressed by Argyris and Schön (1978: 18-26), who assert that individuals, by questioning organizational behavioural systems (*single-loop learning*) or systems of norms (*double-loop learning*) make their own knowledge evolve, consequently provoking a modification in the knowledge of the entire organization:

> Just as individuals are the agents of organizational action, so they are the agents of organizational learning. Organizational learning occurs when individuals, acting from their images and maps, detect a match or mismatch of outcome to expectation which confirms or disconfirms organizational theory-in-use. In the case of disconfirmation, individuals move from error detection to error correction. [...] But in order for organizational learning to occur, learning agents' discoveries, inventions, and evaluations must be embedded in organizational memory. They must be encoded in individual images and the shared maps of organizational theory-in-use from which individual members will subsequently act (19).

Argyris and Schön utilize the concept of *organizational memory* and underscore some form of organizational knowledge retention. However, this reflects individual memory ('*individual images and maps*') and can be developed only if there is first an evolution of individuals' knowledge.

2.2.5 Limits of the Cognitivist Paradigm

To sum up our discussion thus far, according to the assumptions of the cognitivist paradigm, organizational knowledge is an evolutionary repository of categories, scripts and causal maps representing significant events. Consequently, *a company's marketing knowledge is constituted by the evolutionary repository of schemas representing market phenomena shared within the organization.*

To design a model for marketing knowledge management, this definition mirrors some of the limitations of the cognitivist paradigm, the assumptions of which allow us to capture only a part of organizational marketing knowledge. An examination of these shortcomings, through a description of the issues which are left unresolved by cognitive theories, will lead into an analysis of the constructivist paradigm, whose assumptions would overcome the inadequacies of cognitivism.

As illustrated in the previous section, according to the cognitivist paradigm, cognition is essentially an individual mental activity consisting of computing symbolic representations of an objective world external to the individual. The aim of this computation is to reach an objective. In management, this typically involves solving a problem by making decisions.

The first issue in this definition, especially when referring to management, is the *relationships between knowledge and action*. Generally speaking, one of the functions of schemas described above was a guide to action. This is therefore seen as successive to – and in some ways subordinate to – cognition. Focusing specifically on managerial models for problem solving and information processing, it is clear that they are substantially shaped by the preceding consideration.

First of all, studies on managerial decision-making processes assume that the solution to a problem (the decision) is the last act in a process in which a series of phases are set up *sequentially*. This means that results of one phase feed the next. And so, information gathering precedes and generates 'raw material' for choosing among various alternatives. This precedes and determines decisions, that, in turn, come before action, greatly influencing it. Action is, consequently, always sequential to knowledge. It is the belief system of the decision-maker that will lead him or her toward a certain course of action with respect to other available alternatives.[19]

Secondly, managerial decision-making models implicitly assume that *the environment is tangible, objective, and external to the decision-maker*, consistent with another fundamental tenet of cognitivism. It is the environment that produces information that the actor has to process in order to come up with the solution to a problem. Actor and environment are, therefore, two separate entities, each constituting a distinct world. Decision-makers can only perceive the environment as it appears to them since they have no way of modifying it. What is more, the environment is the same for all actors. Differences can only exist in the perceptions of decision-makers, and are evidence of more or less finely honed processing competences, which, through successive adaptations, should give rise to correct representations of the same environment.[20]

What, then, is the role of action?

Without question, action takes the backstage with respect to processes of representing problems and selecting among alternatives. Though it does play an instrumental role, with the aim of finding a satisfactory solution, the heart of the model lies in the phases that precede action. As stated by Simon (1973: 105): 'Solving a problem simply means representing it in such a way that the solution is obvious.'

Knowledge, therefore, precedes action. This serves to produce results which are then compared to expectations. In case of a divergence between the two, it allows the decision maker to change her/his behaviour to the point where a solution is coherent with her/his aspiration level.

However, empirical evidence does not wholly corroborate the concept that knowledge precedes action. Often, in fact, subjects and organizations act in an inconsistent manner with respect to the repository of knowledge they possess. Individuals believe in certain principles yet behave in a way that actually negates them. As Argyris and Schön (1978: 11) point out, there exists a divergence between the espoused theory and the theory-in-use, between models that managers claim to use as points of reference and those that they actually adopt in the course of their actions. Also, it often appears that managers, rather than thinking before deciding and acting, think to justify decisions and actions already taken.

A further confutation of certain assumptions is the fact that often decisions and actions by managers are taken with the goal of generating the environment (creating a market, shaping consumers' preferences, challenging competitors, and so on). This happens both out of necessity, because often the environmental information needed is lacking, and out of desire. Thus managers make decisions by intuition or foresight, claiming they need no information beyond their experience.

More problematic still is the second point to a certain extent left unsolved by the cognitive theories: *the relationship between individual knowledge and collective knowledge*. As we have seen, while some authors admit that there is a basis of 'residual' knowledge with respect to individual repertories, cognitive models take on the viewpoint of individuals inside the organization, observing the organization through the eyes of its members. Hence, the individual perspective predominates. In any case, the central tenet of the paradigm does not question the relationship between individual and organizational knowledge: individual knowledge generates organizational knowledge by means of combinatory mechanisms, and, in so doing, it affects its evolution.

However, I believe this position gives rise to several *ambiguities* which must be addressed in order to propose a model for effective management of organizational marketing knowledge. Despite their diversity, these ambiguities have a common origin (which will be detailed at the conclusion of our analysis): the definition of knowledge exclusively as a set of representations, which makes it difficult to take on differing individual viewpoints, and which traces the knowledge generation process back to information processing.

The first area of ambiguity has to do with the initial assumptions of many studies that deal with organizational knowledge: *collective knowledge exists because, even when members change, the organization is able to preserve its knowledge base* by means of some sort of mechanism. This sensible affirmation, however, is easily refutable with other equally sensible observations. For example, if there is variation in an organization's members, the fact that the knowledge base remains may be because some members stay on; in such a case individual knowledge comes once again to the fore. If one supports the notion of continuity where there is a change of personnel, one must assume a change in the entire set of members. In such a situation, it is difficult to argue that knowledge remains intact.

Secondly, often the argument is made that *knowledge resides in organizational procedures and managerial and information systems*. But this assertion can be easily confuted with a further cognitive-laden statement: no information, no procedure is part of organizational knowledge if it does not become a part of individual representations of organizational members.

In addition, consider the notion that organizational knowledge differs from individual knowledge in that the former is *fruit of social interaction*. This is the result of an arbitrary distortion of reasoning. In fact, if it is true that individual knowledge derives from experience, it is also true that individual experience acquired within an organization is by definition the fruit of social interaction, as it is through daily interaction with other organizational members that experience is generated. So this notion does not seem particularly solid either.

Another ambiguity, in my opinion, arises from discordant views regarding the definition of organizational knowledge. In fact, some authors argue that the knowledge of an organization can be inferior to the sum of the knowledge of its members (for example Hedberg, 1981: 6). Others, instead, claim that organizational knowledge is necessarily greater than the sum of individuals' knowledge (for example Langfield-Smith, 1992). Beyond the innate ambiguity of the term 'sum', this disagreement depends on the *ambiguity of the concept of 'sharing'*. If by shared we mean 'common to all or many members' of the organization, then organizational knowledge must be inferior to the set of individuals' knowledge. If, instead, sharing means 'placed in common', or available to all members, clearly organizational knowledge exceeds the sum of individuals' knowledge because the process of intersection is substituted by a process of aggregation, linked to a multiplicative effect due to interaction.

The issue of sharing brings up another area of ambiguity in studies on organizational knowledge. *Empirical research necessarily utilizes limited samples.* Furthermore, often such studies focus on top management knowledge (Bartunek, 1984; Fahey and Narayanan, 1989; Ginsberg, 1989), a choice which, in theory, is supported by the notion that executive power allows this group to influence organizational knowledge exclusively. In this way, however, confusion is created on how knowledge evolves and the impact that this can have on organizational change. This reductionism is clear in all empirical studies. In fact, when an attempt is made to construct organizational cognitive maps, *considerable simplification* is necessary. Such is the case with the typical maps drawn up by Bougon and colleagues (1977), Eden et al. (1981), Hall (1984) and Bougon (1992) – all are made up by a very limited number of nodes and relationships. Hence, the richness and complexity of the concept of organizational knowledge is not given its due. The need to use small groups as units of analysis brings to light the *substantial difficulties in empirically capturing organizational knowledge.*

This appears to be a real phenomenon, but one which can not be empirically investigated unless a serious choice is made by assuming the analogy between organizational knowledge and small groups knowledge or by introducing explanatory variables which are not cognitive (for example, power). In my opinion, it is unlikely that this limitation can be overcome with research methods commonly in use.

In conclusion, the areas of ambiguity described above all revolve around a common source. To think of knowledge (individual or organizational) as a set of representations obliges us to reify knowledge: it is taken as a synonym for information, and simply considered the explicit part of knowledge, the part which is codified in schemas, structured, and as such transferable within the organization. In this view *knowledge is the product of information processing* implemented by individual members or, through interaction, by several members of an organization. Consequently, the connection between the individual and organizational level is based on an isomorphism which leads us to consider the residual area of individual knowledge, the contribution of the organization that makes collective knowledge greater than the sum of individual knowledge, as a further piece of information retained in databases, procedures, routines, and so forth.

In my opinion, with the theoretical tools of the cognitivist paradigm, these areas of ambiguity cannot be clarified. To provide a richer interpretative viewpoint in order to see through this haziness, one must first make a stand, choosing a perspective (either individual or organizational) which offers an escape route through the impasse: *individual knowledge and organizational knowledge are two mirror-like entities, each a reflection of the other.*

For the individual, organizational knowledge is knowledge available in the organization (from other individuals or in the form of data in managerial systems) that can be accessed to enhance her/his repository of representations. For the organization, individual knowledge is a potential that can be activated by organizational mechanisms when necessary. For each, knowledge generation implies recognizing the existence of the other level; each one must deal with the other. A solid epistemological basis for this view of knowledge is provided by studies rooted in the constructivist paradigm which will be analysed in the next section.

2.3 THE CONSTRUCTIVIST PARADIGM: ORGANIZATIONAL KNOWLEDGE AS COLLECTIVE MEANING SITUATED IN A SYSTEM OF INTERACTIONS

The constructivist paradigm has permeated several research fields in the past few years – from management to systems theory, sociology to cognitive sciences, biology to physics.[21] What brings such different disciplines so close together is the concept of *complexity*. Certain discoveries and theories developed in the fields of physics (thermodynamics and quantum physics), biology (molecular and evolutionary), and cognitive sciences (especially artificial intelligence) have led to the realization that complexity marks many phenomena in physical, biological, social and managerial systems. In epistemological and methodological terms, this recognition has also given rise to the conviction that these phenomena cannot be studied with a reductionist approach (attempting to trace the complexity of a phenomenon to the aggregated simplicity of its components). Rather, an interpretative stance must be adopted which is consistent with complexity. The study of these complex phenomena has given rise to the *epistemology of complexity*,[22] which is at the basis of the constructivist paradigm and shapes (implicitly or explicitly) all of the studies discussed below.

There are two initial assumptions of the constructivist paradigm which help mark the distance from cognitive theories of organizational knowledge:

- knowledge generation is, as the term suggests, a generative act, one that is not purely representative. Contrary to the cognitivist view of representation, constructivists believe that for an actor generating knowledge is actually creating a reality,[23] and is actively affecting his or her relationship with the surrounding world. Knowing is a creative act, not merely the revelation of an objective reality; it is an act by which the actor establishes generative relationships, shaping (in-forming) the surrounding environment;
- understanding the generative capacity of a specific actor entails choosing the same actor as unit of analysis. Hence, if the phenomenon to be analysed is the generation of individual knowledge, the viewpoint of the single individual must be adopted; however, if the phenomenon to be analysed is the generation of knowledge of an organization, therefore the perspective of the organization must be chosen. With constructivism, the assumption of an isomorphic relationship between individual knowledge and

collective knowledge fails, and this relationship becomes a problematic one.

The aim of this section is to provide a detailed look at the concepts of the constructivist paradigm that contribute to defining a theory of organizational knowledge. The presentation will take into account both different topics and fields where they have been developed so as to shed light on the ambiguities of the cognitivist paradigm described in the preceding section.

To begin with, I will focus on the connectionist paradigm, developed in cognitive sciences and artificial intelligence, for two reasons. The first is that connectionism puts forth hypotheses on cognition and generative mechanisms of human knowledge that differ radically from cognitivism. The second is that the connectionist view of knowledge as a network of connections offers extremely interesting ideas, useful for the interpretation and theorization of collective knowledge.

The doubt that may arise concerns the relationship between two theoretical systems, both defined paradigmatic: constructivism and connectionism. This doubt, though, can be allayed by thinking of the second as a restricted sphere within the broader scope of the first. Based on the assumption that reality (both psychic and social) is a construction of the actor who interacts with it, constructivism has a wider magnitude, and can be seen as encompassing connectionism too, as this last paradigm focuses solely on cognition.[24]

2.3.1 The Connectionist Paradigm: Knowledge as a Network of Connections

Connectionism is certainly not a new scientific paradigm, since the first studies that defined its basic assumptions were carried out in the 1950s. The relative 'rediscovery' was spurred by the publication of 'PDP' by Rumelhart and McClelland (1986), in which the authors give a detailed presentation of the new approach to parallel distributed processing (PDP) and its application in interpreting various cognitive and biological phenomena.

Connectionist research attempts to provide a solution for those aspects of cognition where cognitivist models fail. In particular, these studies begin with empirical evidence that the individual is capable of performing complex operations (even when faced with numerous constraints) much more effectively and rapidly than any model of information processing performed by a computer. In other words, evidence shows that the sequentiality of the said models cannot produce results equal to those of an individual's mind. What is more, when faced with even greater constraints, human cognition becomes more efficient, while it takes much more time for computer programs to find solutions to problems.

Further empirical evidence consists in the ability of the human cognitive system to adapt, with respect to computer models. In fact, if a sequential program is interrupted at any point it cannot move on; it stops because each phase produces input for the successive one. The human cognitive system, instead, even in the presence of some defect (though clearly not a completely debilitating one), can still carry out most of its functions, demonstrating its capacity to activate multiple pathways.

Connectionist researchers begin with epistemological premises different from those of cognitivists to provide an interpretation of human cognition. The first of these premises is that *the mind cannot be studied separately or independently of its physical support – that is, the brain and the nervous system.* Precisely through the study of these last two elements connectionism draws its fundamental propositions. The brain is made up of a tightly woven web of nerve cells (neurons) connected to one another by links called synapses. Each cell is stimulated by the state and behaviour of the others, giving rise to a network of connections. In fact, the paradigm in question gets its name from the importance attributed to the role of these connections. Connectionists use computer programs to reproduce these networks, which take the name neural networks because they are similar to the neural system of the brain.

The study of the functioning of the brain, and the simulation of cerebral activity through neural networks, has demonstrated how the brain is capable of carrying out extremely complex operations (perceiving objects, stimulating language, guiding motion) even though the single cells that make up the brain are very elementary units. The capacity of the brain derives then from the network; that is, from connections that link neurons which are able to produce different configurations through activation processes.

This result, added to the evidence that a defect in one part of the network does not interrupt the functioning of the brain, leads connectionist researchers to claim that information processing does not happen sequentially, but rather through parallel processes, hence the acronym PDP. The brain and neural networks are able to carry out complex tasks, often jointly, because they can process information in a parallel way.

From this the second epistemological premise of connectionism takes form, which contrary to cognitive theories maintains that *knowledge is not a symbolic representation but a state which emerges from the network, based on sub-symbolic elements.* In the brain, neurons are physical elements; in the same way, in a neural network nodes are physical since they are numerical expressions. In both cases, therefore, symbols (things that stand for something else) do not exist, but rather simpler elements do (which is why they are called sub-symbolic). Each unit does not contain knowledge in itself (instead according to cognitivism, units, categories and scripts, are forms of knowledge). Instead, there exists *knowledge distributed* in connections that link the units themselves.

Thus, knowledge is a state or a configuration that the system (the network) takes on when, stimulated by certain input, connections are activated to perform a specific task. In this sense, networks can learn (and knowledge can evolve) by changing the 'weight' of the connections – in other words, by giving greater importance to certain connections rather than others. Once again, we can confirm that knowledge is in the connections rather than the units.

Summing up, then, connectionist assumptions offer an extremely useful clue for constructing a model of organizational marketing knowledge: *the distributed – rather than localized – nature of knowledge* (Tsoukas, 1996). In connections between actors there is a different form of knowledge than that generated at an individual level. Groups of elementary units are able to perform complex tasks – hence, produce knowledge. This is done not only by aggregating individual knowledge, but by producing collective knowledge that is found in joint activities. In this sense, the relational context provides not only an instrumental contribution ('sets up the conditions for') but a constructive one ('in-forms', 'gives shape') for the generation of knowledge itself. In conclusion, when analysing knowledge generation processes, it is important to consider the context in which knowledge is generated, because creation is in the interaction among individuals and the interaction between individuals and the context.

If this is the great lesson connectionism can teach us, moving on to analysis of and theories on organizational knowledge generation, there are three research themes that echo the assumptions described above and that completely differentiate constructivist from cognitivist studies: the active role of the actor in generating knowledge; the view of the organization as a subject that possesses knowledge as well as specific cognitive processes; the formative role of action in producing knowledge. The following sections are dedicated to these three notions.

2.3.2 From Sequentiality to Circularity of Cognitive Processes: The Concept of Enactment

One of the concepts which lays the foundation for the view of 'knowing' as a generative act is *enactment*, proposed by Weick (1969; 1977; 1979). Central to Weick's theory is the concept of *equivocality*, or ambiguity. Signals from the environment are equivocal; that is, an actor cannot easily attribute them to a precise source. Hence their significance is not univocal: potentially, each signal has numerous meanings. When faced with equivocal signals, the actor sets a series of cognitive processes in motion in order to make sense of these signals. A characteristic of sensemaking is *continuity*. Referring back to Neisser's (1976) concept of the perception cycle, Weick argues that an individual's schemas guide his/her perceptual exploration, which takes place through action. This exploration involves choosing which part of the environment to pay attention to and gather data on; this data then modifies initial schemas by means of a circular process.

Action as such is not a secondary element; it does not merely play a functional role. Action is a vital part of cognition. Without action, sensemaking is not possible; the perception cycle lacks a crucial element. One cannot comprehend individual or collective cognition unless they are interpreted according to a circular logic. In this sense, then, Weick puts forth a more realistic hypothesis than that of traditional problem-solving models, by which cognition can be considered linear sequences: problems → solutions.

Weick argues that *the complexity of the environment is such that it is unknowable to the actor.* In this way, the author also undermines the other strong assumption of cognitive models. The environment is not objective, nor tangible, nor independent of the actor. Each subject, through his or her own actions, activates different portions of the environment than other subjects do, and in this way, constructs a personal environment. Weick names this process *enactment* (Figure 2.3).

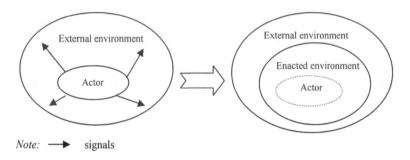

Note: ⟶   signals

Figure 2.3   The enactment process

Action, then, plays a unique role. Through enactment, the actor makes a distinction between that which is part of his or her environment, and that which instead is part of the unknown environment which does not exist in cognitive terms.

To explain how these processes come about, Weick proposes an evolutionary model based on four interconnected processes (Figure 2.4).

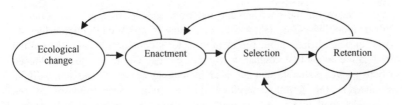

Source: Weick (1969).

Figure 2.4   Weick's evolutionary model

The environment produces continual streams of experience which, every so often, undergo variations. The author calls such variations *ecological changes*. These stimulate actors who, consequently, pay attention to a certain part of the environment, highlighting and focusing on it. This is what Weick calls *enactment*, a process which produces 'raw data' that are assigned meaning, which consists in separating streams of experience before making sense of them. This last element has to do with the *selection process*, which in turn consists in imposing an actor's knowledge structures (schemas) on raw data produced by enactment. Among the various forms schemas can take, Weick gives particular importance to causal maps, maintaining that sensemaking involves constructing causal relationships between events. Schemas which are valuable in reducing ambiguity are memorized by means of a *retention process*. Actors store a number of schemas in their memory that represent enacted environments, or knowledge structures made up of causal relationships that have proven useful in sensemaking and which, circularly, influence successive enactment processes.

It is clear that Weick's model offers some key innovations with respect to traditional cognitive models. In fact, most importantly Weick argues that *meaning is assigned retrospectively*. As highlighted in the previous sections, traditional cognitive theories claim that meaning precedes action. Sense is created by knowledge structures which function as a guide to action, following the sequence: sense → action. Weick says the sequence is inverted: action → sense. In his opinion, given environmental complexity, the actor can make sense only of actions already taken, not actions to be taken in the future. Only by acting, scanning raw data, can actors understand what environment they have constructed, and how a previously indistinct portion of the environment has taken form around their actions.[25]

Secondly, Weick introduces *the distinction between data, information and knowledge*.[26] These terms refer to the different forms that any event-related signal can take. In the previous evolutionary model, the three forms refer to different phases in the cycle. Data are produced by enactment, thus by the actor's action in the environment and by scanning streams of experience. Information, instead, is data to which meaning is attributed through selection. It is 'enriched' data, more useful to an actor's cognition because it is fitted into causal maps that connect it to other events. The information produced which proves valuable can be used in making sense of data that will be scanned in the future. Therefore, the retention process determines the interaction and integration of new information with previous information, generating knowledge.

This last point highlights substantial agreement between Weick and consolidated cognitive models on the *critical role of the actor's experience* in influencing his/her cognition. In the evolutionary model, experience takes on the specific form of retained, enacted environments. This also helps to confirm that in this approach *the environment is inside, not outside, the actor.*[27] Experience influences enactment, guiding action toward known portions of the environment. In this case, therefore, the actor becomes as a consistency seeker. Moreover, experience affects the selection process, stimulating the use of the same interpretative schemas; this is consistent with the profile of the individual as an economizer of cognitive resources. Both cases justify the existence of what Weick calls self-fulfilling prophecies – predictions that are constructed in such a way that they must necessarily come true, since both enactment and selection occur in a 'distorted' manner, and meaning is attributed retrospectively. From these considerations derives the concept that retention stimulates stability of schemas. Consequently, enacted environments tend to be inertial.

The preceding reflections underscore how Weick implicitly introduces a breakthrough hypothesis: *from the viewpoint of information-producing processes, individuals (and organizations) are closed systems.* In fact, if the environment is inside the actor because it is constructed by the actor him/herself, if what comes from the outside is only data activated by the actor, and if the transformation of data into information and knowledge is a process entirely internal to the actor, then we can only conclude that cognizant actors 'function' as closed systems.

The distinctive characteristics of Weick's ideas show a surprising analogy with some concepts developed in systems theory. In particular, two Chilean scholars, Maturana and Varela (1980; 1987), studying the operational mechanisms of the nervous system, have developed a theory that distinguishes the properties of living systems as compared to non-living ones. They assert that the most significant difference lies in the capacity of living systems to reproduce both their components and the relationships between these components. In this sense, living systems are defined as *autopoietic*. Cognitive systems are typical autopoietic systems. Reflecting on some of the properties of these systems,[28] analogies with Weick's proposals surface.

The first property of cognitive systems is *operational closure*. This term refers to the capacity/necessity of the system to make the results of its actions revert back within the system itself. An autopoietic system does not function in terms of stimulus–response, input–output, but rather through a circular process of self-organization. The system acts on the basis of current components and the relationships between them. It keeps its organization stable, that is, it is capable of producing and re-producing components and relationships. This process permits the homeostatic functioning of the system.

Closure from a cognitive viewpoint does not, however, mean isolation. In fact, the system, to assure its survival, *imports energy from the environment and discharges entropy there*. Energy is imported in the form of signals that the system picks up from the environment and transforms into information. This information is then organized in knowledge needed to sustain the process of self-production of the system's survival.

In addition, a cognitive system is characterized by *the definition of its boundaries in contraposition to an environment*. The system defines its own identity and contextually distinguishes itself from something external, represented by the environment. From this observation, we can deduce that the environment does not exist in objective terms; rather it is generated by the system through a process of distinction. Every single system produces its own environment. This production process works in such a way that an alteration of distinctions activated by the system provokes a corresponding change in the environment.

These three properties square with Weick's hypotheses. A cognitive system imports data from the environment, but the process of sensemaking is entirely internal, based on internal components and mechanisms. The environment does not give instructions; the cognitive system operates circularly, and is operationally closed. Then, typical of a cognitive system is the ability of enactment[29] of raw data, scanning streams of experience so as to distinguish between what is internal and what is external. The system cognitively constructs its own reality, a reality which is different from that of other systems.

2.3.3   The Organization as a Cognitive System: Interaction as a Form of Collective Knowledge

One conclusion that can be drawn from the analysis of the constructivist approach to the study of organizations is that organizations can be theorized as cognitive systems, that is, systems able to survive and prosper by continuously generating new knowledge. Knowledge defines the very essence of the organization (Daft and Weick, 1984; Smirchich and Stubbart, 1985; Weick, 1969; 1979; 1995; Rullani, 1987; 1994; Vicari, 1991; Nonaka, 1991;

1994; Nonaka and Takeuchi, 1995; von Krogh and Roos, 1995; 1996b; Spender, 1996; Boisot, 1998).[30]

Theorizing organizations as cognitive systems means considering them organic, living systems.[31] As such, organizations are autonomous systems, whose goals and inputs are set by the system itself and do not derive from any external agent. Organizational knowledge is the source and the engine of the organization's operations, thus becoming its fundamental resource which must be continually reproduced so that the organization can survive and develop. As a consequence, a radical difference between the cognitivist and the constructivist paradigm is that the former posits that the organization *has* its own cognitive systems (database, procedures, routines), while the latter maintains that the firm *is* a cognitive system.

As a consequence, if a researcher or a manager wishes to analyse organizational knowledge, an isomorphic model that begins with the individual cannot be adopted. On the contrary, *it is necessary to adopt the point of view of the organization*. Therefore, generating organizational knowledge does not consist in shifting from an individual level to a group or system level, but in a truly collective generative process. This has been termed 'conversion' (Nonaka, 1994; Nonaka and Takeuchi, 1995: Chap. 3), 'absorption and impacting' (Boisot, 1998: 58-62), 'sensemaking' (Weick, 1995).

The collective process of knowledge generation is a central tenet of the theory of organizations as cognitive systems, hence it is worthwhile to examine in detail how such generation comes about. To discuss this topic, I will leverage on the findings of some empirical investigations that have surfaced from the ambiguities of cognitivism in order to emphasize once more the innovative contribution of the constructivist approach.

The first issue that needs to be brought again into the debate is that of knowledge sharing, and, more precisely, that organizations need shared knowledge structures to function effectively.

Langfield-Smith (1992) attempted to reconstruct a collective cognitive map for a group of six people – members of a team of firefighters who work together on a regular basis –basing her investigation on the premise that 'collective beliefs may encompass more than the beliefs which are common to the individuals of the group' (1992: 353). The experiment failed when it came time to draw up the collective map, because group members shared neither language nor meaning attributed to events. This failure proved contradictory with respect to the initial hypothesis. In fact, a group of people who share daily experiences do not share explanations for those experiences in the same way. The author gives her own interpretation of this contradiction, concluding that 'co-ordinated actions and decisions may take place without there necessarily being an extensive body of shared beliefs (or a collective map)'

(1992: 362). Hence she draws the opposite conclusions of the classic cognitivist notion of shared knowledge structures.

Along the same lines, Eden et al. (1981), in attempting to construct a collective map for a group of managers, showed how difficult it is to come to share schemas, and therefore beliefs. This evidence led these researchers to support the idea that collective knowledge is generated by means of a process of social construction of reality (Berger and Luckmann, 1969). This construction comes about through interaction and negotiation of what the authors call an inter-subjective view between members of the group, that is a view that does not belong to any one individual, but to the group as a whole. In summary, therefore, groups of managers (and by extension entire organizations) may act together in an effective way, though they do not always continually clarify the convictions that are the basis for their actions.

Once again Weick's theory proves useful. In fact, Weick's proposition that what holds the organization together is concerted behaviour rather than shared knowledge shifts attention from organizational shared representations to organizational action.

The hypothesis that can be developed, then, is that *process counts more than structure* (that is, representations).

Socialization, in other words, is actually a process of joint action that is not only instrumental to generating collective knowledge, but is also a very particular form of knowledge in and of itself. I argue, therefore, that *action embodies a form of knowledge that is not present in the representations of actors*.

Once again, it is Weick who offers a series of extremely stimulating considerations in this regard. Beginning with the premise that 'an organization is a body of thought thought by thinking thinkers' (1979: 42), Weick's notion of organizational knowledge can be traced to two strong propositions.

The first is that collective structures, hence organizations, *form around a common means rather than a common end.* This implies (1969) that initially individuals who are unable to attain their specific ends on their own, converge their actions and means. Once a certain convergence is created on actions, common ends emerge for the group (for example that the structure survives and is perpetuated) so as to ensure the attainment of diverse ends. At this point, the group will find it convenient to divide up work internally, utilizing different actions and means. This will foster the attainment of diverse ends and hence the entire cycle, as represented in Figure 2.5.

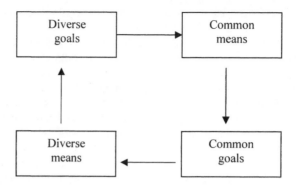

Source: Weick (1969).

Figure 2.5   A model of group development

The second proposition is that *shared meaning emerges after shared action*. Individuals attempt to assign meaning to their collective experiences after taking action, or after having 'placed in common' their means. Sense is established retrospectively, and collective action precedes collective knowledge. Weick in particular, distancing himself from other scholars in this field, maintains that a great deal of sharing is not necessary *ex ante*, because the fundamental point is sharing actions.[32]

Besides the ones just described, other theories support the relevance of joint action in collective knowledge generation. Specifically, research on group competences and on managerial practices provides us with remarkable insight into organizational knowledge generation, with positive emphasis on empirical investigation.

As for research on *competences of work groups*, Weick and Roberts (1993) investigated the existence of a *collective mind* in a work group responsible for handling flight operations. For such a group, reliability is an indispensable requirement. The fundamental concept proposed by the authors is that of heedful interrelating. Weick and Roberts' premise is that a characteristic of groups that are very reliable in their performance is that group members carry out interrelated activities, paying disproportionate attention to their relationships. These particular types of relationships define the collective mind. Two fundamental elements of this concept are joint action and quality of interrelations. As the authors state: 'We portray collective mind in terms of method rather than content, structuring rather than structure, connecting rather than connections' (1993: 365). The collective mind is an *emerging* property of group actions if they are carried out in a heedful way. It is a type of intelligence which is shaped by joint action.

Weick and Roberts believe that for this quality to emerge, the actors must act (contributing), imagining the existence of a system of joint actions of the group (representing), and connect their own action to the imagined system (subordinating). A collective mind emerges if the actors have the ability to imagine the overall functioning of the system, hence the actions of the other members of the group, *as if* the group knew how to operate in the expected way. Secondly, it is necessary that the actors feel they are a fundamental part of the system, acting *as if* their contribution were fundamental to shape the system itself. The concept of mind, therefore, refers to interrelated actions, not to single members of the group: 'We conceptualized mind as action that constructs mental processes rather than as mental processes that construct action .... To connect *is* to mind' (1993: 374).

Weick takes up on some of these concepts and discusses others in the analysis of the Mann Gulch disaster (1993). This case involves the organizational failure of a team of firefighters which ended in the death of most of its members. Demonstrating the reasons for this failure, Weick suggests that an organization should possess certain properties to be more reliable and more elastic to change: two of them (the ability to improvise and the existence of a system of virtual roles) recall the capacity for action and representation typical of a collective mind as previously described. The other two, instead, are of greater interest for our purposes: wisdom and respectful interaction.

As for *wisdom*, Weick bases his reasoning on the fact that whenever individuals acquire new knowledge, they become more ignorant at the same time, because knowledge gives rise to new doubts, new uncertainties. Wisdom is the disposition of a group to have reasonable doubts about its own knowledge. Citing Meacham, Weick states: 'Wisdom is an attitude taken by persons toward the beliefs, values, knowledge, information, abilities, and competences that are held, a tendency to doubt that these are necessarily true or valid and to doubt that they are an exhaustive set of those things that could be known' (1993: 641). In essence, to be wise means to recognize that one's own knowledge refers to the past, to meaning created retrospectively, so it may prove inadequate when dealing with a complex environment. In order to be reliable, a group must cautiously doubt what it knows so as to be attentive to the unexpected.

The second property is *respectful interaction*. Since a group is formed by the interaction of its components, reliability comes about when members come to trust one another, express their ideas and intentions honestly, and tend to respect their own perceptions and integrate them with the perceptions of others (1993: 642-643). What makes a group reliable and flexible in the face of change is a mingling of dispositions, behaviours, and the will of group members who, interacting, continually recreate these variables.[33]

The studies described above highlight two relevant points: first, if one wishes to investigate group competences, the group must be the unit of analysis; second, knowledge is tightly linked, or better still, connatural to action. Groups and organizations are formed on interactions, and knowledge is formed in interactions.

In research on *managerial practices* a fundamental concept is that of *activity*. It consists in the means by which individual knowledge and the work context merge.[34] Activity is the basic unit of analysis for understanding how knowledge develops.[35] From this, researchers also conclude that there is a need to define and utilize new methodologies for studying knowledge and learning that are based on researchers' direct observation and participation in activities carried out in the workplace.

Scribner (1984), for example, analyses practical knowledge of a group of warehouse employees of a milk and dairy producer. The objective of the author was to ascertain the existence of common patterns among workers for performing certain activities. Focusing on a number of specific tasks which required a minimal ability in mathematics, in optimizing physical space, arranging objects in order while working within a time limit, the author identifies a sort of *working intelligence*, constituted by a set of rules adopted in performing tasks, different from prescribed rules or standard calculating procedures, but which optimized both physical and cognitive effort. From this evidence, Scribner concludes that work activity provides a number of contributions to the development of knowledge; thus analysing the two separately is not possible. Moreover, conceptually speaking, this demonstrates how abstract and practical thought are necessarily connatural and indivisible.

A second fascinating study was carried out by Orr (1990) on *collective memory* of a group of Xerox maintenance technicians. Directly participating in activities, the author observed that the technicians, who had maintenance manuals which did not cover every possible type of problem, were able to transmit information, and in this way develop a set of shared knowledge. They did so by telling 'war stories' – anecdotes about their daily experiences when they succeeded in finding an adequate solution to a new, unforeseen problem.

The primary feature of these war stories is that, unlike manuals which only give information on the machine, these accounts describe the machine in the utilization context and in the repair context. For this reason, they only relate episodes which are not banal (to capture the listener's interest, stories cannot be predictable) and draw attention to a much broader field of activity than the simple technician–machine relationship – that is, a 'technician-machine-user-use activity' context. From this, the author concludes that transmitting 'rich' information through stories facilitates sensemaking, determines group membership, and allows collective knowledge to be generated.

The final study of interest here was conducted by Brown and Duguid (1991),[36] who take up on Orr's ideas, placing their central focus on *communities of practice*. These are groups of people who emerge from performing a series of activities jointly, going beyond the boundaries and ties established by formal organizational structure. The authors posit that any theoretical definition of roles, responsibilities, or procedures, will never succeed in predicting or forcing into pre-established confines the complexity of real situations, nor of the work activities with which this complexity must be addressed and managed. This provokes the emergence of communities of individuals linked by the execution of complementary activities, capable of developing their own work methods, rules, and collective knowledge – like Orr's technicians.

Brown and Duguid provide a definition of learning which comes out of these considerations, one which is extremely innovative: *learning consists of membership in a community*.

This occurs when actors gradually move from the periphery toward the centre of the community, becoming fully-fledged members. One develops knowledge by 'learning to belong' to the community, sharing behaviours, rules, stories. This knowledge is not theoretical or abstract, but rather *situated in the context* of the community.

Studies on managerial practices propose convergent notions with research into group competences, and further develop some of them.

First and foremost the centrality of the group, of the community, as a primary unit of analysis is confirmed in the study of organizational knowledge.

The critical role of action also emerges as it gives form to knowledge and permits learning to take place. What is more, however, these studies emphasize how the knowledge of a group of individuals primarily *resides in relationships and interactions between members*, and is nourished by the reinforcement of group participation.

The *relevance of context* for knowledge creation also finds confirmation. If the barrier between theoretical thought and practical thought falls, the merging of the two brings context to the fore, highlighting its role in determining opportunities for creating and disseminating managerial intelligence. From this one can conclude that, besides action and interaction, context becomes a critical factor in the generation of organizational knowledge.

2.3.4   Summary and Conclusions

To conclude the preceding sections, we can sum up the findings of investigations which share a constructivist background with three main achievements.

The first is that a systemic perspective is necessary to describe, interpret or theorize on collective knowledge, and the *unit of analysis must be the community of individuals, that is, the organization.* Beginning with the concept of individual knowledge and attempting to use various sorts of combinatory approaches to arrive at collective knowledge, the transition from one to the other creates a number of problems, both from a theoretical and methodological standpoint. Instead, research into group competences (which underscores the emergence of collective mind as qualifier of interaction between members), and studies on communities of practice (which propose the concept of knowledge as participation), and also connectionist theories (by which knowledge is distributed in the connections between elementary units of a system), converge on the notion that *collective knowledge is different from individual knowledge.* For this reason, the starting point must be the community, not individuals. In this sense, studies that maintain a view of the organization as a cognitive system are very clear. Only if we adopt the viewpoint of a system, of a group of individuals, can we understand knowledge generation and evolution at a more aggregated level than the individual one. Obviously, this does not deny that knowledge represented in cognitive structures of single organizational members is part of collective knowledge. It instead emphasizes that such structures denote only a part of collective knowledge, since there exists a tacit, social dimension that is not represented by individual schemas.

Consequent to this affirmation, the second relevant achievement is that *interaction plays a knowledge-generating role.* Empirical research shows how groups of individuals that interact effectively and efficiently do not necessarily share the same set of representations. Moreover, both studies on group competences and managerial practices prove that in joint action a form of sensemaking emerges which is inseparable from the specificity of the action itself. Highly reliable groups and communities of practice are created around specific activities, and through those activities knowledge is enhanced. Evolution of knowledge – learning – can be considered a form of membership. In the same way, connectionism posits that every unit in the network takes on meaning only as a function of and in relation to all the others. What is more, action is measured by the evolution of importance placed on connections.

The third and final achievement is that *all knowledge is situated in a context*, and context is formative of this knowledge.[37] It is not useful to describe abstract, theoretical knowledge in an organization because significant knowledge is that which 'comes to be' in activities performed by the organization itself – in other words, knowledge 'embodied' in a real-life, social context. Studies on communities of practice highlight how significant knowledge is transmitted by telling war stories because this knowledge is situated. Connectionism roots knowledge in the functioning of its physical support: the brain. Both emphasize, in different ways, the critical nature of context.

From these three achievements, we can deduce that *action carried out in a social context – hence, interaction – embodies a form of knowledge that is not necessarily present in representations of those who interact.* This knowledge is not present prior to the action but *emerges* from the system of interactions. Moreover, it is connatural to the context in which the interaction takes place, or, in the words of Varela and colleagues (1991), it is *embodied.* Action generates context according to a circular process, by which one and the other are simultaneously active and passive elements in the generation of knowledge.

The conclusions listed here represent basic assumptions of the marketing knowledge model that will be described in the following chapter.

NOTES

1. Actually, a number of scholars claim the two theories are complementary. They point out that with either theory it is difficult to demonstrate (in an empirical and exclusive way) the relationships between independent variables and performance. In this regard, see: Barney (1991); Amit and Schoemaker (1993); Henderson and Mitchell (1997).

2. After more than twenty years from its original proposal, very detailed reviews of this theory are provided in the international literature. In most of them both strengths and drawbacks of the theory are highlighted. See the works of Conner (1991), Schulze (1994), Barney (2001b) and the debate between Foss (1996a; 1996b), Conner and Prahalad (1996) and Kogut and Zander (1996); and between Hunt and Morgan (1995; 1997), Dickson (1996) and Deligönül and Cavuşgil (1997); lastly, between Priem and Butler (2001) and Barney (2001a).

3. Among the first studies aimed at highlighting the value of such resources are Itami (1987), Winter (1987) and Vicari (1989).

4. In this case, too, for an in-depth analysis of the literature on this topic see studies listed in note 2.

5. This is the reason why, as Verona (2000: 36) also affirms: 'Studies on resources have turned into studies on organizational knowledge' (my translation), and the resource-based theory has slowly evolved toward a knowledge-based theory of

the firm (Conner and Prahalad, 1996; Grant, 1996b; Spender, 1996; Grandori and Kogut, 2002; Nickerson and Zenger, 2004).

6. A detailed examination of cognitivist assumptions in management literature can be found in Stubbart (1988), and Stubbart et al. (1994: xi–xv).

7. '[...] "the thinking organization" is a rich metaphor chosen to recognize the view that there is no essential difference between organizations and their members. According to this position, people *are* the organization' (Gioia and Sims, 1986: 1).

8. Reference must be made to studies by Simon (1947; 1955), March and Simon (1958) and Newell and Simon (1972). See also: Hitt and Tyler (1991), Eisenhardt and Zbaracki (1992) and Spender (1992).

9. Obviously, this does not happen exclusively since, as stated before, schemas are multi-faceted and composite, and so the same signal can be assimilated by different schemas.

10. Here, action is considered in a broad sense, so a decision or communication are forms of action.

11. Some of the more representative are: Lyles and Mitroff (1980), Dutton et al. (1983), Isabella (1990), Milliken (1990), Thomas and McDaniel Jr. (1990) and Gooding and Kinicki (1995).

12. In psychology, the first reference to cognitive maps is made by Tolman (1948). A study that is often used as a reference by scholars of social psychology is Neisser (1976).

13. This dual utility has, however, caused some ambiguity and even brought about criticism in light of epistemological and methodological considerations (Cossette and Audet, 1990; Eden, 1990a).

14. For a summary of exhaustive commentaries on the topic, refer to Huff (1990), the two monographic issues of *Journal of Management Studies* (1989; 1992), and Eden and Spender (1998).

15. For a summary of the two positions, refer to: Hedberg (1981), Shrivastava (1983) and Fiol and Lyles (1985).

16. In fact, March and Olsen draw a distinction between *role-constrained* learning, when the link between individual cognitions and individual actions is interrupted; *superstitious* learning, when the sequence between organizational actions and environmental responses is interrupted; *audience* learning, when there is no connection between individual actions and organizational actions; and learning *under ambiguity*, in cases where there is no relationship between environmental responses and individual cognitions.

17. Articles referred to are: Glick (1985), James et al. (1988) and Glick (1988).

18. Regarding the evolution of collective schemas, management literature abounds with studies that offer a wealth of reviews of previous works (Argyris and Schön, 1978; Duncan and Weiss, 1979; Hedberg, 1981; Shrivastava, 1983; Fiol and Lyles, 1985; Levitt and March, 1988; Huber, 1991; Dodgson, 1993; Jelinek and

Litterer, 1994; Glynn et al., 1994; Walsh, 1995). Most of the debate revolves around opposing views of organizational learning as a modification of an organization's schemas, or of an organization's behaviour (cognitive change vs. behavioural change). For our purposes, this debate does not prove very useful, in the sense that behavioural changes are, in any case, based on modifications in decision-making rules and organizational routines. As such these changes can be traced back to schemas. The emphasis placed on one or the other of these modifications is linked for the most part to the research domain of the scholars in question.

19. This view has always enjoyed wide popularity in management research. Consider strategy studies which posit that environmental analysis and company resources assessment (when threats, opportunities, strengths and weaknesses are identified) must come before strategy formulation and this, in turn, must determine strategy implementation (Hofer and Schendel, 1978; Hax and Majluf, 1984; Grant 1991). Similarly, marketing management studies maintain that the starting point for any strategic or operative marketing decision must be the analysis of customers and competition (Kotler, 2000).

20. Here, too, previous reference to marketing and strategy literature provide good examples of how this assumption is rooted in management research. In particular, consider how intrinsic to the concept of marketing is the assumption that customers' needs are objective and independent of companies' actions.

21. For an in-depth discussion of constructivist epistemology, see the volume edited by Watzlawick (1984) and in particular the two works by von Glasersfeld (1984) and von Foerster (1984). For the purposes of this book, an equally meaningful definition is 'socio-cognitivist paradigm', as this term would clearly underscore the role of collective cognition. However, I still prefer the term 'constructivist' to highlight that the creative rather than representative nature of individual knowledge is the more crucial distinction between this paradigm and the cognitivist one. Some references on the debate about the two paradigms and their effect on management research are: von Krogh et al. (1994), von Krogh and Roos (1996b), Tsoukas (1996), Venzin et al. (1998) and Mir and Watson (2000).

22. For a detailed discussion of the epistemological impact of the theme of complexity in different research fields, see Bocchi and Ceruti (1989) and Walldrop (1992). As far as its effects on the theory of the firm and management, see Vicari (1991), Stacey (1995), Brown and Eisenhardt (1997) and Boisot (1998).

23. Reality is 'invented', as Watzlawick argues (1984).

24. In fact, few management studies make explicit reference to the connectionist paradigm (Vicari, 1991: 138-141; Weick and Roberts, 1993; Vicari and Troilo, 2000). Many, however, draw attention to the critical nature of connections for the purpose of generating knowledge, and so can be considered implicitly connectionist.

25. This position is also clearly expressed in Hedberg (1981: 3): 'Organizations increase their understanding of reality by observing the results of their acts.'

26. This is a fundamental distinction for all studies that draw on the constructivist paradigm. See: Vicari (1991: 63-68), Fransman (1994); von Krogh et al. (1994), Nonaka (1994) and Boisot (1998: 10-13).

27. Hedberg (1981: 8) once again, states: 'In a sense, the environment is inside an organization. The real world provides the raw material of stimuli to react to, but the only meaningful environment is one that is born when stimuli are processed through perceptual filters.'

28. For a broader description of the evolution of the systems theory and the properties of autopoietic systems, see Vicari (1991: 22-29) and Kickert (1993). For a more general discussion of self-organizational systems, see also Drazin and Sandelands (1992), Stacey (1995; 1996) and Boisot (1998).

29. The term enactment is also utilized in research on autopoietic systems, as we can observe in Varela et al. (1991: Chap. 8).

30. Interesting literature reviews on the topic are Schneider and Angelmar (1993) and Walsh (1995) who provide noteworthy ideas for analyzing these theories.

31. Nonaka et al. (2000b) define an organization as a 'knowledge-creating *entity*' (italics added), giving a sense of a spiritual and transcendent content as well as a living one – this in keeping with the philosophy that also shapes the oriental managerial culture.

32. It is interesting to note how some researchers, without abandoning the traditional cognitivistic assumptions, have recognized the relevance of joint action in constructing both collective knowledge, and the organization itself. For example, Jelinek and Litterer (1994) attempt to unite the tradition of managerial problem solving with the concept of sharing knowledge. In fact, their initial assumption is that individuals belonging to an organization, thinking in organizational terms, produce organizational knowledge and behaviour. The two authors take up on the tradition which holds that organizational knowledge consists in the knowledge of individuals who operate inside an organization, but maintain that, 'Separate, autonomous individuals thinking with an organizational perspective, and choosing behaviors to achieve an organizational outcome, together produce collective, organizational level behavior. The choice of organizational perspective level, as contrasted with individual level, enables them to bridge from individual to organizational cognitions and actions' (1994: 15). What is significant here is that Jelinek and Litterer's starting point is the opposite of Weick's, as the first two authors assert that there must be prior sharing of objectives by members of the organization. However, despite having begun with two very different premises, Jelinek and Litterer (just like Weick) come to the conclusion that from joint action (directed toward common objectives) shared knowledge emerges.

33. McGrath et al. (1995), leveraging on the concepts set forth by Weick and Roberts, propose the existence of two antecedents to the development of organizational competences: understanding and deftness. The capacity for understanding is defined in quite a deterministic way as the ability to identify necessary resources for reaching objectives. Deftness is identified as a property of the group that emerges when the group begins to function through the interrelated activities of its members and become reliable.
34. Regarding the relevance of activity for generating organizational knowledge, see also contributions by Blackler (1993) and Spender (1996; 1998).
35. Such a choice fosters the use of researchers' participant observation as the most appropriate methodology for investigating knowledge and learning.
36. For an in-depth analysis of the role of communities of practice in generating collective knowledge, see later studies by Brown and Duguid (1998; 2000) and Lee and Cole (2003).
37. A position consistent with this is expressed by Polanyi in numerous works (1958; 1967), which refer to tacit knowledge as that particular type of knowledge constructed by the relationships of a subject with a context.

3. Marketing Knowledge: A Model for Management

3.1 ORGANIZATIONAL MARKETING KNOWLEDGE

The analysis in the preceding sections consolidates the statement which concluded Chapter 1: the market orientation theory is based on a highly traditional view of knowledge-generating processes. This theory is rooted in the cognitivist paradigm and is, in fact, greatly influenced by the managerial information processing model and its basic assumptions. Information processing is considered instrumental to taking action on the market (intentionality). In addition, it is seen as a process of selecting alternatives, depending on the results to be obtained (computation). Thirdly, the main source of information – the market – is presumed to be objective, stable, and external to the subject carrying out the analysis.

This last aspect, moreover, has played a substantial part in shaping the concept of marketing knowledge from the origins of this research field (Myers et al., 1980). In fact, if the market is considered objective, *marketing knowledge is essentially knowledge of the market*. A market oriented company is one that knows the market in which it operates or intends to operate. This knowledge, in turn, *consists of information about market phenomena captured through market research.* From this statement we can deduce that the larger the repository of available information, the broader the knowledge, and the more market oriented a company is.

Moreover, the market responses to actions taken by the company enable that company to *adapt its behaviours* by extending its repository of information; this is made possible through a process of trial and error.

If one wishes to design a model for marketing knowledge management in a constructivist mould, clearly such considerations are excessively reductionist. First of all, to regard market knowledge solely as information provides a limited view of the concept, because the complexity with which this information is represented by actors is not taken into account. For example, companies that have access to a considerable quantity of information (for example those that invest heavily in market research) may have insufficient means for interpreting this information. On the contrary, companies with little information might have notable interpretative competences, or possess considerable behavioural ability (scripts) and be able to represent their markets in a more structured, comprehensive way. Therefore, in order to provide a more complete view of the concept of marketing knowledge, we must first move from one level to the next: from information to schemas representing market phenomena.

A further consideration is that a company's knowledge of the market does not completely encompass its marketing knowledge because if this were so, all knowledge represented in scripts of events and behaviours and causal connections between them would be excluded. Therefore, a broader view is needed which also takes into account all of these elements. This is why I prefer the term marketing knowledge rather than market knowledge or market-based knowledge.

Thirdly, the evolutionary nature of knowledge must be considered, in particular the processes that influence the generation and development of knowledge structures. If, in fact, market orientation consists of marketing knowledge, then assessing a company's market orientation entails evaluating the potentiality of organizational marketing knowledge. To do so, we cannot neglect to include procedural knowledge within the repository of knowledge, in other words the heuristics and biases that guide the creation and evolution of this repository.

All this, however, places emphasis exclusively on the structural components of knowledge, highlighting only *knowledge localized* in individual schemas. These represent only *potential knowledge* (Vicari and Troilo, 1997): knowledge available to the actors and which can be translated into actual behaviour. But in taking such a view, the risk is that no importance is given to the most relevant part of marketing knowledge: *knowledge situated* in interactions among organizational members involved in marketing activities, and in interactions between organizational members and market actors (customers, competitors, distributors, and so on). This represents the company's *knowledge in use,* and generally finds only marginal expression in the knowledge structures of organizational members.[1]

To sum up, therefore, the marketing knowledge of a company is made up of:

- evolutionary representations, both individual and shared, of organizational members involved in activities that impact market relationships;
- evolutionary knowledge situated in interactions within the community of practice which carry out activities that impact market relationships, and lastly;

- evolutionary knowledge situated in interactions of organizational members with market actors.

Marketing knowledge, in other words, has three components: one consisting of representations, the other two of interactions – in communities of practice within the organization and, externally, with market actors. The configuration of marketing knowledge is, therefore, a network, where a part of the knowledge resides in nodes, represented by individual actors, while another part is *distributed in stable interactions* between actors.

Asserting the existence of knowledge distributed in interactions, however, does not imply that all individual knowledge is structured while only collective knowledge is distributed. On the contrary, and consistent with the constructivist paradigm, a part of individual knowledge is also situated, in the sense that it is distributed in the activities that an individual (a single manager or employee) performs when interacting with the organizational context: artefacts, symbols, systems of norms, and, finally, other organizational members (Homburg and Pflesser, 2000).

Referring once again to the definition, I believe mine has noteworthy advantages over others found in the literature (cf. Menon and Varadarajan, 1992; Sinkula, 1994; Li and Calantone, 1998; Rossiter, 2001).

First of all, it emphasizes the existence of potential knowledge localized in individual schemas (or collective, if shared) still not used by the company, which can be captured through appropriate emersion processes, as we will see in the following chapter.

Moreover, it leverages on the indications of the constructivist paradigm, and suggests that the boundaries of the organization extend to all portions of the environment enacted by the company. One part of organizational marketing knowledge, therefore, resides in interactions with actors outside the company: market components (customers, distributors, competitors, and so on) and all actors who possess knowledge which is necessary for managing market relationships (for example, market research institutes, communication agencies, and so on). In addition, this definition highlights the importance of inter-departmental relationships within the organization, underscoring how a relevant portion of marketing knowledge is distributed in the interactions of Marketing with other departments (Research & Development, Engineering, Manufacturing, Sales, and so on). Again, the boundaries of organizational marketing knowledge do not correspond with those of the department that has specific responsibilities for building and developing market relationships (Krohmer et al., 2002).

Last of all, this definition further accentuates how not all marketing knowledge is structured in schemas, hence not all marketing knowledge can be consciously communicated by those who possess it. As a consequence, if a company wishes to make marketing knowledge an engine to fuel its competitive advantage, the use of specialized tools for its capture and management is necessary.

This implies a clear understanding of the nature of the components of marketing knowledge, as detailed in the next section.

3.1.1　The Localized Component of Marketing Knowledge: Marketing Mental Models

Taking up on the categorization made in section 2.2.2, the localized component of marketing knowledge of a company can be traced to *mental models which represent market phenomena.* Specifically, this component consists of:

a) descriptive models representing market actors' identity;
b) descriptive and interpretative models of market relationships;
c) descriptive models representing the company's self-identity;
d) marketing behavioural models;
e) marketing decision-making models;
f) heuristics and biases.

a) The first component of marketing knowledge is the set of categories used by company personnel to represent market actors. At a first level, these categories are abstract, and are made up of a small number of attributes. As a consequence they tend to give rise to prototypes; hence, they can better be referred to as *macro-categories*. Traditionally, marketing literature identifies three main macro-categories: customers, distributors and competitors. In strategy studies, more focused on industry analysis than market analysis, suppliers and newcomers are included (Porter, 1980). Other models might refer to government agencies, consumer groups, trade associations, research institutes, advertising agencies, and so on. These models are a first-level rough description of the market and the identity of market actors. They are characterized more by width than depth, since sub-classes of individual actors (that is specific customers, individual competitors, and so on) are not represented. This first component broadly represents the set of actors thought to influence market phenomena.

For example, consider an industry that is undergoing a transformation from an oligopoly to a more competitive system. Descriptive models used by the company in the recent past would exclusively represent government agencies and the few competitors in place, in other words, the only actors perceived as able to affect market dynamics. With the industry opening up to competition, new identity models emerge regarding domestic competitors, international competitors, key clients, and others. Thus, the set of identity models enlarges to incorporate new actors, guaranteeing a broader view of the market.

At a second level, macro-categories are then structured in taxonomies representing the identity of individual market actors. In other words, for each single category, actors which are perceived as similar in terms of specific attributes are grouped together. These are *micro-categories*, because actors pertaining to the same category share a higher number of attributes. Typical mental models of this kind represent strategic groups, market segments, key accounts (cf. Dickson, 1997: 93-99).

Figure 3.1 presents a taxonomy shared by managers of the Scottish knitwear sector reported by Porac et al. (1989), representing different product categories offered on the market.[2]

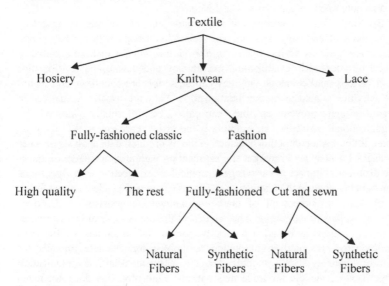

Source: Porac et al. (1989: 407).

Figure 3.1   A taxonomy of the Scottish knitwear sector

b) Descriptive models of market actors' identities provide a static picture of marketing knowledge which is made dynamic through the inclusion of causal relationships that link macro- and micro-categories. Such causal maps represent managerial perceptions regarding the responses of single market actors (or a group of actors) to other actors' behaviours. The maps of relationships can be thought of as the set of *descriptive and interpretative models* of reciprocal influences among market actors. A typical example of these models is elasticity to price or advertising of certain customer segments, which maps managerial perceptions regarding the sensitivity of customers to price or advertising changes.

c) The third component of marketing knowledge is constituted by models with which organizational members represent the company itself – its distinctive *identity* with respect to other market actors. The competitive positioning of the company as perceived by its members is a good example of these categories, as well as the distinctive values of the organization. These categories have a two-fold value: on one hand they highlight the position of the company in the taxonomies describing market actors' identity, and on the other they distinguish the company from the prototypical attributes of its category. The process this derives from can be defined *self-categorization* and its outcome is organizational *self-identity*.

d) Marketing knowledge is also made up of models representing behaviours of company personnel in their relationships with market actors. These are basically scripts regarding *behavioural models* that are adopted or could be adopted in establishing, maintaining and developing relationships with various market actors. Obviously these scripts are countless, and regard all activities related to market relationships. They are usually formalized in organizational procedures, but can also be informally adopted by organizational members. An example is the script representing actions to be taken following a competitor's launch of a new product: data analysis on sales to check for changes in market shares; meeting with area managers to assess the differential impact in various geographical areas, meeting with Operations personnel to analyse the distinctive attributes of the new product and so forth.

e) Another component of marketing knowledge consists of *decision-making models of marketing*. They represent the map of causal links between company actions and market actors' responses. These models are the ones traditionally presented in marketing textbooks: for example, models for market share analysis, models for the assessment of communication effectiveness, models for trade negotiations. Evidently, this does not mean that marketing knowledge is constituted only by models prescribed in the literature, but rather by any decision-making model that connects company actions to expected responses of market actors in the perceptions of company personnel.

f) While factors presented till now concern the content of marketing knowledge, this final fundamental component involves the *heuristics and biases* that influence both marketing decision-making processes and behaviours. These represent procedural knowledge and constitute the basic assumptions underlying organizational marketing decision-making and behaviours. By this I do not mean that one generic heuristic (for example representativeness) is a component of marketing knowledge rather than another. Instead, my belief is that given the existence of such thinking strategies, the particular forms they take on are part of an organization's marketing knowledge. For example, a company could make sales forecasts just by analysing key accounts' intentions to buy (representativeness), or exclusively by elaborating on its past market performance (illusion of control). Hence, even if two companies have the same data about the market, they will possess different marketing knowledge simply due to the different heuristics they put into place.[3]

Figure 3.2 summarizes the model of organizational marketing knowledge structures.

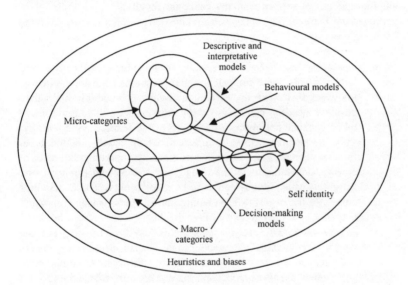

Figure 3.2   Marketing knowledge structures

3.1.2   The Distributed Component of Marketing Knowledge: Marketing Competences

A sizeable part of organizational marketing knowledge is situated in interactions of communities of practice which are involved in marketing activities within the organization, and secondly in interactions of company personnel with market actors. This is what I define as marketing competences.[4]

Categorizing all distributed marketing knowledge would require that we single out specific activities undertaken by a company in its interactions with the market. This would be an impossible task. However, there being a consensus on which processes a market oriented company effectively exercises (Kohli and Jaworski, 1990; Narver and Slater, 1990; Ruekert, 1992; Vorhies et al., 1999; Slater and Narver, 2000; Weerawardena, 2003; Hooley et al., 2005), a set of typical marketing competences can be identified. I argue that there are two different categories of marketing competences: procedural and behavioural. The difference between the two is not in their nature, since both are situated knowledge, but rather in their scope: *procedural marketing competences* refer to specific marketing processes of market oriented companies, while *behavioural marketing competences* refer to generic activities and can be applied to all marketing processes.

Procedural marketing competences are knowledge which is situated in the following processes:

- *marketing knowledge management.* In the language of Argyris and Schön (1978), these competences represent deutero-learning, that is, knowledge situated in learning activities. The ability to satisfy customer needs systematically and continuously resides, above all, in the organizational ability to learn from the market systematically. This, in keeping with the constructivist approach adopted here, requires competences in terms of making marketing knowledge emerge, generating new knowledge, and sharing and using it in all activities which impact on market relationships. These activities constitute the process of marketing knowledge management, which is the focus of the remainder of this book.

- *market relationship management.* In this case, I refer to competences which are embedded in interactions between organizational members and market actors – typically clients, distributors, competitors, government agencies, media and so on. This competence refers to all those activities essential to building, maintaining and developing relationships with market actors, relationships which obviously differ depending on the macro-categories of actors   (that is customers vs. competitors), and subsequent micro-categories (key customers vs. non-key customers). For customers, for example, reference can be made to that set of activities that is more often defined as customer relationship and loyalty management (Boulding et al., 2005; Payne and Frow, 2005; Ryals, 2005; Verhoef, 2003). Distributors call for trade marketing activities. As for competitors, instead, activities are to be found along the *continuum* that runs from pure competition to collaboration, and encompasses forms of co-opetition (Brandenburger and Nalebuff, 1996). Finally, building and maintaining relationships with mass media requires the development of integrated marketing communication activities (McArthur and Griffin, 1997; Low, 2000).

- *inter-departmental relationships management.* Reference, in this case, is made to interactions between organizational units involved in any process that contribute to customer value generation. Since specific marketing activities are exercised jointly by different departments (Krohmer et al., 2002), this knowledge is situated in the interactions between those departments. However, the interactions that result in competences do not refer to formal or spot interfaces (for example, inter-departmental communication via reports or documentation or meetings to pass on research data). Rather, marketing competences emerge when a set of joint actions between different departments are systematically carried out, giving rise to effective managerial practices.
- *innovation management.* A company that learns from the market is not only able to gather data from the market and shape organizational processes accordingly, but can also generate continuous innovation in its interactions with the market (Atuahene-Gima, 1996; Kahn, 2001; Im and Workman, 2004; Baker and Sinkula, 2005). Continuous innovation requires specialized knowledge as well as integrative knowledge (Henderson and Cockburn, 1994). Both the first and second forms of knowledge emerge from the interactions of various communities inside and outside the company and are fundamental for the innovation success (Lee and Cole, 2003).

Marketing behavioural competences, instead, are knowledge situated in:

- *listening activities.* This refers to activities involving the systematic monitoring of expectations, perceptions, preferences, behaviours, and satisfaction of actors with whom the organizational members interact. It means being on the same wavelength of such actors in order to focus attention on their explicit knowledge and also on tacit components, which can be observed in joint activities, so that an intersubjective view can emerge (Eden et al., 1981; Weick, 1993; Weick and Roberts, 1993). In addition, listening improves the quality of interrelations, augmenting effectiveness and performance of the group. Clearly, listening is the basis for both interactions with customers or other actors outside the company, and with organizational members with whom joint activities are carried out.
- *caring activities.* Though the term 'care' usually refers to customers (Johansson and Nonaka, 1996: Chapter 2), I believe that its meaning

can be extended to any set of interacting actors. Caring is a multi-dimensional activity that goes beyond satisfying expectations of people involved in interactions. It is a combination of respect, trust, commitment and attention which is focused not solely on the content of the activity but rather on the quality of the relationship (von Krogh, 1998). Enriching interaction through caring means paying attention to the human needs of the other person without taking into account hierarchical links or process relations. In this way, the interaction takes place on a higher level than a simply professional one.

- *educating activities.* As stated repeatedly, since interaction always generates knowledge, it requires co-specification of needs, co-determination of solutions, and therefore co-evolution of interacting actors. For each subject, therefore, it is necessary to educate the other parties involved through a recursive process of enactment, sensemaking, and retention which begins by trying out an initial direction, and then through listening, proceeding to a joint definition of the route to follow. Hence, this is a process in which all parties let their own knowledge emerge in the interaction.

Clearly, knowledge situated in the activities of listening, caring and education is transversal to that regarding procedural marketing competences. In fact, in marketing knowledge management, market relationship management, inter-departmental relationship management and innovation management, each actor involved must purposefully listen to others in order to see their point of view, care about others in order to enrich and enhance the relationship, and co-specify one's own expectations and needs together with those of other parties.

Equally evident is how marketing competences are closely interconnected. The company, seen as a socio-cognitive system, evolves if it is able to generate new knowledge systematically. In this sense, therefore, the first procedural competence – marketing knowledge management – is a sort of meta-competence, on which all others stand. At the same time, however, a company that wishes to learn from the market to attain sustainable competitive advantage must implement a marketing knowledge management process that engages the whole organization, and that also encompasses all actors considered critical for reaching that objective. In this sense, therefore, organizational members must be capable of interacting competently with one another and with market actors in order to reinforce and enrich market relationships and allow them to continually evolve. A considerable part of organizational marketing knowledge derives from these activities.

The following chapters are dedicated to an in-depth description of the marketing knowledge management process. Specifically, the next chapter addresses the marketing knowledge emersion process, the subsequent chapter to the marketing knowledge generation process, and the last to the dissemination of market information and its use in customer value-generating processes. Before detailing each single phase, though, I believe a premise would clarify certain basic assumptions of the model's design.

3.2 FROM A DESCRIPTIVE MODEL OF ORGANIZATIONAL MARKETING KNOWLEDGE TO A PRESCRIPTIVE MODEL OF MARKETING KNOWLEDGE MANAGEMENT

The objective of the remainder of this book is to propose a model for marketing knowledge management which separates the process into different phases and allows the recommendation of specific managerial tools for effectively and efficiently managing marketing knowledge. This proposal requires a transition from a descriptive approach to a prescriptive one that must be founded on clearly stated assumptions.

First of all, as often reiterated, a *systemic view of knowledge* is adopted. In epistemological terms, this means that the system itself is the perspective from which we observe organizational knowledge. It is the system, through self-observation, that makes potential organizational knowledge emerge. However, as the objective of this book is to propose a model for managing marketing knowledge, *the point of view adopted here is that of the manager charged with designing a marketing knowledge management process*. Therefore, to be even more precise, the viewpoint is that of a manager who must have a systemic view of marketing knowledge.[5] Assuming this systemic view means that organizational potential knowledge is constituted by knowledge localized in nodes of the network and by knowledge distributed in the connections, so that one complements but does not substitute the other.

The second consideration is that in the model, *organizational marketing knowledge is linked to specific activities*. This assumption has a dual meaning. From an epistemological standpoint, once again, it means that since a considerable part of organizational marketing knowledge consists in competences (that is knowledge situated in managerial practices), an attempt to make marketing knowledge emerge without focusing on specific activities would be contradictory. In methodological and operational terms, it is useless (if not impossible, given the web of interconnections) to make a company's 'entire' marketing knowledge emerge. Bringing to light this knowledge seems more sensible when the process is limited to specific activities which can be analysed with appropriate tools. Otherwise, enlarging the map would result in a very sketchy picture of the territory.

Thus, adopting a specific activity (or a series of activities that take place during a process) as the unit of analysis, the assumption is that we can come to an understanding of the entire system of marketing knowledge inherent to this activity in a holographic manner. For example, consider a company with a marketing culture characterized by intense aggressiveness toward competitors. In the language of the proposed model, this trait is a constituent element of the company's self-identity, as well as the perceptual biases of its managers, who tend to interpret competitors' actions as 'attacks' on their own market positions. Therefore, such a cultural trait does not refer to any specific activity in that it shapes all market behaviours of the company. The assumption is, in any case, that traces of this form of knowledge can be found in every marketing activity of the company. Analysis of these activities, then, would bring this knowledge to light. For example, in the case of defining pricing policy, there is a very good chance that managers set product prices according to a competition-based approach, with the goal of damaging the position of competitors, or even forcing them out of the market. In identifying the system of knowledge at the basis of price setting, the market aggressiveness trait will again come to the fore.

A further consideration has to do with *the issue of the boundaries of organizational marketing knowledge.* In fact, if a manager wishes to design a marketing knowledge management process, she/he must decide on the boundaries of the territory to be analysed. According to the perspective adopted here, if the viewpoint is that of the system, the difference between internal and external knowledge no longer exists. Hence, knowledge possessed by customers, distributors and partners proves to be an integral part of the knowledge repository of the company. In keeping with this assumption, to elicit marketing knowledge regarding a series of activities it would also be necessary to capture knowledge possessed by these actors. Theoretical consistency, however, contrasts with operational requirements, seeing as the difficulties with eliciting 'external' knowledge are much greater, and such a study often requires the use of different methodologies and techniques. For this reason, and because of managers' tendency to consider this part of knowledge external, in the proposed management model I consider *organizational marketing knowledge only that possessed by organizational members.* It is also assumed that knowledge of external actors becomes a part of a company's knowledge repository following a process of enactment. For this reason, such knowledge will be taken into consideration in the phase of marketing knowledge generation.

Lastly, since managing marketing knowledge is useful to organizational decision-making, it can be assumed that whatever the form, *the content of knowledge regards relationships between the company market behaviours and consequent responses from the market.* In this sense, therefore, the view of knowledge adopted here gives emphasis to purely cognitive as well as behavioural aspects. In fact, marketing knowledge available to a company in a specific time frame allows the company to exploit a set of potential market behaviours (cf. Huber, 1991), even though these are not necessarily 'actual' market behaviours. A marketing manager's knowledge of benefit segmentation, for instance, gives the company the chance to segment the market accordingly, despite the fact that at that very moment this is not the segmentation strategy being followed.

Also for the *structure and sequence of the phases that constitute the management model*, a brief description of the assumptions adopted may be helpful.

First of all, the model, as illustrated in Figure 3.3, is made up of three sequential phases: making marketing knowledge emerge, generating new knowledge, sharing and using this knowledge.

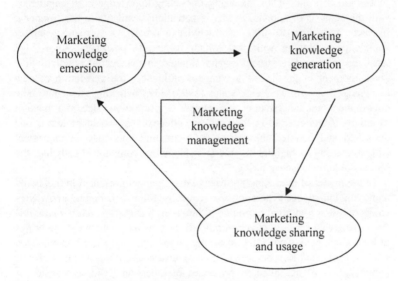

Figure 3.3   The model of marketing knowledge management

The adoption of a sequential structure is coherent with models of knowledge management proposed in the literature (cf. Nonaka, 1994; Leonard-Barton, 1995; Nonaka and Takeuchi, 1995; Davenport and Prusack, 1998). The distinguishing characteristic, however, is the emphasis placed on the different phases. In traditional models the phase that generally predominates is knowledge generation. In fact, it is a company's ability to do so systematically which is linked to the possibility of attaining sustainable competitive advantage. Emphasis on knowledge creation has not only met with enthusiasm among scholars, but has also concentrated the efforts of a considerable number of companies which have invested in knowledge management systems. In research done by Ruggles (1998) on different processes related to knowledge management in 431 European and American companies, processes rated as best performing regarded the generation of new knowledge. Interesting to note, as the author quite rightly emphasizes, is that despite being the top rated process, less than half the interviewees stated that they had achieved high performance in creating new knowledge, proof of the challenges this process entails. Given the prevalence of the generation phase, other typical stages in the process (dissemination, retention and utilization of knowledge) are assigned a supporting role. For this reason, most knowledge management models begin with the knowledge generation phase.

From what has been stated in previous chapters, it seems instead that the first phase of a model for managing marketing knowledge must commence with the analysis of knowledge that is potentially available to the company. In fact, according to the constructivist approach, a system generates knowledge beginning with that which it already possesses. Knowledge localized in cognitive structures and situated in managerial practices in a given moment in the life of a company influences the generation of new knowledge because, as Weick states (1995:133), 'believing is seeing'. The environment that the system enacts depends on prior knowledge, as a function of environments enacted in the past. So, effectiveness would be lost if one described and handled the process of marketing knowledge management without starting by highlighting the knowledge that company already has: the process of knowledge capturing.

In the model of marketing knowledge management presented in this book, marketing knowledge generation, consequently, follows marketing knowledge emersion. It is important to point out, however, that *there is often a very fine line between emersion and generation.* In fact, as the emersion phase brings to light a company's potential marketing knowledge, and since this emersion is often connected to processes of gaining awareness, the generation of new knowledge is often linked to processes of emersion. Simply consider a manager who, when reflecting on market share results obtained following a change in advertising strategies, formulates the hypothesis that these new methods enable the company to broaden the target market. As repeatedly stated by Schön (1983), reflection on a completed action and on an action being completed produce results which are difficult to differentiate.

As for the creation of new knowledge, the basic assumption of the model is that *generating marketing knowledge requires intention by the company.* By this, I do not deny that new knowledge can be created by chance. Nonetheless, as will be discussed later, either at a cognitive level or at a behavioural level, an effort (attention, reflection, or action) must necessarily be undertaken by the company. The theoretical justification for intentionality lies in the theory of self-regulatory cognitive systems. These systems, in fact, naturally tend toward homeostasis – they continue to confirm prior knowledge that produces expectations regarding the occurrence of action–result connections. Whether knowledge is observed at the level of an individual, a group or an entire organization, cognitive systems tend to keep their own reproduction mechanism stable, which is their basis of knowledge. Only effort made by the company, hence intention, will allow the introduction of disturbances within the system capable of driving the system from one model of equilibrium to another, generating new knowledge and making it evolve.

Secondly, *generating marketing knowledge is considered the change in potential marketing knowledge available to the company following a process of sensemaking.* This assumption, which concurs with Huber's position (1991) on organizational learning, reiterates the fact that organizational knowledge generates competitive advantage only if it translates into behaviours (Senge, 1990; Vicari and Troilo, 2000). At the same time, emphasis is placed on the fact that new experiences do not always necessarily generate immediate reflection, nor do new knowledge structures instantaneously induce new behaviours. However, if the potential of organizational behaviours is extended, both elements are capable of generating sustainable competitive advantage and should, consequently, be taken as new knowledge.

From this discussion, and from the descriptive model of marketing knowledge developed in this book, marketing knowledge generation can be attributed to changes in knowledge localized in cognitive structures, and to changes in knowledge situated in interactions – among components, and between components and market actors. In other words, the variation in knowledge of both individuals and groups, and of both structured and situated components, generates new marketing knowledge.

The last assumption at the basis of marketing knowledge generation, is that *there exists a difference between the concepts of data, information and knowledge.* These three concepts refer to the different forms that a signal associated with an environmental event can take on. Data represent the state of an event, and are therefore a characteristic of the event itself. As Vicari asserts (1991: 63), this does not mean that data are objective. They are, after all, collected by an actor, and the activity of data collection is marked by subjectivity as it involves the selection of the event to be analysed, the choice of the data gathering method, and so on. Information, instead, as Boisot suggests (1998: 12), is a relationship established between a subject and an event. In other words, it is data which are given form; meaning is associated with it from the individual point of view of the actor. Information is, therefore, data enriched by a system of meaning. Knowledge, on the other hand, is the integration of current information with previous information obtained by the actor. Hence, knowledge is organized information. The difference between these three concepts is a fundamental one since the generation of new knowledge involves a transition of the forms taken on by an event from one level to the others.

The third phase of the model deals with sharing and utilizing marketing knowledge. Stated another way, after making potential knowledge emerge, and generating new knowledge wherever possible, the company must work to guarantee that that knowledge is made available and is utilized by all those who make marketing decisions and carry out activities which impact market relationships. As it was stressed in the first chapter, in the debate on market orientation there is substantial consensus regarding the fact that a company can not be defined as market oriented unless it disseminates and utilizes information on at least two macro-categories of actors: customers and competitors (Shapiro, 1989; Kohli and Jaworski, 1990; Narver and Slater, 1990).

In Chapter 2, the ambiguity of the concept of sharing was debated, as well as the theoretical problems that arise from this concept. For this reason, it is necessary to clarify the use of this term. I consider *sharing as the distribution of data concerning marketing phenomena*, from those who have data to those who need it. In fact, according to the theoretical background espoused here neither knowledge nor information can be transferred, but only generated. What happens, then, is that the actor who has knowledge, in an attempt to transfer it to another actor, transforms it into data which are received by the other actor according to his/her schemas. Such a transfer, therefore, involves a transformation of the state of the knowledge, which reverts back to the form of data. Data will acquire the status of knowledge once again when the receiver assigns meaning to them and integrates them into his or her prior knowledge (cf. Hansen, 1999). Summing up, then, sharing requires a greater effort by the receiver than by the possessor of knowledge. With respect to the concept of knowledge transfer, which is the focus of a large part of knowledge management literature (cf. Davenport and Prusak, 1998: Chapter 5), the concept of sharing used here is intended in more restrictive terms: knowledge as such can not be transferred. The transfer of knowledge, instead, causes a disturbance for the receiving system, the effects of which depend more on it than on the possessor of knowledge.

In addition, as far as the use of knowledge is concerned, the position adopted here is that *to attain sustainable competitive advantage, a company must utilize marketing knowledge.* Generating knowledge which is not employed in marketing decisions and activities does not produce competitive advantage. To clarify this assumption further, it must first be said that the use that knowledge can have is not only instrumental, but also conceptual and symbolic (Menon and Varadarajan, 1992). Instrumental use is when knowledge is actually utilized in problem solving, decision-making, and interacting with the market. Conceptual use happens in cases where knowledge amplifies the set of potential knowledge of the company (for example its representations) but is not translated into behaviours. Symbolic use is when knowledge is utilized for the purpose of reassurance, to confirm previous hypotheses, to support one's own position, to legitimize the organization (Feldman and March, 1981). In all three cases one can refer to the use of knowledge, but the assumption made here is that only the first two can contribute to generating sustainable competitive advantage. In fact, if as stated in Chapter 1 market orientation contributes to improving organizational performance by increasing both innovativeness and learning capability, clearly it is not so much symbolic as instrumental and conceptual uses that impact these two factors.

Confirming this assertion, a study by Moorman (1995) proves that there is a positive relationship between the success of a new product and the use of both conceptual and instrumental knowledge. However, success is not influenced by simply acquiring or disseminating market information. In brief, if in managing marketing knowledge the company focuses exclusively on generating and sharing, there is no guarantee of an increase in the probability of attaining a competitive advantage, for which stimulating the use of marketing knowledge is also required.

An additional consideration, essential to the model design so as to render it more functional in managerial terms, is that *the organizational unit which possesses marketing knowledge is the Marketing Department (or its equivalent), while the units which must share and utilize this knowledge are all the other organizational departments.* In fact, if marketing knowledge is constituted by a set of representations and interactions, we can easily assume that this knowledge is possessed for the most part by those who are responsible for market interactions, that is members of the Marketing Department. Obviously, this assumption holds in most cases, both because representations are also widespread among members of other organizational units, and because, as often reiterated, a part of knowledge lies in interactions of Marketing with other departments. But since members of the Marketing Department are generally responsible for market relationships, and interaction that affects the market almost always involves marketing personnel – while not all members of other departments necessarily participate – we can assume that market representations of marketing personnel are more complex than those of other organizational units.

With these assumptions in mind, the next chapters are devoted to the description of every single phase of the marketing knowledge management process.

NOTES

1. This distinction is comparable to that between the espoused theory and the theory-in-use by Argyris and Schön (1978).
2. An extensive body of literature (Porac and Thomas, 1990; Reger, 1990a; de Chernatony et al., 1993; Reger and Huff, 1993; Day and Nedungadi, 1994; Hodgkinson and Johnson, 1994; Reger and Palmer, 1996; Clark and Montgomery, 1999; Rosa et al., 1999; Cillo and Troilo, 2002) confirms the tendency of managers to view industry structure in terms of competitive taxonomies.
3. Marketing researchers, however, have traditionally devoted very little attention to the basic assumptions that constitute organizational marketing knowledge, unlike strategic management scholars who have focused a great deal on analysing perceptions and strategic issues (Dutton and Duncan, 1987; Dutton and Jackson, 1987; Dutton et al., 1983; Dutton et al., 1989; Thomas and McDaniel, 1990; Dutton, 1993; Schneider, 1994).
4. Von Krogh and Roos (1996a) also arrive at a similar definition through empirical research aimed at identifying the concept of competence shared by a sampling of Scandinavian human resource managers.
5. An orthodox reading of the theory of autopoietic systems could contrast with this position, as such a literal interpretation negates the possibility that individuals who operate within the system can determine behaviours, and that, in the final analysis, there can be communication between these two levels. I believe these positions can be reconciled assuming that the designers of a knowledge management process only cause a disturbance for the system, the effects of which are not predictable in a linear sense, but are adaptable as the process is being set up and learning occurs.

4. The Emersion of Marketing Knowledge

4.1 THE OBJECTIVES OF THE MARKETING KNOWLEDGE EMERSION PROCESS

The process of marketing knowledge emersion is critical to identifying the scope, content and evolution of such knowledge. If the organizational knowledge repository is what determines its potential for achieving sustainable competitive advantage, then this advantage is dependent on three factors: the magnitude of the repository, the type of knowledge it is made up of, and its systematic renewal through the accumulation of new knowledge.

In this sense, therefore, the emersion of marketing knowledge is a crucial step in evaluating the potential for achieving competitive advantage. The following specific objectives can serve as guidelines for the emersion phase:

- to assess the magnitude of potential knowledge regarding one or more marketing activities;
- to verify the extent to which basic assumptions which guide marketing activities are shared;
- to evaluate the degree of change in the marketing knowledge repository;
- to detect possible rigidity within the system of knowledge;
- to transfer useful marketing information inside and outside the organization.

To assess the magnitude of potential knowledge regarding marketing activities or processes essentially means to ascertain what structural and situated components the actors can utilize in performing these activities. In other words, the aim is to discover what mental models actors use to represent activities, and which practices they utilize in performing these activities. The focus on magnitude derives from the assumption that the greater the knowledge potential, the more the organization is able to represent and effectively accomplish the activity in question. For example, the magnitude of marketing knowledge relative to a given market segment is constituted by the number and variety of:

- descriptive models (categories and taxonomies) of the identity of actors that constitute that segment, both those belonging to it (customers) and those relating with it (the company itself, competitors, distributors, and so on);
- interpretative models of relationships between these actors (for example the elasticity of different market segments to marketing mix variables);
- decision-making models that the company utilizes to build its positioning in the segment (for example how decisions are made on pricing, product range, and so on);
- decisional heuristics (for example systematic analysis of certain key customers as representative of the segment);
- relational competences (for example those involving customer care, competences of salespeople serving the segment, and so on).

The second objective centres on *the extent to which basic assumptions that guide marketing activities are shared.* In fact, there being a need for a dominant logic (Prahalad and Bettis, 1986), or a basic common view to avoid conflicting positions within the organization and to spark strong motivation to reach a goal, the company has to ascertain whether or not the people involved share common assumptions. For instance, say a company is about to design a new product for a market segment. In such a case, management could find out if members of the Marketing and Engineering departments have the same representation of the segment. If they have different ideas on which variables carry the most weight, the two departments will not be able to join forces and work together.

Also, the company may be interested in *evaluating the degree of change of its marketing knowledge*; that is, its own capacity to enrich the structural and situated components of this knowledge over time so as to evolve and maintain its competitive advantage. Referring again to the previous example, imagine that the company discovers major differences between the models that members of the two departments use to represent the market segment, and so decides to run a training programme to bring the knowledge repositories of the two groups into line. *Ex post*, it would be interesting to assess whether this alignment has actually come about in joint activities.

Closely linked to the preceding objective comes *detecting rigidity in the marketing knowledge system.* As numerous authors have pointed out, organizational knowledge can become fossilized, morphing into competence traps (Levitt and March, 1988), core rigidities (Leonard-Barton, 1992), or cognitive inertia (Reger and Palmer, 1996). This being the case, the company in our example would do well to heed Hamel and Prahalad's (1994) warning on the need to escape from the tyranny of served markets. Imagine that the company decided to start competing in another market segment, but found it could not duplicate the success it had in the first. The emersion of marketing knowledge used by managers could expose gaps caused by applying the same interpretative and decision-making models in the new market segment that are not effective at all here.

The final objective is *to transfer marketing information* inside and outside of the organization. To make this transfer possible, the company must first gain awareness of the marketing knowledge available to it, and then be able to assess the extent to which this knowledge can be codified, so as to implement the most effective methods to make it emerge. To conclude the example, imagine that the company decided to involve some key customers from the segment in a joint new product development process. To do so, a number of development-related competences need to be shared with these clients. Making these competences emerge, then, is the prerequisite for being able to transfer them.

In the description of the objectives that guide the process of marketing knowledge emersion, it is taken for granted that this emersion is possible and non-problematic. In actual fact, the emersion phase is a formidable one precisely because it is very difficult to make some knowledge emerge due to its particular configuration. This is the topic of the next section.

4.2 THE CONFIGURATION OF EMERGING MARKETING KNOWLEDGE

To make marketing knowledge emerge, the organization must observe itself: the system has to reflect on itself and gain awareness of the marketing knowledge potentially available to it.[1] At first, one might think that all this process requires is running some interviews with the actors involved in performing the activities in question in order to make the knowledge explicit. In actual fact, however, the marketing knowledge emersion phase proves to be extremely challenging because, in Polanyi's words (1967: 4), 'We know more than we can tell'.

Put another way, marketing knowledge emersion would be a simple process if one adopted a purely cognitivist view of knowledge. But the limitations of this view, described in Chapter 2, are exactly what greatly reduce this simplicity. It is the tacit, implicit, embedded, embodied nature of knowledge[2] which makes marketing knowledge emersion a process that requires a great deal of care and attention in the use of self-observation techniques.

To have a better understanding of the challenges a company must overcome, the taxonomy proposed by Winter (1987) can be used in describing the various types of knowledge-based assets (Figure 4.1).

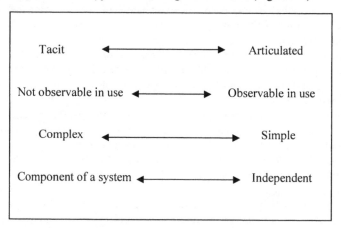

Source: Adapted from Winter (1987: 170).

Figure 4.1   A taxonomy of properties of knowledge assets

Winter points out how different knowledge assets are characterized by their differing positions with respect to certain properties placed along a *continuum*. The farther left an asset is positioned on the continuum, the less transferable it is among actors inside and outside the organization. The most important distinguishing feature of assets is *tacitness*; on the opposite end of the spectrum we find those which can be articulated. Winter accentuates the fact that many assets are based on actors' idiosyncratic knowledge, so making such assets explicit is no easy task. On the other hand, there are assets based on knowledge that can be fully articulated, in which case actors are able to express this knowledge and communicate it to others. Similar to the tacit dimension, the author also refers to the characteristic of observability during use. With this property, Winter draws a distinction between those assets based on knowledge that can be revealed through observation of the asset itself (for example, the technology that characterizes a new product can be discovered through reverse engineering) and those for which even observation during use can not give relevant clues. Thirdly, according to Winter some knowledge is connoted by a sizeable amount of information, and as such is complex; other knowledge instead has less constituent information.

In a very similar way, the last property Winter describes is belonging to a system of knowledge as opposed to being independent from the knowledge base of the asset. The first dimension of the property implies that transferring the asset means being able to transfer the entire system of knowledge to which it belongs, while in the opposite case it would be sufficient to transfer the knowledge base alone. Assets based on knowledge which is tacit, difficult to observe, complex, and slotted into a system are hard to transfer because of the difficulty in articulating the set of action–result relationships that this knowledge denotes. Since this set of relationships is the very heart of organizational knowledge as defined in this book, it is easy to see how the existence of knowledge characterized by these properties makes the emersion process extremely problematic.

In summary, Winter's proposition taken together with Polanyi's words calls attention to the fact that there are essentially three types of barriers to overcome in the phase of marketing knowledge emersion:

- communicability;
- context dependency;
- consciousness.

The *barrier of communicability* can essentially be traced to the fact that a substantial part of knowledge that individuals, groups or organizations consciously learn over time is retained in memory and utilized automatically. Put another way, eventually some knowledge is transformed into routines, as Nelson and Winter point out (1982). So, when facing a problem that has already come up in the past, actors immediately apply the solution retained in their memory. The more routinized the knowledge, the harder it is for the actor to communicate it, that is codify and transfer it to another. What is more, actors often experience complex problems which they learn to associate with complex problem-solving methods, but this relationship is not easily expressed by means of verbal language.

As clearly demonstrated in studies on managerial cognition, often managers are surprised by the complexity of their cognitive maps, because the decisions in which they apply their knowledge constitute an enormous reduction in complexity. Moreover, at a collective level, very often knowledge becomes common sense (Boisot, 1987). In other words, this knowledge is shared inside the group or organization, but it is hard to make the network of connections among the nodes that constitute this knowledge emerge. Basically, it is as if individuals or organizations internalize action–result relationships, but at the same time forget the causes of those relationships. Put another way, these actors apply know-*how* without knowing *why*.

Secondly, evidence that some knowledge is distributed in the relationships between actors and not necessarily retained in individual memory proves that a barrier may arise because of *the strong contextual nature of knowledge*, even where communicability poses no problem. Knowledge, in other words, is related to an activity that is made up of a system that connects people, technologies, artefacts and symbols. In this case knowledge cannot be de-contextualized without losing pieces of it. For example, consider a company that wants to duplicate the knowledge of a new product development team made up of personnel from Marketing and Research & Development, which has turned out to be a huge success. It is possible to discover and effectively transfer managerial models utilized in the development phase by each department, but it is tremendously complicated to figure out and articulate what practices the group uses when running creative meetings, or the informal roles that create an atmosphere which inspires new ideas, and so forth. Therefore, context-dependency barriers come up because it is hard to duplicate practices accumulated during socialization processes (Nonaka, 1991; 1994; Nonaka and Takeuchi, 1995), since it is in socialization that a part of knowledge lies.[3]

For some time now these first two barriers have captured the attention of researchers, and much has been written about them. On the contrary, very little emphasis has been placed on the last, the *barrier created by unconsciousness*, with which some knowledge is acquired and utilized. In fact, most of the scholarly debate on knowledge has centred on the problem of codifying and then communicating portions of knowledge. Generally, and often implicitly, the assumption is that people who possess knowledge are aware they possess it, so the challenge for the company is simply to identify the most effective techniques for making this knowledge explicit, and then to convert it from individual to organizational knowledge.

However, as Nelson and Winter have already pointed out, tacit knowledge is often 'not consciously known' (1982: 134). Members of an organization (both individually and as a group) acquire knowledge not only through a process of reflection on and abstraction from life experiences, so as to highlight action–result relationships, but also by means of a process that takes place at a sub-conscious or unconscious (that is implicit) level. As clearly explained by Sparrow (1998: 185), these processes can shed light on the difference between skills (the routines mentioned previously) and what the author calls *tacit feels*: 'Skills are acquired consciously but proceduralized to a point where information is no longer represented declaratively, and is thus difficult to articulate. Tacit feel is defined as mental material that is represented non-declaratively, but has never been conscious. It was acquired implicitly.'

The distinction drawn by Sparrow brings a historically neglected issue back into the heart of the debate on managerial knowledge. If the study of knowledge and learning implies the use of theories and models which derive from psychology, then we cannot forget that individual learning, in psychology, is traced both to explicit learning (that is fruit of reflection on experience by the actor), and implicit learning (that is rooted in the subconscious and the unconscious levels of the individual). This is linked directly to people's experiences and influenced by their emotional state, as well as positive reinforcement and negative consequences. It is easy to see how in the marketing knowledge emersion phase, the unconscious component of individual and group knowledge plays a vital role. What is more, eliciting and capturing this component can give rise to serious problems.

In conclusion, the emersion phase is when the organization gains awareness of marketing knowledge potentially usable and actually utilized in activities and processes that impact on market relationships. This knowledge is both localized in mental models of individuals and in those shared by work groups inside the organization, and is also situated in individual and group competences (Figure 4.2).

	Individual	Collective
Localized	Individual marketing mental models	Shared marketing mental models
Distributed	Individual marketing competencies	Organizational marketing competencies

Figure 4.2   Different configurations of organizational marketing knowledge

The process of marketing knowledge emersion consists in selecting and applying methodologies and techniques which are suited to the specific configurations of marketing knowledge, so as to overcome the barriers described. These methods, then, must take into account the differing degrees of communicability, context dependency and consciousness which characterize marketing knowledge, bearing in mind that the total emersion of the entire knowledge is still a decidedly difficult task, if not impossible in extreme cases.

The next section gives an in-depth description of the most appropriate methodologies for capturing the different types of marketing knowledge available to an organization.

4.3 METHODOLOGIES FOR MARKETING KNOWLEDGE CAPTURING

Numerous methodologies can be used to foster the emersion of marketing knowledge. For this reason it is crucial that when choosing a methodology, managers take into account the consistency between the configuration of the specific region of the knowledge they want to elicit, and the characteristics of the specific methodology. Naturally, since portions of knowledge utilized in marketing activities are closely interrelated, it is possible to come up with a rich description of those portions if various methods and techniques are used in a complementary way.

In order to come up with a categorization, it is useful to distinguish between methodologies on the basis of their effectiveness in overcoming barriers of communicability, context dependency and consciousness.

Communicability of marketing knowledge is facilitated in two basic ways: by articulating it into a number of components, and by codifying it using codes shared by actors other than those who possess it (for example Zollo and Winter, 2002). As stated before, seeing as the content of knowledge can be traced back to a number of action–result relationships, *articulating* a portion of knowledge enables us to reconstruct the map of the network of connections that knowledge is made up of, so it can be reduced into a set of simpler relationships.

For example, a marketing manager's knowledge may consist of a descriptive mental model, based on 'market sensibility' accumulated over the years, which can be summarized as follows: 'Market demand increases if the company increases the price of its products'. Now, this concept might seem very idiosyncratic and difficult to fathom for a colleague in Operations who has been trained to think in terms of a conflicting model: 'We need to systematically reduce costs because that way we can lower our prices and improve our competitiveness'. If the model is broken down into a series of cause–effect relationships, such as: 'Raising prices triggers customers' perception of higher quality, and this in turn generates higher sales volume', the model becomes more communicable even to those who do not have firsthand experience of market relationships.

Secondly, communicability is improved if marketing knowledge is *codified*. This means that it is 'translated' into constructs (that is codes) which function as data economizers (Boisot, 1998: 45), making knowledge content more comprehensible (Cowan and Foray, 1997). Codes serve as vehicles for information, and make the communication process more efficient and effective. For example, describing a market segment in terms of traits such as socio-demographics, behaviours, cultural characteristics and values makes communicating about that segment quite tiresome. Instead, by utilizing the category 'lifestyle', and labelling each type of lifestyle, we can slot a customer into a segment more simply and rapidly.

So, *methodologies that encourage the articulation and codification of marketing knowledge allow the company to overcome barriers to communicability and to make marketing knowledge localized in individual and collective mental models emerge.*

As for the *context dependency* of marketing knowledge, context can be determined by a set of technologies, norms, symbols and cultural elements with which organizational members usually interact. An example is a marketing manager's competence in evaluating the market potential for a new product, which derives from the ability to analyse market test results and the capacity to use a software that generates sales forecasts based on these results.

The context of marketing knowledge can also be shaped by other members of the organization, giving rise to knowledge situated in interactions among them. This is the case, for instance, when one considers competences of a cross-functional new product development team. In both circumstances it is extremely complicated for the actors involved to realize how relevant context actually is. To be more specific, it is difficult to give a detailed description of roles, habits, customs and routines which make up context and which come into play both at an individual and group level when activities are carried out. To capture this knowledge, the context must be allowed to emerge, so as to bring to light its formative influence. Storytelling, involving key episodes in individual learning of a specific competence, observation of work habits of an individual or a group within the organization, narratives of critical events in the evolution of a group – these all provide a representation of the co-evolution of actors with the context and in the context of performing an activity.

In conclusion, *methodologies that highlight the role of interactions in generating marketing knowledge allow companies to overcome barriers of context dependency, and to make individual and group marketing competences emerge.*

As far as the last barrier – *consciousness* – is concerned, Schön's (1983: 243) comments are extremely insightful:

Managers do reflect-in-action, but they seldom reflect on their reflection-in-action. Hence this crucially important dimension of their art tends to remain private and inaccessible to others. Moreover, because awareness of one's intuitive thinking usually grows out of practice in articulating it to others, managers often have little access to their own reflection-in-action.

It is exactly this tendency not to reflect during an action nor on a finished action (often because there are organizational mechanisms that do not encourage such reflection) that makes internalization of some marketing knowledge a phenomenon that is as tacit as it is inaccessible.

Schön suggests that the emersion of the unconscious part of managerial knowledge is favoured by the habit of 'conversing with the situation'; in other words, questioning oneself during an activity and after it is completed:

> on the norms and tacit considerations that are at the basis of an opinion, or on the strategies and theories implicit in a certain type of behavior. [The manager] can reflect on the 'feeling' for a situation that led her to adopt a particular line of action, on the way she structured the problem that she is trying to resolve, or on the role that she has constructed for herself in the sphere of a broader institutional context (1983: 62).

In this sense, therefore, by reflecting on one's own actions a person can make sense of them retrospectively (Weick, 1979) and become aware of action–result relationships. Even though Schön is interested in individual knowledge in particular, his propositions can easily be extended to work groups. In fact, reflecting during an action is a method that can highlight divergent positions based on different assumptions, or create collective meaning through joint reflection by members of the group.

Summing up, then, *methodologies that encourage reflection on activities while they are being carried out or when they are completed permit companies to overcome barriers of consciousness and make individual and group marketing competences emerge.*

After having delineated the properties needed to overcome different barriers, the most useful methods for the emersion of organizational marketing knowledge will be described. The principal characteristics and configurations of marketing knowledge for which each methodology is most appropriate will be indicated.

What should be mentioned beforehand, however, is that while some can be utilized directly by managers who have the knowledge in question (either individually or as a group) with an eye to self-management, most require intervention by an external actor who gathers and interprets data on emerging knowledge.

4.3.1 The Repertory Grid Technique

The repertory grid is a technique proposed by Kelly (1955) with the aim of making his personal construct theory operative. Very briefly, according to this theory every individual represents the surrounding reality by means of a series of interconnected elements which serve to construct theories on why things happen. Kelly's objective was to design a technique that would avoid imposing researchers' pre-defined schemas on respondents, and instead elicit the constructs they actually utilized. The technique is essentially based on three phases: defining constituent elements of a representation; eliciting constructs (that is dimensions by which elements are associated with one another); and revealing perceptions of elements with respect to constructs. This final phase culminates in the construction of a grid representing the personal theory of the actor.

The first phase is usually implemented through semi-structured interviews in which respondents are asked to describe the fundamental elements of the phenomenon being studied. For the second phase a number of variants have been proposed (Fransella and Bannister, 1977; Reger, 1990b). Generally elements are written on cards and respondents are encouraged to express an opinion on the degree of similarity/dissimilarity of these items. Variations may involve the number of alternatives respondents must rank[4] and the sequence of comparisons (rotating all the elements in every evaluation, or changing the order of elements). In the third phase a grid is set up highlighting what specific constructs best represent single elements.

From this brief description it is clear that the *repertory grid technique is useful for the emersion of marketing knowledge localized in individual and group mental models*. In fact, the technique proves to be a very powerful one in bringing to light representative categories of market phenomena, and hence mental models that represent customers, competitors and other market actors.

A valuable example of this technique for marketing knowledge emersion can be found in a study by Reger (1990a) on competitive positioning in Chicago's banking industry. The research objective was to reconstruct the grid of competitors' positioning by comparing the perceptions of a number of bank managers who competed on that market. In this case the elements were single competitors, the constructs were the distinctive positioning variables, and the grid provided a map of positioning. The constructs were elicited by asking each respondent to group together or divide up competitors by comparing them in sets of three.

For our purposes, the results of the study are also interesting. First of all, very few constructs were shared among managers for the representation of positioning, confirming that they each had a highly idiosyncratic and subjective view of the competitive arena. Secondly, the constructs tended to be quite different from those proposed in the literature, supporting the theory that in order to make organizational marketing knowledge emerge, it is more appropriate to adopt the point of view of the organization instead of attempting to impose pre-determined models.

4.3.2   Q-methodologies

This label is given to a number of methods and techniques all having the common goal of soliciting respondents to make sense of events and situations they are involved in, making explicit their 'inner worlds'. Though often such practices have different characteristics, all make use of *Q-sorting*. With this technique, respondents are asked to sort through a series of statements, sentences, descriptions of events or viewpoints, and then select and rank the ones that best represent their view of reality or their way of performing activities.

The original Q-methodology was proposed by Stephenson (1935) as a psychometric method for analysing individual behaviour. In this tradition, therefore, the aim of the methodology is to quantitatively measure the distance between positions of different actors questioned (cf. McKeown and Thomas, 1988). These positions are often proposed to respondents by researchers on the basis of prior analysis of documents or secondary data.

In managerial studies, instead, a more qualitative approach prevails for the purpose of encouraging actors to reflect on their actions. The most commonly used method is called the *Self-Q* because it prompts participants to ask themselves about their experiences. It was proposed by Bougon (1983), who clearly underscores its specificity (Bougon et al., 1990: 328): 'Self-Q rests on the more productive principle: *How do I know what I think until I see what I ask myself?*'

With *Self-Q*, in an initial interview the respondent is encouraged to reflect on the activity being studied, so as to reveal underlying models. In successive interviews (usually two) sorting is done: the interviewee is asked to evaluate knowledge nodes in order of importance. Relationships between them are highlighted, so as to come up with a representation of the knowledge the actor brings into play during the activity in question.

From this description, it is clear that *Q-methodologies constitute a set of methods which are especially useful for the emersion of implicit and explicit marketing knowledge localized in individual and group mental models.*

An interesting application of the methodology is described by Bougon and Komocar (1990). The aim of their study is to highlight the presence of loops in managers' representations of reality, and to verify how change in a system (hence in a company's strategy) necessarily entails intervention on the knowledge of the system. The authors utilize the *Self-Q* to construct a congregated cognitive map of managers in the organization being studied, showing how change calls for intervention on the loops themselves more than on the nodes.

4.3.3 The Biographical Method

The objective of the biographical method is to identify ways in which an individual personally represents reality, acting on reality itself. The focus of study is the cognitive biography of the individual, defined as 'the (multi-faceted) identity of our mind that surfaces when we question ourselves, or when we are questioned, about this identity' (Demetrio, 1994: 211; my translation).

The basic assumption of the biographical method is that knowledge is accumulated not only through cognitive mechanisms and operations, but also on the basis of influential factors which may be affective, emotive, or sensorial.[5] Techniques utilized with this method tend to make the style with which individuals acquired their knowledge emerge. This way, particular situations that hinder or enhance learning come to light.

As Demetrio stresses (1994: 200), what these techniques have in common is the special attention given to 'life stories', experiences the person has had during times of learning (a characteristic very similar to storytelling, detailed further on). Also, a series of stimuli is used that allows individuals to distance themselves and then re-involve themselves – that is, to gain awareness of the elements that make up their own history and mental models, and to utilize them in further cognitive experimentation. Generally, data-gathering techniques are the in-depth interview and diaries for self-observation, both focusing on the specific activities which are the object of the knowledge emersion process.

The biographical method, therefore, proves particularly useful for the emersion of marketing knowledge localized in individual mental models, and specifically in heuristics and biases that connote these models.

4.3.4 Cognitive Maps

Cognitive maps are representations of the knowledge structures of an individual or a group.[6] They allow managers to identify the concepts that actors use to represent reality and phenomena that they have knowledge of, and the relationships between these concepts.

The methodologies for constructing a cognitive map are numerous[7] but all follow a series of specific steps: producing 'cognitive material', codifying that material, defining the relationships between concepts. The cognitive material utilized is usually verbal. In substance, drawing up a cognitive map means analysing the contents of a text; this is why both the repertory grid[8] and Q-methodologies are often utilized.

The most common data-gathering technique is the semi-structured individual or group interview, but cognitive maps can also be constructed on the basis of documents, for example company reports or autobiographical diaries mentioned previously. The second phase in constructing a map – codifying material – is done by selecting portions of text which have some functional aspect in common with respect to the type and purpose of the map. For example, for a map meant to represent perceptions of the degree of collaboration of distributors, one would choose categories that actors utilize to group together or distinguish between various distributors who operate in the industry based on the actors' concept of collaboration. In the final phase, relationships perceived between identified and codified elements are reconstructed. This is done either by directly asking actors to point out these connections, or by analysing opinions given by actors on the topics being studied. As already mentioned, there can be many kinds of relationships, from denotation or connotation to membership in a category to simple or weighted causation.

Collective cognitive maps can be constructed in two different ways: either by drawing up individual maps first and then aggregating them or directly drawing up a collective map, gathering data from the group and not from individuals. Clearly in the second case difficulties arise due to the need to obtain a consensus both on the nodes and on the relationships of the map. Often the interpretation of the person who constructed the map is extremely insightful.

Summing up, then, *cognitive maps prove very useful for the emersion of explicit individual or group marketing knowledge localized in mental models.* On the contrary, maps are not a valid tool in cases where we want to elicit knowledge situated in interactions, or unconscious knowledge.

Beyond the examples given in sections 2.2 and 2.4, two more works can be cited on the application of cognitive maps in capturing knowledge. The first is a study by Cillo and myself (2002) based on in-depth interviews with a number of key actors. We show how in verifying the existence of an industrial district (in this case the production of songs in the Neapolitan language), knowledge shared by the actors contributes to the identification of the boundaries of the district itself. Our proposition is that in order for a district to be recognized as such, it is not enough that collaborative relationships exist among the actors throughout the production process; these actors must also see themselves as a district. In other words, it is necessary that in their system of knowledge they possess a series of action–result links that make the substance of the collaborative relationships between actors in the district emerge, and that this knowledge impels them to behave in a collaborative way.

A second noteworthy study is by Johnson et al. (1998). These authors, again utilizing semi-structured interviews, analyse the degree of shared managerial representations of competitors in the automobile industry. They also examine the influence of two factors on the degree of shared representations: there is only a moderate degree of shared representations among managers within the same company, while very different perceptions come to the fore among those who hold the same position in different companies.

4.3.5   Storytelling

The storytelling methodology is based on the assumption that the perception of phenomena by an individual and the social construction of reality by a group happen in a narrative way. What is meant by this is that individual or collective experience is given meaning by interpreting a set of events through piecing together stories (Rosa and Spanjol, 2005).

With respect to a simple, linear description of a phenomenon or a series of phenomena, a story represents a much richer and complex way of sensemaking. Storytelling, in fact, is a framework within which equivocal events are interpreted, events are generally interconnected toward well-defined ends, and a diachronic and evolutionary sense is given to phenomena. In this way action–result connections are reinforced. Moreover, in the case of collective storytelling, the events marking the evolution of joint activity are positioned on different levels of relevance and coloured with different shades of interpretation.

In operational terms, a story is told individually or collectively, beginning with a series of events or situations that the narrator considers key (generally defined as 'themes') regarding the activity in question. On the basis of these themes the overall flow of events is constructed. So usually there is no explicit reference to the knowledge that comes into play; instead it comes to light after interpreting the themes and the stories as a whole.

From this description, clearly *storytelling is a useful methodology for the emersion of marketing knowledge – especially implicit – which is individual or collective and distributed in interactions.*

An example of the application of this method is provided in a study conducted by Boyce (1995) on the construction of fundamental values (in the language used in this book, descriptive models of identity) and how these values are shared in a moment of transition in a non-profit religious organization. The author utilizes two 'storytelling events' which each last four hours. During this time some people in the association (members and managers) are encouraged to narrate a series of stories about the organization, first individually and then as a group. Some of these stories are then selected as exemplary of the values on which the organization was founded, and compared to those that top managers chose. Results of the study show that, in that moment of transition, there is a clean break between knowledge systems used by top management in redefining strategies and those utilized by members of the organization in daily activities.

The *critical incident technique* can also be considered part of the storytelling methodology, as it is based on the same assumptions and narrative data-gathering techniques. This technique differs from orthodox storytelling in that the stories only recount incidents, that is, events which in the perception of the narrators did not match with expectations or the normal flow of events. In this case, therefore, the system of knowledge to be captured is limited to events that are the exceptions to the norm in the context of an activity or a series of activities.

4.3.6 – The Workshop

In implementing this method, the group being studied is asked to reflect on the activities where their marketing knowledge is applied, so as to gain awareness of it. The objective is not necessarily to reach a group consensus, unless this is actually the purpose of the emersion phase.

In a workshop, the focus group technique is used, where participants discuss various topics proposed by a moderator. The role of the moderator is to stimulate the debate so that the system of knowledge associated with the activities in question emerges.

The unit of analysis of the workshop is two-fold. On one hand there is the single participant with whom the group interacts to stimulate reflection, making the assumptions, prejudices and idiosyncratic viewpoints unique to that person emerge. On the other hand, however, there is also the group as a whole which (as a unit in and of itself) reflects on being a group and on how it acts as a group, shedding light on joint actions, the meaning assigned to them, and the ends which emerge.

In conclusion, *the workshop method proves very useful in the emersion of implicit marketing knowledge, situated in the interactions between single individuals and the context, and in interactions among members of the group itself.*

Boisot (1998: Chapter 10), in his study of knowledge underlying the operations of two English companies, provides an interesting example of the application of the workshop method. For each organization, the author plays the role of moderator in a two-day workshop with the goal of arriving at a map of the knowledge system utilized by the two companies. With the help of a groupware system, managers are asked to identify the key competences at the basis of Operations, and to evaluate each one, drawing distinctions in terms of degree of codification, dissemination within the organization, and impact on performance. Results show that managers perceive the importance – indeed, the very existence – of differing competences. In addition, a misalignment also surfaces between the system of knowledge described as distinctive to the company in official internal communications, and that perceived by its managers. This shows little awareness, both on an individual and collective level, of available knowledge.

4.3.7 Simulations

Simulations reproduce the activities being studied in a sort of laboratory. Participants are asked, individually and as a group, to act 'as if' they actually had to perform these activities. This way, they put their knowledge into play when carrying out the tasks at hand.

As in any experimental situation, participants know they find themselves in a pseudo-reality, so there is no guarantee that they will not behave in an opportunistic way, or simply will neglect to tap into all their competences. However, the setting of the simulation is very similar to reality, hence without overt intrusion, both individual and joint action can be observed firsthand.

The most commonly utilized techniques are *role playing* and the *business game*. As for the first, participants are asked to act 'as if' they held a certain role, either their actual position or a different one: each case provides different indications. The former gives evidence of the system of knowledge habitually brought into play by the actor or the group (depending on the unit of analysis). In the latter, instead, we gain fascinating insight on the effects of the recombination of the actor's (or group's) knowledge of carrying out interrelated operations and performing activities following role-swapping.

The business game, on the other hand, usually involves a group of individuals acting 'as if' they were a decision-making body inside the company. Contrary to role playing, the organizational choices regarding the functioning of the group (dividing up roles and responsibilities, defining operative processes, and so on) become a dependent variable of analysis, so that related group competences can emerge.

Consequently, *simulations provide a useful contribution for the emersion of situated collective marketing knowledge, with particular emphasis on implicit knowledge.*

In this regard, Clark and Montgomery (1999) utilize the business game to identify the system of knowledge regarding a competitive arena. Using Markstrat2, the authors analyse the choices made during a business game to understand how the groups (made up of students and managers) select the companies to compete with directly. The results obtained in this study highlight how groups make use of the variables 'firm size', 'success', and 'aggressive behaviour' with reference to the other companies in the industry in identifying competitors.

4.3.8   Protocol Analysis

This methodology too can be considered simulative because it is based on an analysis of performing an activity to make the underlying knowledge emerge. I prefer to mention it separately because there are some peculiarities in this method that make it suitable for specific situations (Ericsson and Simon, 1980; 1993). First of all, typically the unit of analysis is the individual rather than the group. Secondly, an individual is asked to carry out an activity, applying two techniques which are distinctive to this method: *talk-aloud* and *think-aloud*.

With the first, the person is encouraged to verbally describe all the operations undertaken to complete the activity, in other words, to say out loud everything that she/he would say to her/himself. With think-aloud, the person is asked to verbalize anything that comes to mind while performing the activity, thus providing information not only on the contents of the cognitive process but also on the process itself.

By analysing protocols, that is reports on the verbalization of the activity, researchers can discern both cognitive and emotional aspects which come into play while a task is being performed. The basic assumption of this method is that the individual, in the verbalization stemming from the two techniques described above, can actually express the wealth of connections that constitute her/his system of knowledge, overcoming perception filters that generally inhibit such expression.

From the description of the methodology, one can conclude that *protocol analysis proves useful for the emersion of implicit and explicit individual marketing knowledge, both that localized in mental models and distributed in the interactions of the individual with the context.*

4.3.9   Script Analysis

This method, like the previous two, is characterized by limited intrusiveness of the researcher in relation to the actors whose knowledge is to be captured. The unit of analysis is typically the individual, who is observed while carrying out tasks linked to the activity being studied. Since the actor knows she/he is being observed, here too there are limitations regarding over-accomplishment or possible lack of sincerity.

The purpose of this method is to reconstruct the sequence of operations which constitute the actor's knowledge structures, and to analyse them to discover the underlying system of knowledge.

In addition, script analysis enables researchers to determine whether knowledge is applied effectively, if there are highly idiosyncratic regions of knowledge that could be socialized with other members of the organization, and if the knowledge utilized is integrated or could be integrated with other systems of knowledge.

Though scripts are knowledge structures, it is extremely difficult for the person who possesses a script to articulate it, since the vignettes that make up a script almost always represent interactions with contexts, constituting a system of knowledge which usually exceeds the actor's capacity for verbalization.

Hence, in this sense, *script analysis enables individual knowledge to emerge – that implicit or explicit marketing knowledge which is situated in individual/context interactions.*

An interesting application of script analysis is described in Pentland and Rueter's work (1994). They study routines of employees in the customer service centre of a software maker. The authors' hypothesis is that underneath routines (that is scripts), one can find grammars of action. In other words, though performing tasks that seem quite varied and variable over time, individuals have a set of rules that work like a grammar for a language system. The authors, observing these operators at work, break down activities into a series of micro-activities, and categorize them according to a system of codes. An analysis of the connections between the codified operations makes the grammars of action emerge.

The results show that scripts are shared to a considerable extent by operators. In addition, (and extremely interesting for the organization) these scripts allow employees to act on exceptions that come up, correcting them when they bring about inefficiencies, or exploiting them when they open the way for creativity in performing a task.

4.3.10 Ethnomethodologies

Ethnomethodologies are imported from cultural anthropology. Their fundamental premise is that 'people within a culture have procedures for making sense' (Feldman, 1995: 8). In fact, the object of analysis is precisely that set of verbal and behavioural mechanisms with which a group of people socially make sense of phenomena. The most common among ethnographic methodologies is *participant observation* (Jorgensen, 1989).

The basic assumption of this group of methodologies is that to understand the sense attributed by a group of individuals to a series of events or activities (and the processes of sensemaking utilized), we must first embrace the viewpoint of these individuals. To do so it is not possible to act from outside the group; one must live the same experiences. This involves firsthand experience of activities while they are being carried out.

The originality of the methodology lies in the absence of temporal separation between the moment an activity is performed and the moment data are gathered. In fact, data are collected while the events producing this data are unfolding.

Clearly, in this way all filters of selective perception, distortion and retention of the respondent are overcome, barriers which arise whenever there is a lapse between these two points in time. By the same token, it is also true that the marketing knowledge emersion phase is greatly influenced by the interpretation of the observer, because those who possess knowledge are not directly asked to express themselves, but rather are observed while they actually carry out their activities.[9]

To sum up, then, *ethnomethodologies are an effective method especially for the emersion of implicit and explicit marketing knowledge situated in interactions between actors.*

The studies on managerial practices described in section 2.3.2 are fascinating examples of the application of ethnographic methodologies. These studies, carried out through participant observation, demonstrate how knowledge situated in interactions between a group of members of an organization produces extremely effective performance. Also, the creative role of groups, with respect to individuals, in the production of knowledge is reconfirmed.

The methodologies described in this section are all suitable for making organizational marketing knowledge emerge. In conclusion, it is worthwhile to recap on two aspects that people responsible for managing the marketing knowledge capturing phase should fully understand.

The first is that each of the methodologies has a preferential field of application and is therefore particularly suitable for the emersion of certain configurations of marketing knowledge and not others. These areas of preference were pointed out in the description of each methodology, and with the help of an adaptation of the matrix in Figure 4.2, they can be summarized as in Figure 4.3.

The second point, which logically derives from the first, is that to make the system of marketing knowledge emerge more fully and accurately, using a combination of methods will most certainly produce the most effective results.

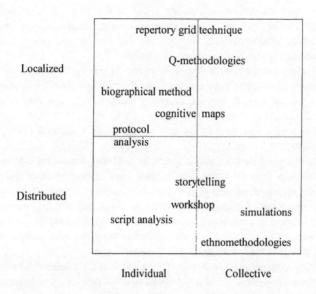

Figure 4.3 *Marketing knowledge capturing methodologies and knowledge configurations*

NOTES

1. Having adopted the viewpoint of managers who deal with designing a marketing knowledge management process, this necessarily means that those managers, by adopting a viewpoint that encompasses the entire system, utilize specific techniques that allow the system to observe itself and gain awareness of available knowledge.
2. As often described by the numerous authors who have addressed this issue: Nelson and Winter, 1982; Winter, 1987; Nonaka, 1991; 1994; Hedlund and Nonaka, 1993; Rullani, 1994; Nonaka and Takeuchi, 1995; Spender, 1996, 1998.
3. Summing up, consider Nelson and Winter's (1982: 105) affirmation in this regard: 'The context of the information possessed by an individual member is established by the information possessed by all other members.'
4. The triad is the most common – called minimum context form – but comparisons can also be made between dyads, between hierarchies of elements through laddering, and in the case of full context form, between all elements combined (cf. Sparrow, 1998: 81-82).

5. In this sense, episodic knowledge, as defined in section 2.2, is a typical example of knowledge rooted in the complex context of affective as well as cognitive factors associated with the episode. For this reason, access to episodic knowledge makes all its components emerge.

6. See section 2.2.2 for a discussion of the differences. In that section the dual utility of cognitive maps was emphasized – both as knowledge structures and as a way of representing the structures themselves. In this part of the book, obviously, I refer to the second use.

7. For a review of the different methodologies, see: Laukkanen (1989) and Huff (1990).

8. Useful ideas for designing a system for marketing knowledge capturing can be found in Brown's article (1992) which compares the repertory grid technique and cognitive mapping to survey the knowledge of a group of managers in the crop protection industry. This research shows that the first methodology is thought to be more boring, more difficult to implement, and further from normal thought strategies of managers involved in the study, who showed much more enthusiasm for constructing causal cognitive maps.

9. Participant observation is one of the most flexible research methods available. Researchers usually use a combination of data-gathering techniques, so it is possible that very structured techniques such as interviews are also used. Moreover, observation is enhanced by an analysis of documents and artefacts.

5. The Generation of Marketing Knowledge

5.1 MAKING SENSE OF THE MARKET AND THE ROLE OF UNEXPECTED EVENTS

As highlighted in the second chapter, the process of sensemaking is one which circularly links action and cognition: by enacting the environment, the organization generates raw data which are interpreted; this interpretation generates a framework for action–result relationships which, in turn, is the starting point for successive enactment. Sensemaking, therefore, means placing actions and cognitions in relation to one another. Consequently the process can begin with either one of these two basic components. As Weick suggests (1995: 155): 'Precisely because beliefs and actions are interrelated, sensemaking can start at any point. Structures of mutual causality mock the language of independent and dependent variables.' Thus, generation of knowledge is not possible unless both components are somehow correlated. Experience of the environment produces data, and previous cognitions allow individuals to integrate the information which is generated from these data giving rise to new knowledge. Obviously, this is true both for knowledge localized in mental models and that distributed in interactions.

However, it may so happen that one of the two components (cognition or action) predominates in driving marketing knowledge generation. In this regard, Weick (1995) draws a distinction between *belief-driven* and *action-driven sensemaking*, identifying two different approaches to each. When the process of creating meaning is primarily guided by cognitions, sensemaking comes about through *arguments* or *expectations*. In the first case, beliefs are tested out through discussions with other members of the organization. It is when contradictions, disagreements, or controversies emerge that the belief system is able to produce meaning. In the second case, instead, cognitions generate expectations and so produce meaning because they make it possible for events to be tied back in to those same expectations. Weick stresses that of the two, expectations are the more powerful drivers, because people tend to seek their confirmation rather than their contradiction. For this reason expectations are more stable than cognitions in the face of argumentation.

In the case of *action-driven sensemaking*, again Weick identifies two different methods: sensemaking by taking direct responsibility for action (commitment) and by explaining action capable of affecting major changes (manipulation). The first occurs when an action is irreversible. In this case, people are prompted to create meaning to find a way to justify what has happened. The more committed one is to an action, the greater the need to justify it and the more effort goes into sensemaking. In the case of *manipulation*, on the other hand, one acts in order to create an environment which is comprehensible and manageable. In other words, sensemaking is done by (cognitively) shaping the environment so that it can be integrated into prior knowledge.

Gavetti and Levinthal (2000), using a simulation model, showed how learning attained through the combination of cognition and experience brings about better performance than that based only on experience. Actually, what is more interesting is the insight the authors provide into how to describe the two types of learning. While mental models (beliefs) produce *forward-looking*, 'off-line' sensemaking, experience produces *backward-looking*, 'on-line' sensemaking. What the authors mean is that mental models give rise to an expanded range of possible actions because they lead actors to imagine alternative hypotheses for action–result relationships. In this sense they are forward-looking. The label 'off-line' refers to the fact that beliefs do not refer specifically to an event experienced firsthand. Experience, on the other hand, generates meaning in a backward-looking way because it stimulates interpretation of events that have already happened. Since meaning relates to those events and not others, this explains why this kind of sensemaking is 'on-line'.

Clearly, Gavetti and Levinthal share a similar viewpoint with Weick: belief-driven sensemaking is forward-looking because it is detached from the bi-univocal relationship with real life experience, while action-driven sensemaking is backward-looking because it produces retrospective meaning relative to previously-experienced events. The fascinating concept proposed by the authors (which is useful in developing a model of marketing knowledge generation) is that the sensemaking process, circularly connecting cognition and action, is based on *leverage* that can be exerted on both components. The set of mental models can be broadened and the set of actions extended. In any case, each one affects the other and new knowledge is generated.

Whatever the context in which sensemaking takes place, it is crucial to understand that in order for new marketing knowledge to be generated, the cognitive system must come up against an event which clashes with current schemas and practices – in other words, it must be in the presence of an *error* (von Krogh and Vicari, 1993; Vicari and Troilo, 1998). Error is defined here as the distance between existing expectations of an event and the event itself (Vicari and Troilo, 1998).[1]

The need for error is at the basis of many interpretations of learning processes, both individual and organizational (cf. Argyris and Schön, 1978; Schön, 1983). The presence of errors is necessary because cognitive systems naturally tend toward homeostasis or inertia, which leads to the reconfirmation of prior assumptions and knowledge. In other words, cognitive systems naturally tend to assimilate signals from the environment within mental models and action models that have worked in the past. What happens is that the system first tries to codify an event according to the current set of models. Only when it is very distant from these models, when it is at odds with them, when it can not be assimilated, does the event cause a disturbance. At this point, the set of models breaks down, so the system has to generate new ones.

Schön (1983) gives an excellent description of the importance of error, pointing out how critical the element of surprise is in the context of reflecting while an action is underway: 'Much reflection-in-action hinges on the experience of surprise. When intuitive, spontaneous performance yields nothing more than the results expected for it, then we tend not to think about it. But when intuitive performance leads to surprises, pleasing and promising or unwanted, we may respond by reflecting-in-action' (1983: 56). Clearly, then, something undesired, or unexpected (either in positive or negative terms) stimulates a renewal in cognitive and action models, switches on the process of sensemaking, and in turn sets in motion the generation of new knowledge.

Using the language of Weick, it is something unexpected, brought about by testing the belief system through argumentation or the generation of expectations, or something surprising, brought about by a very committing or ground-breaking action, that elicits a sense of inadequacy in terms of current mental models and competences. This is what prompts the individual, the group, or the entire organization to mobilize its capacity to make new sense and learn from the events it experiences.

All this is what drives individuals to come up with new theories on why things happen in the world. Again Schön's words prove useful:

When the phenomenon at hand eludes the ordinary categories of knowledge-in-practice, presenting itself as unique or unstable, the practitioner may surface and criticize his initial understanding of the phenomenon, construct a new description of it, and test the new description by an on-the-spot experiment. Sometimes he arrives at a new theory of the phenomenon by articulating a feeling he has about it (1983: 62-63).

Error, then, is a 'unique case' which requires an *ad hoc* theory, that is the generation of new meaning that can make the error understandable and allow people to interact with it, transforming it from negative to positive. When there are no incoherent events, no unique cases, the individual, group or organization will tend to repeatedly apply cognitive and action models that are 'tried and true'.

That is not all. When people are not willing to put incompatible events to the test, the creation of new meaning or the generation of new marketing knowledge is highly unlikely (cf. Daneels, 2003). So, when seen in this light, sensemaking is a process that demands intentionality, an intentionality that does not simply or necessarily mean action, but attention, perception, reflection. The process of creating meaning, as stated many times before, is a circular phenomenon which produces an accumulation of cognitive as well as behavioural material, both critical for the generation of new knowledge. The next section focuses on this process.

5.2   THE MARKETING KNOWLEDGE GENERATION PROCESS

From the initial assumptions and the theoretical framework adopted in this book, the model proposed below has been designed to preserve two elements that are strongly connotative of the sensemaking process: the circularity that ties together cognitions and behaviours,[2] and the transformation of signals from the environment into elements with more substantial information content.

The model is based on four phases; the output of each one provides the starting point for the phase that follows. The end result (in a given moment in time) is a system of marketing knowledge consisting of mental models and interactions. The model is illustrated in Figure 5.1.

The *action* phase involves the enactment of the company's market environment (cf. Daneels, 2003). Whatever organizational member interacts with the market enacts a portion of the environment that might already be retained in the organization's mental models (customers who are already in the portfolio, well established distributors, long-term rivals, and so on), or may not be known (new clients, new competitors, and so on). Furthermore, since marketing knowledge is also distributed in intra-organizational interactions, market enactment is exercised also when the company changes its internal interfaces that can impact market relationships.[3] Consider, for instance, the case of a company setting up a customer service office. From now on this company will gather firsthand data about problems customers are experiencing with its products and services and so it will have a different representation of the market. Also in this case an action that enacts a new portion of the market environment is implemented.

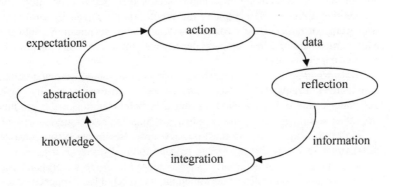

Figure 5.1   The model of marketing knowledge generation

Another consideration to make is that action must not be thought of in a limited way, exclusively as behaviour. Action should be more broadly understood as interaction which can be communicative or even merely cognitive, such as attentive perception of some environmental signals. This way it is possible to encompass the wide array of events that do not derive from intentional activity of the organization but from *chance*.[4] These events, in fact, can be seen as organizational actions as they produce a cognitive effect only if the organization perceives them and pays attention to them.

From the discussion thus far, four different strategies can be identified for error (and thus marketing knowledge) generation (Vicari and Troilo, 1998).

Experimentation takes place when the company enacts a portion of the market environment which has not been previously enacted, and so is 'unknown'. The aim is to produce relevant information for acquiring knowledge which differs from current knowledge. Examples of this strategy are launching a new product on a market that is not yet explored; using a new distribution channel; extending a brand to products outside the traditional competitive arena; involving members of departments other than Marketing to interact with the market.

Recombination happens when the company modifies its market interactions in order to create distance between the already enacted market and its own expectations. For example, enriching the system used to monitor customer satisfaction with new indicators brings to light a different perspective on customers' perceptions, attitudes and behaviours in such a way that they do not necessarily meet previous organizational expectations.

An *alteration* occurs when signals come from a part of the market that does not belong to the organization's system of expectations: examples of this are changes in technology in another sector that pervasively affect the competitive arena of the company, the product is purchased by customers who were not targeted, new competitors from other sectors move into the market, members of other company departments make proposals for product or service improvement.

Transformation comes about when, all interaction activities being equal, non-habitual events take place: for example, customers modify their perceptions and/or buying habits, some distributors eliminate the product from their assortment, competitors radically change their strategies.

In all these cases, the firm must put new processes in place and generate new marketing knowledge in order to respond to the disturbance triggered by inconsistent data. Error is the raw material needed to produce learning. Each time the organization realizes that something unexpected has happened which is far from its system of expectations (even if this differential is caused by intentional actions) a new system of representations, new interactions, and thus, new knowledge must be generated.

Combining the four alternatives, a matrix can be drawn up (Figure 5.2) which serves to classify the various means of action that allow errors to occur, resulting in the generation of new marketing knowledge.

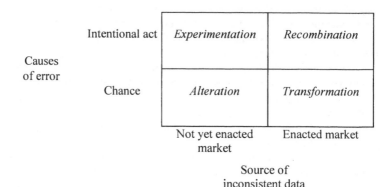

Source: Vicari and Troilo (1998 : 213).

Figure 5.2   Different strategies for market enactment

The output of the action phase is *data*, which constitute the raw material for creating meaning. These data are the focus of the *reflection phase*, which primarily requires paying attention, or selecting data on the basis of some criteria.[5] Reflection begins with careful observation of data so that a portion of the environment can come to the fore. The less this portion can be traced back to previous portions, the greater its information content. Hence, observation is effective if it spotlights inconsistency, incompatibility. Consider the case of a new product launch in a well established market (an example of recombination, using the language of the matrix above). Total sales are in line with forecasts, yet the sales breakdown among market segments differs from expectations. Observation limited to an initial 'first glance', concluding with a comparison between actual and forecast total sales, generates no error because it confirms the system of marketing knowledge prior to the product launch. Taking a closer look, though, by delving deeper into the data generated, incongruity emerges due to the breakdown among various segments which is not in keeping with forecasts. This kind observation highlights the difference between a portion of the environment that stays in the background (total sales), and a portion that emerges (sales in various segments). The greater the incongruity, the richer the content of potential information, and the stronger the stimulus for new sensemaking.

Once again it is clear that observation is not passive, but consists instead of activity (cf. Ocasio, 1997). If the criteria are changed, there is a consequent change in the relationship between background portions and emerging portions. For this reason, reflection means not only paying attention, discerning, but also generating hypotheses, structuring data by 'framing the problem' (Schön, 1983: 128-133).[6] Reflection materializes in the generation of experimental hypotheses that provide an explanation for the data. With respect to the previous example, the unexpected sales breakdown among segments might lead us to surmise that competitors have simultaneously taken action on some segments and not others, or that some retailers have an obstructionist attitude, others collaborative, and so on.

Obviously, the hypotheses generated produce limited information content if they are linked to the specific situation; in other words, if they produce what Gavetti and Levinthal (2000) refer to as 'on-line' learning. In such a case, in fact, these hypotheses would be good candidates for episodic knowledge generation, but they would not work in the subsequent phases for generating cognitive or action models. To do so, they have to be able to stimulate a re-adaptation of the network of connections that make up the system of marketing knowledge. In addition, for the same purpose, reflection must be able to stimulate a chain of hypotheses that is a complex series of action–result connections, in order to have a strong impact on the previous network. In other words, it is the intensity of the signal, expressed in terms of distance from expectations, which spurs the generation of new knowledge (Vicari and Troilo, 1998).

The result of the reflection phase is *information* that constitutes the input for the successive phase: *integration*. During integration, this information is slotted into the network of connections retained by the firm, modifying that network and generating new marketing knowledge (cf. Anand et al., 1998).

The impact on the network of connections can take on different configurations. This information may simply create a new node in the network, or it might cause the relationships between nodes to be modelled in a new way.

As a consequence, two possible configurations can be identified. There may be an *extension of current marketing knowledge* when consolidated interpretative models (that is those that already make up the network of connections) are applied to new kinds of information. In this case, the boundaries of the network are expanded, encompassing more extensive portions of the environment. Referring again to the previous example, the unexpected sales breakdown among different market segments can add information to the current system of market representations such as, for example, 'competitor X is extremely aggressive', extending the descriptive mental models of the market.

The creation of entirely new marketing knowledge comes about when new interpretative models are applied to new information. Here, the process of generating new marketing knowledge is more radical since new nodes appear along with new links among nodes. Moreover, this network immerses the company in a completely new environment, fruit of an enactment process that broadens and deepens the organization's cognitive territory – thus its range of possibilities in terms of market behaviour. Referring once again to our example, imagine that information on the sales breakdown in various segments prompts the creation of a new market segmentation model (for example, on the basis of benefits introduced by the new product). This would require transforming the network in a more complex system.

The result of the integration phase is marketing *knowledge*: a new network of connections that constitute the system of organizational mental models and interactions – that is marketing knowledge. This knowledge serves as input for the successive phase: *abstraction*. This phase is closely linked to the previous one because it generates new knowledge, though it does so in a very different way.

Abstraction, in fact, is when generation is *beliefs-driven* or *forward looking*, that is it is directed by the set of beliefs that are used to simulate experience (March et al., 1991). In the abstraction phase, reasoning is made up of 'as if's'. This is when a 'virtual reality' is created (Schön, 1983: 157-162) in which, beginning with the set of retained structures and interactions, new cognitive and action models are generated. As Boisot (1998: 48-52) suggests, by means of abstraction, new hypotheses arise for action–result relationships; these are put to the test of experience through action, thus closing the loop and activating a new cycle of sensemaking. Seen in this light, abstraction is a form of *vicarious learning* (Gioia and Manz, 1985), in which knowledge maintains its hypothetical form and is susceptible to modifications after reflection on experience.

The abstraction phase consists in *enriching current marketing knowledge*, which can be done in two ways: either by focusing on the details of experience, or by changing the perspective with which one reflects on experience, again to make different, hypothetical relationships emerge between actions and results. Taking up on the suggestion of March et al. (1991), we can say that with abstraction, a unique case (deriving from the reflection phase and integrated into the network of connections) is put back into play and used as inspiration, as an incident for inferring more general relationships. The same authors recommend two techniques for the abstraction process: *near-histories* and *hypothetical histories*. With the first, one begins with real life experiences and moves on to generate hypotheses on other events that might have given rise to incidents, or factors that may have prevented the occurrence of an event or conditioned it in some way. A near history suggested by our example would lead to a model of the causes of an uneven distribution of sales in various segments, or ways this situation might be avoided, or possible courses of action which could drive this unequal distribution in a profitable direction for the company. With hypothetical stories, on the other hand, one speculates on a set of events which has not yet occurred, and uses it as a stimulus for creating scenarios. Such stories, then, are composed of alternative action–result relationships based on an 'and if ...?' correlation. Our example easily lends itself to a hypothetical story based on the question: '... and if the sales breakdown stays the same as it is now, could we launch new products that would satisfy the specific needs of each segment?'.

Clearly, the abstraction phase is not necessary for the model of marketing knowledge generation, since a new cycle of sensemaking could be triggered off directly from the integration phase, based on knowledge retained up till that time. However, the ability to envision 'alternative worlds' is one of the unique characteristics of a company with a high learning orientation (Hurley and Hult, 1998), since the capacity to continually generate new hypotheses is fundamental to the organization's creativity and hence its evolution (Vicari and Troilo, 2000).

The abstraction phase generates a series of *expectations* which are simply marketing knowledge that induces action. Expectations are what guide action, in the sense that they stimulate enactment of parts of the environment, which then gives rise to errors, which in turn supply the raw material for generating new knowledge.

Taking the two phases together, integration and abstraction, we can summarize the different configurations of marketing knowledge generation on the basis of two aspects: how new the information and the models used are (Figure 5.3).

	Current	*Consolidation of current marketing knowledge*	*Enrichment of current marketing knowledge*
Information			
	New	*Extension of current marketing knowledge*	*Creation of entirely new marketing knowledge*
		Current	New

Interpretative models

Figure 5.3   Different configurations of marketing knowledge generation

In addition to the categories described above, the matrix includes a fourth configuration, but here there is no actual generation of marketing knowledge because action generates neither errors, nor new information content. This is the case of *consolidation of current marketing knowledge*: mental models and interactions where knowledge is situated are confirmed without adding any further information. Knowledge consolidation can be seen as a natural homeostatic process which all cognitive systems tend toward when there are no disturbances (Vicari and Troilo, 1998; 2000). To conclude with the example used till now, consolidation occurs when a new product launch on a consolidated market produces both the forecasted sales levels, and a sales breakdown which is true to expectations, confirming pre-existing mental and action models.

The marketing knowledge generation phase, as described thus far, involves a process of sensemaking regarding market phenomena, and produces a system of knowledge localized in mental models and situated in social interactions. Since the content of knowledge structures is market phenomena, and interactions come about with market components, in order to understand and model the marketing knowledge generation phase it is essential to clarify just how these representations and interactions come to be. To do so, our attention must focus on the subject who is at the heart of the concept of market orientation – the customer. The next section analyses the customer's contribution to the generation of marketing knowledge.

5.3 THE ROLE OF THE CUSTOMER WITHIN THE MARKETING KNOWLEDGE GENERATION PROCESS

Some theoretical premises are necessary in order to identify the role of the customer within the marketing knowledge generation process.

First of all, having embraced the view of organizations as socio-cognitive systems, the customer must also be thought of as such. Therefore, *the customer is a socio-cognitive (autopoietic) system and the interactions between company and customer must be interpreted as interactions between cognitive systems.* As a consequence, the customer[7] (like the organization) possesses some resources and behaves in such as way as to guarantee his or her survival and evolution. In other words, the individual as a multi-faceted social actor can be analysed from an economic standpoint: as one who undertakes activities which generate value in order to attain physical, psychological and social well-being.

From the organization's perspective, the customer is a component of the market environment. This might be a previously-activated portion of the environment, if the company already knows of the customer, or non-activated portion if the opposite is true. In any case, the customer is a generator of signals and disturbances, and as such is basically a source of data subsequent to the company's actions. Conducting marketing research on current or potential customers, 'listening to the voice of customers', analysing their satisfaction: all are typical examples of actions that generate data which serve as input for the reflection phase. In this sense, therefore, *the organization can not import information or knowledge from customers. What it can do is to enact the market to produce data which are then subjected to sensemaking, from which new marketing knowledge is generated.* This does not mean that customers' knowledge cannot be utilized by the company, but simply that in order to do so the organization must activate this knowledge, making it emerge, and after a process of sensemaking, integrate it with prior marketing knowledge. This is why it can be said that customers are nodes of knowledge *within* the organization.

Moreover, the company has recursive interaction with some customers. In such cases knowledge situated in these interactions is generated. This knowledge, as discussed in previous chapters, is not necessarily represented in the mental models of the organization or of the customer, nor is it consciously generated.

The conclusion of this epistemological premise is that *for the company, integrating customers' knowledge means both slotting customers' mental models and their interactions (i.e. their competences) into its own representations, as well as establishing interactions with the customers where additional forms of knowledge are situated.*

5.3.1   The Customer's Knowledge System

In the exact same way as with the company, the customer's knowledge system is made up of knowledge localized in mental models and situated in interactions (Busacca et al., 1999).

As regards *mental models*, these consist of the following:

- *Categories and taxonomies used to represent personal identity.* For the most part, these have to do with terminal or instrumental values (Gutman, 1982), categories regarding self-perception that describe the customer's position within the social context, and lastly, descriptive categories of the image that the actor expects to project.
- *Categories and taxonomies used to represent market phenomena.* These models describe the structure of the market from customers' perspectives, that is companies and products retained in the evoked, negative, or latent sets – other customers they have relationships with; opinion leaders and sources of information; and so on. In other words, this system is the map of the market used by customers to make up their minds on what to buy or how to utilize goods and services.
- *Descriptive and interpretative models of the relationships with other market components, and heuristics.* These categories represent the relationships between the customer and the company or its products/brands, and between the customer and other customers. So in this case reference is made to traditional constructs like attitudes and beliefs; in other words, those constructs used when weighing alternatives in order to make a choice. The means–ends chain (Gutman, 1982) is a good example of this set of models: the customer's system of connections between values, benefits and attributes of the product/service. This system, often acquired implicitly, defines the perceived value.
- *Behavioural models related to purchasing and using processes.* Here reference is made to scripts that typically involve:
  - shopping: finding information needed to create a set of alternative goods/services to choose from;

- procuring: getting hold of financial resources, or tapping into current or potential resources;
- buying: looking for information where the purchase is made, procuring goods/services, negotiating terms of sale, exchanging information with the retailer, etc.;
- using: manipulating, transforming, combining goods and services in order to extract utility;
- gifting/bartering: exchanging goods/services for reasons of friendship/affection or negotiation/finance, for the purpose of obtaining social benefits or other goods/services;
- dismissing: handling a product which is obsolete or used up, or selling it, for example at a flea market.

As far as customer's *competences* are concerned, these involve knowledge situated in interactions with market and social environments. Such competences typically involve:

- *Arranging a set of information.* This is linked to interactions undertaken in order to collect information regarding companies, products, brands, retailers, and so on, which is useful in choosing which product/service to buy. Some examples are data-gathering strategies that the customer implements (from interactions with sources of information to interactions with other customers), methods for exploiting various channels of communication, surfing the web, selecting relevant data (by assigning importance, verifying sources, and so on), strategies of utilization and sensemaking (that is methods for combining data, integrating them with previous information, and so on).
- *Interacting with the context of consumption.* This involves activities undertaken for the social construction of the context itself, where context refers to a set of goods, actors, and the relationships between them in very general terms. Constructing a context involves building a 'system of consumption' of a given product with other actors (Douglas and Isherwood, 1979). The individual consumer interacts with the system of consumption of a product and participates in the evolution of that context. For example, the system of consumption for garden plants for a certain consumer might have to do with taking a course in gardening, subscribing to a specialized magazine, visiting gardens of historic homes, and so on.
- *Using goods or services.* These competences regard activities that the customer carries out in order to extract utility from goods or services. Typically such activities involve manipulating and/or

transforming the product so it can be used; integrating the product within a set of other goods to generate a system of consumption which is meaningful to the consumer; or making an emotional or functional assessment of the results of the product's utilization.

5.3.2   Customer Knowledge Capturing Methodologies

To integrate customers' system of knowledge, the first step is to collect data regarding this system. The obvious reference, consequently, is to the world of marketing research.

From the perspective adopted here, however, research takes on a different role from that of a traditional market analysis tool which precedes action. The purpose of research is not to import customers' knowledge, but rather *to stimulate the creation of new representations of market phenomena and the creation of new systems of interactions with critical actors.* It follows that research proves useful for the purpose of sensemaking if it is conducted after action is taken, so as to favour the reflection phase and to transform data into information more effectively. This does not mean that the traditional use of research (prior to marketing action) is not useful. Rather its usefulness depends on the awareness that such research provides data on events and situations which have already come to pass and which are therefore results of enactment processes previously implemented by the company and its competitors in that market (cf. Rosa and Spanjol, 2005).

To provide some indications on the most effective kinds of research to integrate customers' knowledge, the knowledge-capturing methodologies presented in section 4.3 prove helpful. But when one attempts to apply categories used for internal marketing knowledge to customer knowledge, two problems immediately surface.

The first is that in the world of marketing research there is a wealth of methodologies that help assess customers' explicit knowledge (whether consciously acquired or not). But this same world is lacking in methods that elicit knowledge situated in interactions. In fact, most methodologies are based on asking customers to express (often verbally) their motivations, perceptions, preferences and behaviours.

The second has to do with collective knowledge. A company is organized around joint action, and so it is possible to make situated marketing knowledge emerge. Customers, on the other hand, do not usually partake in collective buying or communal use of goods and services in any organized way. Thus, research methodologies must overcome higher barriers compared to those which are encountered when analysing organizational knowledge.

The most immediate effect of this phenomenon is that a very common methodology used in qualitative marketing research, the focus group, does not reveal situated knowledge when used with customers. In fact, customers who participate in such research have usually never met each other before, and so have never interacted. A focus group of customers, then, becomes an effective method for capturing knowledge that is possessed by a group of people, but that is not collective. As a consequence, such a group simply represents an analogical reproduction of interactions that occur on the market.

The two problems described above are mitigated by the interconnections now possible thanks to the rise of the Internet. As numerous authors have already noted (Hagel and Armstrong, 1997; Hagel and Rayport, 1997; Kotler and Sawhney, 1999; Prahalad and Ramaswamy, 2000; Sawhney and Prandelli, 2000a; Urban and Hauser, 2004), the dissemination of technological competences in wider market segments and the ease with which customers generate their own knowledge repositories due to relatively low-cost access to experiences of other customers or actors both come to help companies in capturing customer knowledge.

All that said, the *customer knowledge capturing methodologies* that prove most effective are (i) those that succeed in giving emphasis to the contribution of context in the generation of customer knowledge, and (ii) those that bring to light the knowledge situated in interactions. A good example of the former (i) are ethnomethodologies. Beyond a description of all such methods (provided in section 4.3.10), at this point it is interesting to focus on the role of *observation* in eliciting customer knowledge. First of all, observation (whether participant or not) has a clear advantage over other marketing research methodologies: it does not attempt to access explicit knowledge repositories of customers outside the context in which they are generated. Rather, observation aims at overcoming barriers to communicability, contextualization and consciousness by gathering data when and where knowledge is generated or utilized.[8] So, customers are observed while they perform typical activities related to buying or using processes. While doing so, they build up and put into play competences involving the arrangement of sets of information, interaction with the consumption context, and usage of goods and services.

As for the second type of methodology (ii), the *creation and management of virtual communities* is worthy of note. This topic has been widely discussed in the literature, with detailed descriptions of why such communities were created and how they have developed, different kinds that exist, and operational aspects related to their management (Hagel and Armstrong, 1997; Hagel and Singer, 1999). Here I will simply point out some of the advantages this tool offers. Virtual communities were conceived as an aggregation of people who exploited the potential for interconnections offered by the Internet to overcome space/time barriers, and to relate to other people who shared the same interests and goals.

Hence, communities sprung up spontaneously and grew along with the spread of Internet, and immediately became points of interest for companies. In fact, communities offer their members the chance to share experiences and information, so they are ideal places for those knowledge-generating interactions which, as mentioned before, have always been lacking in the context of consumption and utilization of goods and services. Taking part in a virtual community enables companies to tap into a pool of knowledge situated in interactions between members that no other methodology has allowed on such a wide scale until today. The creation and management of virtual communities lets the firm integrate collective customer knowledge by means of interaction in the community itself, which thus becomes a community for the creation of situated knowledge (Sawhney and Prandelli, 2000b). In order to do this, the company must first be able to identify which customers are potentially most interesting for co-generating knowledge, and then design a system of incentives to encourage these people to interact (Sawhney and Prandelli, 2000a).

A third methodology for customer knowledge capturing which can also lead to integration of non-explicit, situated knowledge, is *participation in joint projects* with the company's own customers. As highlighted in particular by the literature on new product development (von Hippel, 1986, 1988; Urban and Hauser, 2004) and on collaborative relationships between producers and distributors (Anderson and Narus, 1990; Gemunden et al., 1996), integration of tacit customer knowledge proves much more effective if socialization processes can be created (Thomke and von Hippel, 2002), or better still co-generation processes. In the latter case, knowledge capturing comes about by performing joint activities, as with internal knowledge generation. Creating a project team made up of a company's employees and customers (to invent new products or services, to re-engineer logistics flows, to define joint offers to propose to other clients, and so on) triggers cycles of collective sensemaking. The result of this process does not regard the competences of the customer or the organization but rather the relationship between the two. In this case too, even more so than in creating and managing virtual communities, two activities are crucial for the company: selecting customers to establish a partnership with, and designing a system of incentives to motivate customers to participate in the joint project.

5.3.3   The Market as a Cognitive Context of the Organization

In light of the considerations made on marketing knowledge generation and the role played by the customer within this process, some points can be raised on one of the cornerstones of the discipline: the market concept.

One of the initial assumptions of this work is that the environment does not constitute a reality which is objective or external to the organization, but rather a subjective reality, fruit of enactment and sensemaking processes. Moreover, it has been stated that customer knowledge can not simply be imported; it represents a set of data generated by the actions of the organization.

Taking these two considerations together, one can deduce that *the market is a cognitive construct of the organization.* It consists of the localized and situated knowledge regarding those actors (typically customers, competitors, distributors, partners, services suppliers, and so on) perceived by the organization as interacting. The construction of the market is the outcome of a process of enactment (cf. Daneels, 2003): the organization, acting in the environment, enacts raw data which it shapes by means of a process of reflection and integration with previous knowledge. This knowledge gives rise to expectations on how the market works, and these expectations guide successive market action following a circular path.

Two consequences logically derive from this line of reasoning which modify some of the basic assumptions of marketing. The first is that *needs are not pre-existent to the actions of companies.* If the customer's needs are essential ingredients of the market, and the market is enacted by companies, then needs necessarily emerge from products/services offered by companies. In other words, the organization, as a cognitive system, is not capable of knowing the environment 'as it is', but can do so only through its own representations and interactions with the environment itself. In this sense, *needs emerge as relational structures between the two partners in an exchange*, and constitute the formative context of marketing knowledge.

The second implication, deriving from the first, is suggested by Smircich and Stubbart (1985): *the company does not adapt to the external market, but rather to its own representations of the market.* Traditional marketing literature, on the contrary, begins with the reverse assumption: that the market is an objective reality, external to the company, which is to be analysed and adapted to. The hypothesis put forth by these authors, instead, is that schemas of the market, when they prove to be effective in reducing equivocality of signals from the environment, are retained by the organization as part of the enacted environment. So, the company can not help but adapt its actions, and thus the products/services it offers, to these schemas. From this we can also assert that when a company competes exclusively in the same markets, it faces the danger that its marketing knowledge could fossilize, which would hinder development and learning (Daneels, 2003).

Essentially, as Hamel and Prahalad (1994) also claim, one of the risks that the company runs is to fall into the 'trap of served markets', that is the inability to generate new marketing knowledge because the context in which the company operates (which is formative of knowledge itself) always stays the same. And that is not all. As stated before, since needs emerge as relational structures, an additional consequence is that customer knowledge also fossilizes when the company repeatedly utilizes the same methods of enactment. In other words, since from the customers' perspective the company knowledge that they interact with is part of their prior knowledge (Busacca et al., 1999), they too tend to stabilize their representations and interactions if the signals they receive are always the same (Rosa and Spanjol, 2005).

Evidence supporting this theory can be found in the scarcity of radical innovation in mature markets. Here, in fact, not only do companies tend to repeat the same behaviours which determined past success, confirming their expectations on how the market works, but also customers 'get used to' the same products and services (that is they confirm their system of expectations). This shows little willingness by customers to modify their representations and interactions when innovations are proposed.

5.4 MANAGERIAL TOOLS FOR MARKETING KNOWLEDGE GENERATION

Having described the process by which marketing knowledge is generated, at this point it is fundamentally important to take an in-depth look at ways in which a company can promote the production of this knowledge. Having asserted the critical nature of errors as generators of change in mental models and competences, it follows that the management of marketing knowledge generation can be substantially configured as *error management*.

If error is the distance between the system of expectations that guides action and the data deriving from action on the market, managing errors must primarily involve defining reference parameters which allow this distance to emerge. In managerial language, this means first *to define a clear, powerful, shared vision*, a medium- to long-term goal toward which market activities must be directed.[9] It is the 'strategic intent' (Hamel and Prahalad, 1994) that has to move the energies which circulate within the organization. It is not so much possessing a vision that favours error generation, as the three characteristics of vision listed above.

First and foremost, the vision must be *clear*. There are two different aspects of clarity. The first is *codification*, that is, the vision must be expressed in a language that is easily understood by the people who must act on it, which allows them to systematically assess their performance. In this sense, the more a vision can be transformed in a system of measurable objectives, the clearer it is. Visions which simply translate into declarations of intent are of little use in producing error or generating knowledge.

Consequently, such visions do not provide valid parameters for comparison with information generated in the sensemaking process. On the contrary, effective visions are those which can be converted into objectives pertaining to measurable market performance (for example increasing annual turnover, augmenting productivity, gaining a position of market leadership, adding to the number of new products launched on the market, and so on).

The second aspect, related to and enhanced by the first, refers to *communication*. As Eccles and Nohria (1992) put it so well, management can be seen as an activity of creating rhetorical universes which are suitable for stimulating action. The more effective the vision (from a communicative viewpoint), the more it will allow the company to build rhetorical images, facilitating the creation of collective meaning. Taking up on the examples cited above, setting a goal such as doubling turnover in three years is easily understood by organizational members, and favours the construction of an 'action epic' capable of circulating the energies of employees.

The second attribute that vision must possess is *power*. Again, in terms of managerial rhetoric, power must refer to the capacity to strongly impact cognitions and actions of the organization. In this sense we can interpret Hamel and Prahalad's (1994) concept of *stretching*. A powerful vision obliges the organization to stretch beyond current boundaries of marketing knowledge. It forces the company to become aware of the incongruity of the current marketing knowledge and act to develop new knowledge.[10] Put another way, a vision is powerful if it creates tension within the organization, where tension opens the way to something new (Vicari and Troilo, 1998). A powerful vision creates a sense of irrevocability which, as Weick emphasizes (1995: 159), triggers action-driven sensemaking. Indeed, if the objective is so powerful as to create tension in the organization, the data generated by action will prompt people to take responsibility and create justifications for their actions (committing). What is more, the power of vision creates that sense of mission and destiny (Hamel and Prahalad, 1994: 129-136) which steers the company to the future and thus toward the development of new marketing knowledge.

The third essential characteristic of vision is that it must be *shared*. Though clarity facilitates the dissemination of a vision, it is fundamental that this dissemination coincide with a collective orientation. As often reiterated, this does not mean that there has to be consensus on the representations of reality or the meaning attributed to them. Instead there must be consensus on objectives. If the goal is truly a powerful one, it can only be achieved if the company is able to mobilize all its resources. In this sense, then, a powerful vision allows the company to select resources, choosing between those who serve to reach the goal and those who do not. For this reason, the goal must be shared. If it is not, people will lose their focus, which in turn will hinder the leveraging process which is crucial for reaching the goal (Hamel and Prahalad, 1994: chap. 7). The possibility to develop new marketing knowledge, essential for achieving the goals which define the vision, presumes that a process of accumulation can be activated which is directed toward those goals, not toward ulterior ends or conflicting objectives.

In conclusion, a clear, powerful, shared vision is necessary because it defines medium- to long-term expectations which are then systematically measured against data resulting from market actions. Obviously, for this type of comparison to be made, the vision has to be linked to the system of indicators used to measure market performance. If, for example, the vision involves becoming the supplier with the highest level of customer satisfaction and customer loyalty in the market, the company must systematically monitor these indicators. Otherwise distances can not be detected nor can actions be guided (cf. Morgan et al., 2005).

Another option for managing marketing knowledge generation is *designing coherent managerial systems.* In fact, keeping in mind that knowledge consists of a network of connections between nodes, managerial systems can contribute both to increasing the variety of nodes as well as modifying the relationships between them (Vicari and Troilo, 2000). In the first case, key systems are recruiting, organizational roles and career paths design, and training. To bring variety into a system of marketing knowledge, one of the most common and useful methods is *recruiting personnel* with different experiences, backgrounds, competences from those traditionally found or promoted in the organization. This decision sets off a process of 'un-learning' (Hedberg, 1981; Hamel and Prahalad, 1994: chap. 3) through the dialectic confrontation between different mental models and competences. In other words, hiring people with divergent viewpoints stimulates sensemaking through argumentation (Weick, 1995), that is, the recombination of the network of connections following dialectic exchange of differing opinions.

In addition to recruitment, the same outcome can be achieved by *designing organizational roles and career paths* to favour job rotation. In doing so, people who have held positions in certain organizational units (so their knowledge has been shaped by interaction with specific contexts) are moved into totally different roles where interaction takes place with completely dissimilar contexts. As a result, the network of connections between nodes of knowledge is modified. For instance, many companies opt to rotate marketing people into sales (Dewsnap and Jobber, 2000, 2002; Rouziès et al., 2005), or trade marketing, or marketing research. Again, the aim here is to integrate these actors with contexts that are different, but still relevant for the department. Furthermore, at the same time the company can prevent competences linked to specific organizational roles from becoming fossilized, which usually causes barriers to communication and hinders the integration of efforts and activities toward a shared vision.

Clearly, high job rotation may have negative effects; dispersion of competences and loss of efficiency in organizational processes are real risks.[11] Consider, though, that in highly dynamic markets, current competences will have to be substituted by others very rapidly. In addition, only some personnel are rotated, so as to preserve memory and innovation by maintaining equilibrium.

The final managerial system is one to which the task of generating new knowledge is traditionally delegated: *training*. The organization, by training its personnel, can impact on the marketing knowledge system by using two approaches which, like the classification used for sensemaking, we can call belief driven or action driven.[12] The objective of the first is to modify individual or collective representations of members of the organization by having them learn new descriptive and interpretative models of market phenomena, or new decision-making models that connect the actions of the company to specific expected results. In the latter case, on the other hand, the aim is to let members of the organization try out different managerial practices, soliciting the generation of new marketing competences. This is typical of learning by doing or by experimenting, often associated with socialization processes regarding knowledge already available in the organization, though only among specific roles or possessed by external actors (key customers, suppliers of specialized services, partners, and so on) with which interactions must take place.

The description above outlines typical managerial systems that can be implemented to modify knowledge nodes. Other systems, instead, are more oriented toward modifying relationships or interactions between nodes. Beyond goal setting and performance monitoring systems, discussed in relation to vision, two other managerial processes prove effective: reward systems and the information system.

Designing reward systems enables a company to give structure to the system of expectations. Some incentives are preferable to others depending on the strategy for market enactment implemented. If for example the company wants to encourage experimentation, a system of incentives could take into account the number of new clients activated or new products launched. Another fundamental factor is who the target of incentives is. If the aim is to stimulate generation of individual marketing knowledge, rewards must be addressed to each single person. If on the other hand the company's intention is to generate collective marketing competences, then rewards must focus on the group. As an example, the goal of a given company is to be number one in the market in terms of customer satisfaction. This company has decided that the quality of its customer service department is one of the factors which most strongly impacts this objective. So, to stimulate the generation of marketing collective competences in customer service, rewards could centre on the entire department and be linked to results of market surveys on customer loyalty.

The *marketing information system* plays a key role in highlighting and amplifying errors (Vicari and Troilo, 1998; Nonaka et al., 2000a). The process of sensemaking works on the basis of recognizing errors and integrating information generated from them into marketing knowledge. Consequently, the marketing information system must be designed to guarantee that built-in sensors can pick up signals from the market. Moreover, this system must amplify errors; that is, disseminate data to all actors who can contribute to assigning meaning to these errors. Amplification ensures 'error visibility' which is more in line with action-driven sensemaking processes, since the more obvious the error, the greater the need to justify its occurrence (Weick, 1995: 159). Lastly, the marketing information system must allow knowledge to be retained. Retention is essential because it formalizes the system of expectations that guides market action. Of course, the only knowledge that can be formalized is that which can be articulated, hence this is only a small part of the sum total. Still, it is important to stress that the information system, in order to capture the richness of managerial representations in all their complexity, must be capable of handling descriptive, interpretative, and decision-making models, in addition to market information. The better it can do so, the more effective it will be. This is the case with information systems that include decision support systems, expert systems, knowledge-based decision support systems, and neural networks. All these allow models to be retained and action–result relationships to be simulated, enhancing belief-driven sensemaking and the generation of errors.

Another means for modifying relationships between nodes rather than the nodes themselves is changing the *organizational structure*. Such action is generally directed toward varying the architecture, the weight and the quality of organizational interactions (Vicari and Troilo, 2000). In other words, the company might intervene on the organizational design by linking nodes of marketing knowledge in a different way, or loosening up some relationships and tightening others. All this would force the network of connections to rearrange itself, generating new representations and new systems of interaction. However, it is a mistake to think that changing the organizational structure determines specific results. Instead, the final outcome of rearranging the network depends on the specific actions undertaken by organizational members. Once again, the relationship between structure and activity is circular, as Eccles and Nohria (1992: 135) remind us: 'Structure is not some reified thing that people take as a rigid given and then act in accordance with. Although structure certainly constrains individual action, it is also always being shaped *by* people as they take actions to address problems and shape their identity.'

As many authors have emphasized (Davenport, 1993; Hammer and Champy, 1993; Crego and Schriffin, 1995), *process-based organization* is what seems to prompt interaction that produces marketing knowledge. In traditional bureaucratic-functional structures, preference is given to specialized competences, and coordination is entrusted to formal mechanisms for articulating knowledge. Instead, structures which are organized by processes promote the construction of collective knowledge accumulated in work teams, which are responsible for planning and implementing a number of activities (cf. Senge, 1990: chap. 12). The effectiveness of this type of organization is enhanced when team activity is based on self-organization, that is, when team members autonomously decide on the rules to follow, the path for reaching objectives, and managerial practices to use in travelling this path (Takeuchi and Nonaka, 1986; Nonaka, 1988, 1990). In fact, if orders were given by someone outside the group, the whole knowledge system of team members would become entrenched along the lines indicated by this external actor, blocking the development of knowledge situated in interactions. Instead, a 'self-organized' approach to organizing activities is complementary and consistent with the idea of the organization as a *federation of laboratories* (Miles et al., 1997). Organizational units, in this case, are seen as a testing ground for managerial practices focused on accumulating collective knowledge. Advocates of this proposal also emphasize the importance and the role of the central units of the organization, adopting the client-server metaphor of information systems. If peripheral units are for experimentation (clients), central units serve as organizational memory, that is collections of repositories of codified knowledge available to anyone who wants to tap into them for their experiments (servers). Regarding marketing knowledge specifically, obviously the Marketing Department is made up of server units, which single work groups within the department (and outside too) can access to obtain the knowledge they need.

In summary, it is helpful to remember that changing the organizational structure to support the generation of marketing knowledge includes any actions that encourage experimentation, in which organizational members involved in market-related interactions are encouraged to interact. The goal here is to enrich the marketing knowledge repository of the organization. Structural change for the purpose of encouraging experimentation and error generation is a necessary condition, but to reach the objective it is not enough. Change is also needed in terms of the *culture* and *organizational climate*. As for the former, it is only natural that error production is facilitated by *tolerance toward errors*. A culture that tends to penalize behaviour that generates results which do not match expectations tends toward conformity and thus has little propensity for experimentation (cf. Atuahene-Gima et al., 2005).

The ability to produce constructive errors depends on the sense of security that organizational members have; they know they are acting in a protected environment where an unexpected outcome resulting from actions is utilized to generate new knowledge. A culture that is tolerant of errors promotes the *willingness to take risks and deal with consequent uncertainty* (Smith et al. 2005). An action that generates unexpected results by definition creates uncertainty, since it forces the organization to distance itself from representations and interactions that have proven valid in the past and have constituted its set of expectations. A tolerant culture, however, ensures that this uncertainty leads to that creative chaos which (through reflection and integration) can trigger a new order, and from which new marketing knowledge structures can emerge.[13]

Beyond organizational culture, an additional element that favours error production, and thus a new network of connections, is an organizational climate that stimulates cooperation and hence interaction. In this regard an essential element is *trust – among members of the organization and in critical actors external to it*. A detailed description of this concept will be given in the following chapter. At this point, simply note the following: where there is no penalty against opportunistic behaviour by members of the organization, or against attitudes which tend more toward owning than sharing market information, or against interactions organized in closed rather than open structures, employees are not motivated to embark on new paths where error production, and its resulting uncertainty, would find fertile ground. From the previous discussion of the concept of caring, both regarding other members of the organization and external actors (especially customers), we can deduce that generating new marketing knowledge can only take place in a particular organizational climate. In such a climate, interaction between members of the organization, and between these people and external actors, is based on respect and the conviction that the contribution of the others is indispensable. In other words, everyone should be willing to cooperate to build up interactions in which new marketing knowledge can accumulate.

In concluding this section, I argue that managing marketing knowledge generation consists of designing some organizational factors – that is visioning, managerial systems, structures, culture and climate – which support the sensemaking process relative to market phenomena. But such tools must be gauged in a particular way: nodes, and the relationships between them, which constitute the marketing knowledge of an organization, must be free to evolve, systematically rearranging themselves (Figure 5.4).

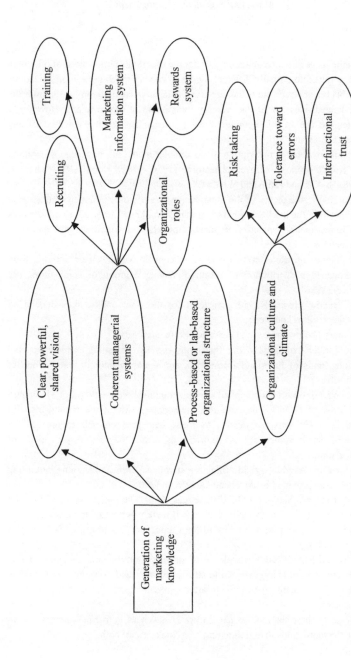

Figure 5.4   Marketing knowledge generation managerial tools

NOTES

1. Despite its negative connotation, I prefer the use of this term instead of others. In fact, it puts into a totally different light a word very much used in organizations to label unexpected events that are given a negative connotation just because the unexpected does not fit the ordinary functioning of organizations. However, I prefer the use of this common word to stress the learning potential of any 'negative' event.

2. For a more detailed description of the circular model of knowledge generation, see Kolb's proposal of cyclical learning (1976; 1984), Boisot (1987: chap. 4; 1998: 58-62), and Zollo and Winter (2002).

3. According to the theory of the organization as a socio-cognitive system adopted in this work, the market is what the organization knows to be so; in other words the representations retained in mental models and cognitions distributed in interactions.

4. For theories on the effects of chance on competitive advantage deriving from heterogeneous distribution of resources among a group of competitors, see Barney (1986).

5. The criteria, obviously, are significant for the actor and so they depend on her/his previous knowledge.

6. For more on this topic, see also Senge (1990: chap. 10).

7. Here I refer explicitly to the final consumer, as industrial customers, being various kinds of firms and institutions, are already economic units in and of themselves.

8. For a case of observation applied to product innovation, see the work of Leonard and Rayport (1997). They use this methodology within the framework of a method called *empathic design*, to create new products able to provide the benefits that customers are not yet aware of, or that they are not yet capable of articulating.

9. On the role played by a rigid vision in fostering experimental learning interesting insights are provided by Atuahene-Gima et al. (2005).

10. In this regard, Senge (1990: 150) argues that: 'The gap between vision and current reality is also a source of energy. If there was no gap, there would be no need for any action to move toward the vision. Indeed, the gap is *the* source of creative energy.'

11. Maltz and Kohli (2000) provide excellent insight on this issue, arguing that an excessive rate of change related to structures, roles and procedures (which they call internal volatility) negatively affects psychological states of middle level managers.

12. Obviously these approaches should not be taken as 'either/or' alternatives. In fact, the more innovative training methods make use of both.

13. On the topic of generating knowledge as order which emerges from chaos, see the work of Nonaka (1988, 1990), Vicari (1991), Stacey (1995, 1996), Cheng and Van de Ven (1996) and Boisot (1998). Interesting to note, though, is the dissenting opinion of Weick (1995: 158) in this regard. His belief is that limited tolerance of errors reinforces sensemaking based on commitment, making action more irrevocable and increasing the need to justify it if results diverge from expectations. However, this position seems reasonable only when one assumes that in a firm with a culture of little tolerance to errors, individuals and groups are still inclined to try new things. Such a position, in my opinion, is difficult to uphold. High tolerance toward errors, as I see it, encourages people to take action, and is therefore the first phase in the process of sensemaking. Though it is true that this kind of culture could reduce the need for commitment, it is also true that the process of reflection and integration can come about in other ways too.

6. The Sharing and Use of Marketing Knowledge

6.1 THE BARRIERS TO MARKETING KNOWLEDGE SHARING

Given the emphasis placed on the relationship between the ability to manage knowledge and the attainment of sustainable competitive advantage, it would seem paradoxical to discover that sharing knowledge among various departments in an organization is such an arduous task. Most likely, the people who are responsible for knowledge management assume (much too optimistically) that simply demonstrating how critical knowledge is will lead people to share it voluntarily, without excessive costs. In the face of evidence of just how problematic knowledge sharing is, the question arises as to why this is so. Once the causes of this problem are clear, solutions can be designed to solve it. There are two categories of barriers to sharing marketing knowledge: *economic* and *organizational.*

Among the economic barriers, first comes the *cost of data transfer*. This is linked to codification and communication processes. The more complex the portion of marketing knowledge to be shared – 'complex' meaning connected to other portions or inserted into a broader system (Winter, 1987) – the more time and effort this transfer entails. In fact, the most suitable codification methods (if any) have to be identified and implemented. Socialization activities may also need to be initiated (Nonaka, 1991; 1994), which call for substantial investments. Where there is no clear breakdown of pay offs, the Marketing Department may decide that costs are too high, and carry on with less-than-optimal transfer mechanisms which might not be consistent with the degree of complexity of the knowledge in question. Another possibility is that marketing knowledge transfer is simply avoided all together.

A second type of barrier involves the *cost of relationship maintenance*. Hansen (1999) clearly illustrates how communication flows set up between two organizational units for data transfer are more effective if the relationship between them is a strong one. However, 'strength' here depends on the energy that the two parties invest in the relationship itself. Consequently, effort is needed to reduce the cultural, linguistic, and often physical distance between the different organizational units (cf. Griffin and Hauser, 1996; Kahn, 1996, 2001; Kahn and Mentzer, 1998). In addition, some degree of commitment is needed on all sides, which generally comes into play through participation in joint projects or activities. Lastly, at a certain point in the life cycle of the relationship, it becomes critical to create joint decision-making teams which govern activities that the organizational units are involved in. All this requires frequent meetings, constant attention to the other unit's needs, flexibility in conforming to the requests of the other unit, rapid change when the relationship requires it. Summing up, then, relationship maintenance, which would guarantee that the transfer process is effective, necessitates major investments which, once again, the Marketing Department may not want to make (or may not have the competence to do so efficiently).

As for organizational barriers, the first to cite is *organizational culture*. Many studies have investigated the impact of culture on the dissemination of marketing information, with contradictory results. Deshpandé et al. (1993) used the categories 'adhocratic', 'hierarchic', 'clan' or 'market' to classify organizational culture. They showed that in highly dynamic competitive arenas, a market culture secured better performance compared first to adhocratic, then clan and bureaucratic cultures. Since both market and adhocratic cultures are believed by the authors to be typical of customer-oriented companies, their results confirm the relationship between this type of orientation and positive organizational performance. Moorman (1995), on the other hand, shows that the process of generation, dissemination and utilization of marketing information connected to new product development proves much more effective in a clan culture.

In conclusion, as I see it the common thread in these studies is that an organization's cultural traits, regardless of what they might be, influence the process of data transfer, promoting the sharing of some types of marketing knowledge rather than others. Boisot (1987: chap. 5; 1998: chap. 6) argues that an important role is played by transactional strategies, that is how information transactions are regulated within the organization. The author outlines four such strategies typical of different company cultures: markets, bureaucracies, clans, and what he calls fiefs, where the authority and charisma of the leader hold together the group. Boisot's hypothesis is that markets and bureaucracies favour the sharing of codified, generic knowledge. Clans and fiefs, instead, support the sharing of tacit, specific knowledge. On the basis of his suggestion, then, it can be posited that organizational culture can constitute a barrier to sharing marketing knowledge when, in the presence of a great deal of explicit, codified knowledge, the prevalent cultural traits are those of clans or fiefs. The reverse is true in the opposite case: where there is a high level of situated, implicit knowledge, transfer will be impeded if the organization has more of a market or bureaucratic culture. In the first case, sharing is highly inefficient because clans and fiefs favour transactional strategies based on personal communication and building relationships over long periods of time. Neither is consistent with an explicit, codified knowledge configuration. In the second case, instead, sharing is ineffective because markets and bureaucracies conflict with the need to transfer relational contexts through which situated marketing knowledge can be shared.

A further organizational barrier to marketing knowledge sharing is *cultural differences between Marketing and other departments*. With respect to organizational culture discussed above, here focus shifts to diverse cultural traits which characterize the members of different departments. Good insights on this issue can be found in research on Marketing integration with other departments (cf. Gupta et al., 1986; Dougherty, 1992; Workman, 1993; Song and Parry, 1997; Dewsnap and Jobber, 2002; Rouziès et al., 2005). As these studies have shown, differing educational backgrounds, various career paths, and diverse institutional contexts bring about belief systems, attitudes and competences which are idiosyncratic, and as such difficult to integrate. A classic example is the contrasting cultural orientation of managers in Marketing with respect to those in R&D. The former are usually oriented toward short-term results; they see themselves as members of the company as a whole, and show a low tolerance for the unexpected and a preference for planning activities. The latter, instead, tend to focus on medium- or long-term results; they share a sense of belonging that goes beyond the organizational borders to a wider scientific community. Their tolerance for the unexpected is high as they research new ideas, and they show little patience for planning as a governing mechanism. The differences between cultural traits make inter-functional integration, and thus marketing knowledge sharing, quite painstaking.

In fact, cultural differences impact on self-perception and the shared sense of identity within the department. This gives rise to the belief that achieving organizational goals is largely dependent on one's own competences and behaviours. Following on from here, one's own departmental performance, processes and responsibilities are all thought to be much more important than those of other departments. All this makes information transfer and decision-making extremely arduous tasks (Frankwick et al., 1994). The study by Fisher et al. (1997) also supports this theory. These researchers utilize the concept of *relative functional identification* to define the degree to which managers identify themselves with their department rather than the company as a whole. The authors verify the impact of this identification on communication processes between Marketing and Engineering, demonstrating that it plays a moderating role between strategies implemented to improve communications between these two departments and results obtained in terms of frequency and bi-directionality of communication itself.

In conclusion, rigid functional cultures limit marketing knowledge sharing because they trigger the perception that the advantages deriving from sharing knowledge are inferior to those associated with protecting it.

Another of the organizational obstacles to marketing knowledge sharing is *perceptions regarding the relative power of Marketing compared to other departments*. By this I mean that the perceptions of a given department regarding its organizational power with respect to others[1] can impact on the willingness to relinquish knowledge. As the saying goes, knowledge is power. And so, sharing functional knowledge from this perspective might be thought of as a loss of power; this may create resistance to sharing. Here too, then, where there are no clear mechanisms for allocation of pay offs, there is no incentive to share.

A department that considers itself very powerful may see its competences and responsibilities as superior to those of other departments. This would lead to a reduction in the importance attributed to knowledge possessed by other functions (cf. Atuahene-Gima et al., 2005). An interesting study in this regard is Workman's (1993) on the role of Marketing in new product development in high-tech companies. He investigates the case of a computer manufacturer, in which organizational power traditionally resided in Engineering and other technical areas. The author shows how the clear perception of this distribution of power provokes two complementary yet negative effects on inter-functional communication. The first is that marketing managers have little inclination to transfer information. In fact, they are convinced that Engineering does not think that customers can give any indications as to what their needs are. What is more, Engineering does not consider Marketing technically competent to translate customer needs into product specifications. The second effect is that engineers staunchly uphold the traditional view that Marketing is only needed when products are not selling. So colleagues in this department should have no say in the design or implementation of innovative projects. Along the same lines, Ruekert and Walker (1987) demonstrate that where there is no perception of dependency of Marketing on resources from other departments[2] (specifically Production, R&D, and Finance) the scope of inter-functional communication flow is diminished. Bringing information resources into the equation, the results of this study coincide with the previous one in highlighting that the distribution of power influences willingness to transfer and receive information at an inter-functional level.

In summary, a commonly shared perception of the distribution of power can lead Marketing to conclude that it would not be advantageous (either for the department itself or for the organization as a whole) to share its knowledge with other departments, even though they are involved in activities that would necessitate the availability of market information.

Closely linked to the previous point is an additional organizational barrier to marketing knowledge sharing: *the perception of fairness and equity of decision-making processes* which arise from that knowledge. This barrier stands on what Kim and Mauborgne (1997; 1998) define *procedural justice*. The authors' initial assumption is that in the debate on cooperation and knowledge sharing, often focus lies on the value of rewards that are granted in exchange for shared knowledge: financial incentives and personal gratification. Kim and Mauborgne, however, claim that willingness to share one's knowledge also derives from the perception that decision-making processes which will result are fair. Attention, therefore, shifts from the justice of the result to the justice of the process.

Along the same lines, Podsakoff et al. (2000), reviewing the literature on organizational citizenship behaviours, highlight how the perception of fairness positively affects such behaviours (that is going beyond fulfilling one's job requirements or respecting organizational regulations). In this sense, transferring data to colleagues in other departments, outside of standardized communication processes, could be seen as organizational citizenship behaviours.

These studies support the argument that when Marketing personnel perceive that marketing knowledge is utilized unfairly by other departments, their willingness to share it deflates. This leads them to refuse to transfer data to other departments, or to transfer strictly what is required by organizational rules, thus limiting the scope of marketing knowledge that can be shared.

6.2 THE BARRIERS TO MARKETING KNOWLEDGE USAGE

Beyond economic and organizational barriers to marketing knowledge sharing, there can be others involving the use of that knowledge. In fact, other departments may not use marketing knowledge even when it is shared by the Marketing department.[3]

Some of the barriers to using marketing knowledge are the same that create an impediment to sharing it. In fact, seen from the perspective of knowledge users (that is other departments) the high transfer cost could require that they too shoulder a part of this burden.[4] The cost of maintaining the relationship also falls to them. Consider too that the distribution of power which influences self-perception and close identification with one's department could give rise to the belief that the marketing knowledge available is of little use. As a consequence, other departments might prefer to continue making decisions and performing activities while utilizing only information generated internally. With respect to the previous barriers, the focus here is on specific

organizational reasons why knowledge is not used, and those associated with
the *characteristics of information.*

The first to cite is *trust in the data supplier.*[5] A considerable amount of
empirical evidence (Moorman et al., 1992; Moorman et al., 1993; Maltz and
Kohli, 1996; Ostillio and Troilo, 2001) shows how this form of trust
influences the use of market information both directly and through the
mediation of two other relevant variables: the *perceived quality of
information* and the *perceived quality of supplier/user interaction.*[6] In other
words, the greater the trust of the potential user in the data source, the more
s/he will associate quality with information generated from those data, and
quality (that is the ability to perform effectively) with user/supplier
interaction. Both these variables, in turn, have a positive influence on the use
of market information. Since trust is a behavioural expectation (cf. Castaldo,
2002), trust in the Marketing Department by other functions materializes in
the expectation that shared marketing knowledge is usable and useful.
Following this line of reasoning, I argue that trust depends on the competence
that Marketing has demonstrated in the past, on the procedural justice that
characterizes inter-functional relationships, and on the organizational climate
which exists between various departments (cf. Maltz and Kohli, 2000). When
Marketing is not seen as being terribly competent, or when it has been given
to opportunistic behaviour in the past, or when there is not a positive
organizational climate among departments, the use of marketing knowledge
by other functions will quite probably be reduced.[7]

One reason why marketing knowledge is not used is lack of trust, not only
where this attitude is directed toward data suppliers, but also *toward
technological infrastructures set up to support knowledge use.* The evolution
of information and communication technologies has prompted many
companies to invest heavily in such systems in the last few years, to
encourage the dissemination and use of available knowledge. Though the
benefits of this technology in terms of connectivity and efficiency can not be
denied, it is also true that some of its features can be counterproductive.

Several studies (Nemiro, 2000; Ostillio and Troilo, 2001; Rice et al., 2000;
Jayachandran et al., 2005), in fact, show that little trust in the basic
information infrastructure (for example Intranet) or in electronic support
systems for decision-making (decision support systems, expert systems,
knowledge-based decision support systems) are factors which restrict the use
of such mechanisms, and as a consequence, the use of data and information
they produce. The reasons for a lack of trust, in the first case, can be traced
back to excessive burden of use in terms of the time needed to deal with
information overload. In the second circumstance, often these systems are
difficult to run (that is, specialized competences are required), which leads
potential users to keep their distance.

Another type of barrier to the use of marketing knowledge is linked to the *organizational structure*. Specifically, there are two elements that research has linked to non-use: *formalization* and *centralization* (Deshpandé, 1982; Deshpandé and Zaltman, 1982; Kohli and Jaworski, 1990; Menon and Varadarajan, 1992; Jaworski and Kohli, 1993). The first refers to the extent to which organizational roles, responsibilities and procedures are strictly codified. The more formalized these are, the less autonomy members of the organization have. The latter, instead, is the extent to which decisions are delegated along the hierarchical structure, in other words, the degree of participation in decision-making processes. As one can easily imagine, the relationship between these variables and the use of marketing information has been shown to be negative: the tighter the formalization and the more centralized the decision-making processes, the more limited the use of marketing knowledge.

The explanation for this lies in the obvious fact that if the members of the organization are not very involved in the decision-making process, and their decision-making autonomy is further limited by extremely prescriptive roles, the perception of utility of knowledge generated in other departments is lessened.

Moving on to an analysis of the second category of barriers, those connected to the characteristics of information, it is obvious that the use of knowledge depends on the *information value* associated with it. From the viewpoint of the user, value depends on the perception of accuracy in generation methods, the ease of understanding, and the possibility to translate knowledge immediately into action[8] (Sinkula, 1990; Deshpandé and Zaltman, 1982; Menon and Varadrajan, 1992; Maltz and Kohli, 1996; Ostillio and Troilo, 2001). These variables generate a perception of credibility and utility of marketing knowledge which enhances the perceived information value, and consequently, the probability that this knowledge will be used.

To provide a clearer picture of this situation, imagine that a project leader responsible for the development of a new product wants to use knowledge relating to the needs of a targeted market segment. Marketing people provide a research report obtained by using focus groups. If these results are depicted as representative of the entire market, and presented by means of a selection of comments made by customers during group discussions, quite probably the project director will disregard this knowledge. In fact, s/he will not recognize the technical accuracy of the data gathering method (in terms of generalizability), s/he will have a hard time understanding customers' intentions (having only extracts of group discussions), and s/he will not see utility in terms of successive action (as no interpretation of data from the focus groups is given).

The two preceding sections have examined the hypothesis that the availability of marketing knowledge is enough to ensure that members of the Marketing Department voluntarily share it, and that members of other functions just as voluntarily use it. This holds true only when there are no barriers associated with economical or organizational factors, or the characteristics of the information in question. Factors that might give rise to such barriers are represented in Table 6.1. Recognizing the existence of some of these in a company is the first step toward designing and creating an organizational environment that favours marketing knowledge sharing and use. Without this type of environment, the company would find its chances to acquire sustainable competitive advantage seriously threatened. The next section is dedicated to a description of the managerial tools that can favour marketing knowledge sharing and use.

Table 6.1   Factors that influence marketing knowledge sharing and use

Factors that influence marketing knowledge sharing	*Factors that influence both sharing and use*	*Factors that influence marketing knowledge use*
Organizational cultural traits	Cost of data search and transfer	Trust in data supplier
		Trust in technological infrastructure
Perception of fairness and equity of decision-making processes	Costs of relationship maintenance	
		Degree of formalization of organizational structure
	Cultural differences between Marketing and other departments	
		Degree of centralization of decision-making
	Perceptions of power distribution of Marketing and other departments	
		Information value

6.3   MANAGERIAL TOOLS FOR MARKETING KNOWLEDGE SHARING AND USE

It would be impossible to argue that all marketing knowledge must be shared within the organization. There are two reasons why. First, one must avoid the temptation of 'the more, the better' – in other words, the more marketing knowledge that is shared with other departments the more likely performance objectives will be met. The risk is that sharing processes become inefficient and ineffective, and that people become demotivated. Sharing as much as possible is less important than sharing and using specific marketing knowledge which is constructive for performing specific activities. Secondly, as mentioned before, the goal of total sharing is not only futile, but very nearly impossible. Given the complexity of marketing knowledge involving specific activities, an attempt to share all of it would entail such an enormous effort in terms of emersion and transfer, that costs of doing so would certainly far outweigh benefits.

In this sense, then, there are two levels of sharing.[9] The first, the *operational* level, has to do with marketing knowledge which is needed in order to perform certain activities. Examples are developing a new product in Engineering, defining how credit is given to customers by Accounting and Finance, setting up standards for service quality by Customer Assistance. In these cases, the essential element for attaining efficient and effective marketing knowledge sharing is the identification of the activity or activities linked to that knowledge.

The second level is *strategic*. Apart from specific activities which marketing knowledge might be linked to, a portion of knowledge exists which must be shared by everyone in the organization. This consists of managerial representations regarding the mission in the markets where the company competes, those which define competitive arena, and those that denote positioning within this arena (Figure 6.1).

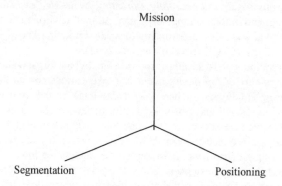

Figure 6.1   Portions of marketing knowledge to be shared with other organizational departments

The mission is what allows the organization to translate the vision into specific market objectives; it enables the medium- and long-term goals defined in the vision to be transformed into a number of short-term market objectives. For this reason, the mission is a reference indicator for error generation. If, for example, the vision is to become the leader in technology, the mission might be 'to become the top-of-mind supplier for the first 20 customers in the market'. If this is the case, people in Marketing as well as those in other departments know that their work must impact on this objective. But in order for each activity to be performed in a coherent way, there must also be shared knowledge of methods for defining the market in which the company wants to compete and the positioning it wants to hold there. In other words, whatever department organizational members work in, *they must all have a clear understanding of which market segments the company intends to serve, what competitive positioning it wants to attain in these segments and which objectives it strives to achieve.* Only then, in fact, can there be a common reference point within the organization that orients all activities of all employees, wherever they work. I argue, then, that what is 'know how' for Marketing becomes 'know why' for all other departments. When this portion of marketing knowledge is not shared, it is very likely that every department will have its own view of customers and competitors.

As far as *managerial tools* are concerned, these must be directed at reaching two objectives: building a positive attitude toward the transfer and acceptance of marketing knowledge, and improving communication processes.[10]

The presence of gaps in sharing and use could be primarily traced back to the absence of a favourable organizational environment. *Building a positive attitude toward transferring and accepting marketing knowledge* essentially involves designing and implementing an organizational environment that encourages Marketing and other departments to make marketing knowledge available and to utilize it (cf. Cabrera and Cabrera, 2002).

The primary requirement is steadfast sponsorship by the organization's executives. This *support of top management* can take various forms. First, statements exhorting employees to share knowledge must be coherent with consequent behaviour (Kohli and Jaworski, 1990). In fact, declarations that encourage sharing which are not accompanied by follow-up action lead others to retain knowledge rather than transfer it. Moreover, both top management and the heads of single departments must act as role models for lower-level employees. Indeed, upper management plays a crucial role in reinforcing behaviour that promotes sharing, and discouraging that which does not. In other words, managerial rhetoric can contribute in a significant way to creating environments which are favourable (or unfavourable) to sharing. For this reason, any communication tools that are beneficial to these rhetorical devices – company newsletters, convention speeches, meetings, formal communications to stakeholders, and so on – are critically important (Kahn, 1996, 2001; Maltz and Kohli, 2000).

In addition, the supporting role of top management is reinforced by any initiative that serves to show the organization's commitment to sharing marketing knowledge. Put another way, any initiative that creates lock-in with employees is helpful to demonstrate commitment. This may include top management's direct involvement in marketing knowledge management projects; investments in technology to support these processes; the creation of roles and allocation of resources specifically for these projects. All these initiatives make managerial rhetoric encouraging sharing concrete; without them this rhetoric would serve no motivational purpose whatsoever.

Of all the initiatives described above, *the creation of ad hoc organizational roles* most strongly demonstrates company commitment. Actually placing roles in the organizational chart is generally a sign of their relevance. To this end, however, there is a question that must be answered – whether such roles should be formalized, or if marketing knowledge management would best be included in the job description of all organizational members.

Those who support the idea of a formal role (von Krogh et al., 1997; Davenport and Prusak, 1998) construct their argument on the observation of organizational processes in some large consulting companies and big multinationals. These researchers emphasize that the presence of a *Chief Knowledge Officer* (who is on the same hierarchical level as other top managers) sends a clear signal about the importance of knowledge management for the company. The CKO is assigned a variety of different responsibilities, such as (Davenport and Prusak, 1998: 114-115): supporting processes of change needed to adopt a knowledge orientation, designing and implementing technological infrastructures to support knowledge generation and sharing, managing relationships with external sources of relevant information, measuring the value of available knowledge, managing human resources allocated to knowledge management.

Following this line of reasoning, within the Marketing Department the role of *Marketing Knowledge Manager* should be created. Due to its similarity with their roles, this title could be given to the Market Research Director or the Head of the Marketing Information System, broadening their areas of responsibility. The Marketing Knowledge Manager, who would refer to the Chief Knowledge Officer, would be in charge of selecting the most appropriate methodologies for marketing knowledge emersion, eliciting knowledge generated in interactions, and designing communication processes to enable knowledge sharing with other departments.

The advantages are clear. Creating a role means assigning responsibility, and this makes it possible to plan activities and evaluate the efficiency and effectiveness of marketing knowledge management processes. There are also disadvantages, however. Generally speaking, the greatest limitation when choosing to formalize a role is the risk of lessening the sense of responsibility of the rest of the organization for consciously managing marketing knowledge.

More specifically, the danger in expanding the roles of the Director of Market Research or of Marketing Information Systems is that marketing knowledge management will be seen as a service activity which can be activated when necessary, depending on various information needs. In this situation, the tendency would be to place greater emphasis on explicit knowledge localized in individual mental models rather than to recognize the relevance of the entire marketing knowledge. As a result, the role of marketing knowledge management in gaining sustainable competitive advantage would be undermined. Lastly, the construction of a knowledge management structure that cuts across company departments brings with it all the challenges associated with managing a matrix organization.

On the other hand, rather than creating formal roles, the organization could opt to make all members (including marketing personnel) responsible for marketing knowledge management. By using various tools (which will be described shortly) individuals, groups and the entire Marketing Department could be motivated to share their knowledge systematically with other business units that might need it. In this sense, people are encouraged to carry out activities involving recognizing and integrating various nodes of knowledge so as to make marketing knowledge emerge and become available for use.[11] As I see it, keeping this role an informal one has the advantage of raising the level of commitment of each individual, making everyone realize how important one's own knowledge repository is for the success of different activities.

Clearly, these options are not either/or alternatives; indeed, the best results can be had with a combination of the two. Formalizing the role guarantees coordination and control of processes involving marketing knowledge management. Informality, instead, stimulates motivation and individual commitment. A good example of a hybrid solution can be found in *tutorship* or *mentorship*, whose aim is the transfer of knowledge at an interpersonal level. When such roles are created, they usually call for a formal job description, along with an informal dimension related to day-by-day responsibilities.

However, there must be *widespread trust among departments and organizational units.* In fact, it is a lack of trust which causes people to activate defence mechanisms against presumably opportunistic behaviour, which usually impedes knowledge sharing (Cabrera and Cabrera, 2002). Such behaviour is again the result of cultural differences between departments, perceptions of the relative distribution of power, and specific organizational cultural traits.

To create an organizational climate based on inter-functional trust and oriented toward cooperation, special attention must be dedicated to *perceived fairness in decision-making processes*. The theorists of procedural justice (Kim and Mauborgne, 1997; 1998) have made it very clear that fairness depends on various factors: (i) individuals (and business units) have to be involved in decision-making processes pertinent to their work, and must have the chance to express their disagreement with others' opinions and positions (engagement); (ii) explanations must be given of reasons behind decisions and why suggested ideas or opinions were not utilized (explanation); (iii) expectations must be clearly defined (before, during, and after a decision is made) based on present or future decisional rules, when applicable (expectation clarity).

Applying this theory to marketing knowledge, we can assert that Marketing personnel will be open to sharing their knowledge if they see fairness in sharing and use of that knowledge. Specifically, this equity depends on the following: some involvement of the department in decision-making and activities that make use of marketing knowledge; explanations on why this knowledge is used or not used in the activities in question; clearly defined expectations of the department.

Consider the following example. R&D is working on a new product development project, and asks Marketing for a report on customers' needs in various market segments. A request like this one lacks involvement, since Marketing is not brought into the process of defining what knowledge would be most useful for the project. There is no explanation, since no one has specified how the requested knowledge will be used. Expectations are not clarified, seeing as no details are given as to successive input required of the department. Under these circumstances, it is unlikely that Marketing would perceive fairness, so the department would not be prone to sharing its knowledge. The result will be a less-than-optimal use of marketing knowledge.

While perceived fairness contributes to raising the level of inter-functional trust, there are other factors which can influence the *degree of interpersonal trust*, which is just as relevant when data have to be transmitted through specific organizational members. As Perrone and Chiacchierini (1999) clearly demonstrate, the variable that most strongly influences trust toward colleagues is their *altruistic behaviour*,[12] while both trust in company executives and in one's direct supervisor have no significant effect on it. Altruism can be measured in terms of the support given by colleagues above and beyond organizational procedures. Helping out when a colleague's workload is excessive, providing support in difficult times, encouraging learning, being willing to cooperate and showing it through actions, not just words – all these behaviours build trust and lay the foundations for effective channels of communication.

Inter-functional trust also encourages the use of marketing knowledge by other departments. As stated before, one of the most daunting barriers to the use of knowledge is the perception that the quality of information is low, which in turn is due to a lack of trust in the information source. Consequently, a high degree of inter-functional trust produces beneficial effects on the use of marketing knowledge, enhancing its perceived quality.

Though the managerial tools discussed so far are suitable for bringing about a positive attitude toward inter-functional and interpersonal cooperation (or reinforcing such an attitude where it already exists), managers can also implement other instruments for *improving efficiency and effectiveness of communication processes*. In spite of the willingness and commitment of single organizational members or units, marketing knowledge sharing and use can be obstructed when communication tools are inadequate or unavailable.

The first element to be taken into account is *the availability of time for transferring and receiving information*. In fact, organizational members hardly share and absorb information if everyone is too busy performing the daily tasks assigned to their unit. So, the company must make time by allowing its members *occasions for social and professional exchanges*, when information can also be shared (cf. Maltz and Kohli, 2000). These occasions can be created in several ways. One method is to organize meetings specifically for sharing marketing knowledge. In addition to the basic function of participating in sensemaking to generate collective knowledge (Weick, 1995: 142-145), such gatherings can be presented as chances to transfer data for the purpose of sharing.

In any case, less orthodox methods can also be used. One, for example, is to allow time (during office hours) for implementing individual or group projects, so that people are free to exchange information spontaneously with the aim of activating projects.[13] Another possibility is to give people time (again, during office hours) simply to socialize. In this case the company recognizes the information value of informal encounters such as coffee breaks, hallway chats and so on. On these occasions, beyond personal information, it is very likely that portions of professional knowledge are also transmitted. Yet another alternative is to arrange social events (conventions, trips, guided tours, and so on) in which to involve some members of the organization. Beyond creating team spirit, this would augment the frequency of inter-functional communication. Lastly, 'knowledge fairs' can be organized in which stands are set up (like at trade fairs) where people with marketing knowledge provide information and transfer portions of knowledge to potential users.

Besides the time the company dedicates to sharing, another essential ingredient is the *availability of physical or virtual space* that favours such activities.[14] As regards the first, it is usually the layout of offices and buildings which promotes or hinders sharing. An open space arrangement rather than individual cubicles, a central location in a single building rather than offices dispersed over a wide area, common areas (talk rooms, in-house cafés, and so on) instead of each unit being physically separated – all this can make information transfer more efficient and effective.[15]

Information and communication technology has shifted attention to the availability of *virtual space*. Newsgroups, chat rooms, forums on the company's Intranet all favour information exchange to an extent that was unimaginable a short time ago. What is more, the huge advantage of these tools is that, since they are often based on the universal protocol of the World Wide Web, they can easily be transformed into Extranet, bringing in external actors considered critical to sharing marketing knowledge. Mention of these tools underscores the role of marketing information systems in this phase of marketing knowledge management.

Designing or renewing the marketing information system for the purpose of sharing marketing knowledge forces the company to focus on specific characteristics of the existing system and certain factors that connote the usage context (Ostillio and Troilo, 2001). In reference to the former, first comes *openness*. This means that several organizational units and also external actors can access the system. Openness also signifies the system's ability to gather and handle different types of data so as to allow diverse knowledge configurations to be shared. Secondly, *interconnectivity* is essential. This term refers to the capacity to interface with other systems, to access different nodes of knowledge, in order to expand the information base and enrich the sharing process. The third key characteristic is the *richness of components*. Given the complexity of the configuration of marketing knowledge, the better able the information system is to reproduce this complexity, the more effective the process of sharing. Therefore, a system that is not simply a collection of knowledge repositories, but which also contains decision support systems, knowledge-based decision support systems, expert systems, neural networks, case-based reasoning (Davenport and Prusak, 1998: chap. 7; Davenport and Klahr, 1998) allows access to richer knowledge, and can have greater impact on how activities and processes are carried out.

However, designing an open system with rich components that facilitates interconnectivity does not guarantee effective and efficient sharing if *trust in the marketing information system* is lacking (Ostillio and Troilo, 2001). Trust essentially consists in users' perception of the utility of the information system structure for the purpose of knowledge sharing. Consequently, trust in the system can be traced back to trust in its components: data sources, types of data, ease of use. The higher the perception of functionality of the system, the more it will be utilized for marketing knowledge sharing and use.

Summing up, then, tools available to management to stimulate sharing and use of marketing knowledge can be classified in two categories: those meant to build up or reinforce a positive attitude toward marketing knowledge transfer and acceptance, and those used to improve efficiency and effectiveness of communication processes in which knowledge transfer takes place. In substance, these two categories can be traced to the organizational environment and the technological infrastructure (Figure 6.2).

As for the organizational environment, the primary aim is to create, reinforce, and disseminate a culture of cooperation and communication. Acting on the infrastructure, instead, serves to improve processes in which this culture takes material form. Research on this topic (Ruggles, 1998) shows how companies invested in technological infrastructure rather than in creating an organizational environment which favours effective use of this technology. The risk in doing so is that dissatisfaction and disappointment may result. This is due to the fact that the potential of such technology can not be fully exploited without creating a suitable environment (McDermott, 1999; Rice et al., 2000).

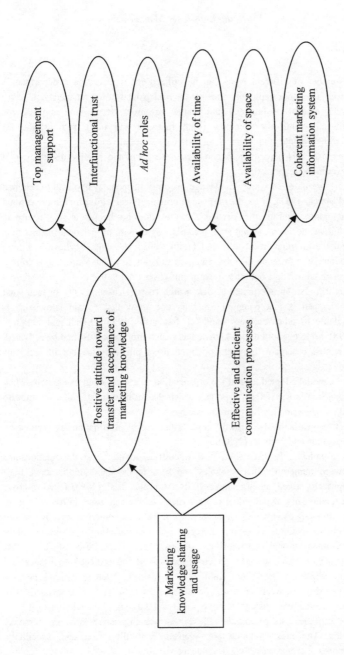

Figure 6.2   Managerial tools for marketing knowledge sharing and use

NOTES

1. A number of different signs can be utilized for representing a department's power. The more traditional ones are the background of top management, salary levels, control of financial and human resources, recognition and rewards achieved within the company (both financial and non), responsibility in coordinating inter-functional or inter-divisional initiatives.
2. Obviously this perception is considered a sign of the relative distribution of power in the organization.
3. There are cases in which knowledge use only happens symbolically (Feldman and March, 1981), or for the purpose of organizational legitimization or personal reassurance. And in other circumstances use does not happen at all, because an 'intuitive' decision-making style prevails, based more on personal instinct than available information (Ostillio and Troilo, 2001). However, I believe it is more productive to focus on the more common situation in which Marketing is willing to share knowledge, but other departments choose not to use it.
4. This can also be interpreted as data search costs (Hansen, 1999). In fact, what can happen is that potential users do not know that certain knowledge is available in other business units (cf. Szulanski, 1996; O'Dell and Grayson, 1998). So to get hold of this knowledge, search processes must first be activated. If related costs are too high, potential users might decide not to seek this knowledge.
5. In the model adopted here of the organization as a socio-cognitive system, when knowledge is transferred, it is data which the receiver must assign meaning to and integrate into her/his prior knowledge.
6. This last variable also directly impacts the use of information, as verified by Deshpandé and Zaltman (1982).
7. To complete this discussion, it is interesting to note that the relationships between numerous other variables and trust in the data supplier have been empirically tested, albeit unsuccessfully. Moorman et al. (1993) failed to prove the relationship of individual characteristics of the data user (in terms of work and company experience), characteristics of the organization as seen by the user (structure, culture, an so on), perceived characteristics of inter-functional or inter-organizational relationships (relative power, culture of the other organization, and so on), and characteristics of the project (importance and personalization). Maltz and Kohli (1996), instead, failed to verify a positive relationship between trust in data suppliers and factors associated with interpersonal relationships (relative power and duration of the relationship).
8. The attributes used to articulate these constructs in prior research are extremely varied. The most common are: realism, credibility, exactness, specificity, comprehensiveness, clarity, relevance, punctuality.
9. From this viewpoint, my position is similar to that of Lyles and Schwenk (1992)

on the difference between *core and peripheral knowledge structures*. These authors, referring to organizational knowledge in general, claim that only a part of knowledge (core) is usually shared by top management, while the more specific knowledge that remains (peripheral) does not have consensus from all personnel. In this sense, the level defined as operational must be shared only by those organizational members who carry out specific activities for which this knowledge is useful, and so it can be considered peripheral. The strategic level, instead, represents the core, and must be shared by everyone in the organization.

10. Davenport and Prusak (1998: chap. 2) use the metaphor of the market of knowledge to suggest tools that can be used to enhance the exchange of knowledge. Though this metaphor is a very powerful one, I prefer speaking more generically of internal environmental conditions for two reasons. First, the emphasis lies on the collaboration needed for sharing, rather than the competitive dimension that the market metaphor suggests. In addition, this metaphor would not bring to light the relevance of altruism and trust which, as we will see shortly, form the basis of transfer processes.

11. In keeping with this position, von Krogh et al. (1997) maintain that a *knowledge activist* should serve as catalyst in generating knowledge and as a liaison for initiatives undertaken to do so. According to these authors, however, the role must be formalized.

12. In this regard, see also von Krogh's work (1998) on the influence of various kinds of caring activities on knowledge management processes. Another way of understanding altruistic behaviour is, as suggested by Weick (1993), 'respectful interactions'.

13. A company that undoubtedly represents an important benchmark in this regard is 3M (von Hippel et al., 1999).

14. Nonaka and Konno (1998) have proposed the idea of Ba (taken from a Japanese philosophical concept) by which physical, mental and emotional space can support knowledge sharing processes by transcending the limited boundaries of individual knowledge. For further insight see the later work by Nonaka et al. (2000b).

15. In this regard, very interesting organizations are advertising agencies, where various departments have to work together to come up with ad campaigns. To encourage the transfer of often implicit knowledge, commons areas are set up for relaxation and entertainment.

7. Conclusion: A Marketing Knowledge Management Strategy and New Roles for the Marketing Function

The main argument of this book is that a market oriented company is one that must make marketing knowledge emerge, generate new marketing knowledge, disseminate it throughout the organization and utilize it in decision-making processes and value-generating activities. This argument has been articulated in two models: a descriptive model of organizational marketing knowledge and a normative model for managing it. The latter is based on three different stages, and for each descriptions were given of the most appropriate managerial tools for efficient and effective marketing knowledge management.

As a conclusion of this work, I believe it is useful to focus on the strategic aspects related to marketing knowledge management which constitute the background in which the processes described must be embedded.

As repeatedly stated, emerging and managing the whole of organizational marketing knowledge is a rather futile exercise, as well as an extremely arduous one. This is why a correct marketing knowledge management process must begin with the identification of activities to which knowledge is connected. This identification will then serve as a platform for activating marketing knowledge emersion, generation, sharing and use. However, marketing knowledge management requires a substantial effort of preliminary analysis; subsequent to this, some fundamental decisions must be taken. The combination of these two stages (analytical and decisional) is what I mean by *marketing knowledge management strategy*.

As often reiterated in describing the three phases which make up the management process, managerial tools to be utilized can be grouped into the areas of organizational factors and communication processes. Consequently, *preliminary analysis* encompasses these two areas.

In terms of organizational factors, it is crucial to carry out an *analysis of the organizational culture and climate*. This study must first be done at a company level. Then, in the case of a very complex organization with departments characterized by diverse competences and responsibilities, it is essential to take on the viewpoint of specific functions interested in marketing knowledge, Marketing *in primis*. Taking up on Boisot's suggestions (1987; 1998), if there is a deep-seated bureaucratic culture, or one that encourages internal competition and the regulation of internal transactions by means of market mechanisms, the generation of marketing knowledge situated in inter-functional interactions and the sharing of functional knowledge require considerable effort. On the other hand, a culture marked by typical clan or fief characteristics favours the generation of the type of knowledge cited above, but requires a great deal of exertion if the aim is to focus particular attention on articulation and formal transfer processes. The energy to invest in the process must be further intensified, and managerial tools duly calibrated, if different cultures and distinctive identities exist among departments. For example, in Marketing a fief culture may predominate, with an unchallenged charismatic leader who handles internal development of knowledge and serves as a liaison between other company departments. In Operations, instead, there may be a bureaucratic culture where norms and standards are scrupulously upheld. In this situation, interaction between these two departments in order to generate situated marketing knowledge will prove extremely complicated. In fact, such interaction would require changes in the organizational structure and in managerial systems (by creating cross-functional teams or designing group rewards, for instance), enhancements in process fairness and reciprocal trust, as suggested in the preceding chapters.

A survey of the organizational climate is equally critical so as to anticipate and assess possible barriers to the willingness to share and use marketing knowledge. The internal climate can be considered a mediating variable in the relationship between the presence of different cultural traits and results deriving from the activation of the marketing knowledge management process. In fact, even where there are conflicting cultural traits, in the presence of an organizational climate open to cooperation which is not based on the 'not invented here' syndrome, and which shows a propensity for experimentation, an environment that encourages interaction and sharing will most certainly be created.

This entire discussion is amplified in scope and complexity if we extend the horizon from internal relationships to external ones: with customers, distributors and partners. The more the culture and climate favour opening and integration of organizational marketing knowledge with that available from these critical actors, the more the management process for this knowledge will be able to aspire to enriching the knowledge repository and consolidating the market orientation of the company. Obviously, in the opposite case the reverse is true: a company with a high opinion of itself which is not open to the external environment will be less sensitive and less reactive toward marketing knowledge management projects that are based on major contributions from external players.

The analysis of organizational culture and climate cannot be complete without an *analysis of the information and communication technology* used to support the process of marketing knowledge management. Throughout the book, attention has been focused on the role played by the marketing information system in supporting the processes of generating and sharing marketing knowledge. While avoiding the trap of hyper-technologization, which seems quite a common one at this point in time, an awareness of the potential of the marketing information system – and more importantly of the reasons why it may or may not be fully exploited – provide extremely insightful indications for the marketing knowledge management process (Ostillio and Troilo, 2001). A comparison between potential and actual use, in fact, is the telltale sign of people's attitudes toward this technology tool. As emphasized in previous chapters, the limited use of technology is symptomatic of a gap in competences linked to its use, or a lack of trust in the information system. Both suggest that there is not a widespread perception of functionality of the system with respect to the ways in which it could be utilized. Secondly, however, such a comparison provides clues to possible action that could be taken so that technology better supports marketing knowledge management. Before making sizeable investments in new information and communication technology, it is undoubtedly worthwhile to verify the existence of unexploited potential of the current information system.

The analysis of organizational and technological factors is a prelude to two *strategic decisions*: the magnitude of the knowledge to be activated, and the configuration of that knowledge (cf. Boisot, 1987).

The first decision entails *defining the portion of marketing knowledge to be activated.* For example, in developing and launching a new product or service, in designing customer care services, in redefining the process of giving credit to customers, in redesigning the process of package quality control, what kind of representations and interactions would it be useful to combine? How broad a region of knowledge should be made to emerge? Should be shared? Should be used? This first decision proves to be a strategic one since it requires designing organizational processes (work methods, project teams, even layout, and so on), managerial systems (rewards systems, communication processes, performance control, and so on) and appropriate motivational systems which have a major, long-term impact on the entire organization. One must not underestimate how the involvement required to personnel affects their commitment and trust in the organization.

The second critical decision to make is *the degree of articulation of marketing knowledge that the organization wants to attain.* In describing marketing knowledge emersion and sharing, much emphasis was placed on the problems associated with the process of articulation as well as the utility of that process. Taking up on these considerations, I believe that the decision regarding the degree of articulation an organization wishes to achieve is a strategic one, because it implies taking a clear position with respect to a crucial trade off: between dissemination and control of knowledge itself. As clearly underscored by various authors (Nonaka, 1991; 1994; Kogut and Zander, 1992; 1995; Boisot, 1998; Cabrera and Cabrera, 2002; Zollo and Winter, 2002), successfully codifying regions of knowledge produces undeniable advantages for the company: greater ease in intra- and inter-organizational sharing, replicability of different artefacts and contexts, recombination and integration with other systems of knowledge. At the same time, however, codified knowledge loses out in terms of appropriability, because anyone who has adequate decodifyng systems can utilize this knowledge for the same operations listed above.

When competitors possess decodifyng systems, the danger is that these regions of marketing knowledge are no longer distinctive, and therefore cannot contribute to generating sustainable competitive advantage. Here the trade off implies a vital decision: the further an organization travels on the path of codification, the more attentive it must be to loss of appropriability. In an economy where industries and competitive arenas are tightly interconnected due to the rise of the Internet (Davis and Meyer, 1998; Shapiro and Varian, 1999), losing appropriability for codified knowledge becomes an even greater risk.

Clearly, these two strategic decisions must be taken jointly. In theory, the larger the portion of knowledge the company wants to activate, the more codified that knowledge should be, so as to make sharing processes more efficient. Throughout this work, though, especially in the description of marketing knowledge emersion in Chapter 4, different methodologies were discussed that enable the company to overcome typical barriers of communicability, context dependency, and consciousness, even when numerous actors are to be involved.

Summing up, then, defining the strategy for marketing knowledge management allows the process leader to make a series of additional decisions: those regarding managerial methodologies and tools to use so that the various phases are implemented effectively and efficiently. This way, the company can construct, consolidate, and make its market orientation evolve.

If, however, the correct implementation of the marketing knowledge management process defines the market orientation of the entire organization, and if the process itself involves all organizational departments, some doubts may arise as to what the actual role of Marketing should be.

In the previous chapters, in fact, the argument was raised that a significant part of organizational marketing knowledge is distributed in the relationships between Marketing and other company departments. In making such an assertion, the assumption is that this knowledge cannot be found only in representations shared within the Marketing department as a single node of knowledge. Moreover, it has been stated that a part of marketing knowledge resides in mental models and competences of external actors, especially customers. Since a company can truly be called market oriented if all its members, whatever their department or role, hold customer satisfaction to be the ultimate objective of all their activities, one might conclude that the role of Marketing in such a company loses much of its relevance, to the point where its very existence could be questioned (cf. Lynch, 1994; Morris and Ritt, 1994; Workman et al., 1998; Webster et al., 2005).

It is my firm conviction, instead, that defining a market oriented company as one that consciously and correctly manages its marketing knowledge highlights *the need for a strong Marketing Department, though one with new responsibilities*. Though every company has its own particular organizational structure, it is always possible to find a specific organizational unit that is assigned responsibility for managing market relationships and consequent performance. From the arguments advanced in this book I think it is clear that Marketing plays a key role, indeed an irreplaceable one, in the process of marketing knowledge management. In fact, when formulating the model, the initial assumption was that the Marketing Department could be considered the repository of a sizable part of the organizational marketing knowledge. This is due to the fact that most customer interactions, where critical marketing knowledge is situated, are concentrated in the Marketing Department (cf. Webster et al., 2005). In addition, as Marketing is usually the generator and foremost user of market intelligence, it is only natural that in this department the mental models representative of the market are more sophisticated than those found in other functions. For all these reasons, it appears that *the fundamental role of Marketing in a knowledge-based company is that of systematically generating marketing knowledge, sharing it with other departments that need it, and promoting its use even outside typical decision-making areas*. Marketing must play the role of 'server' to various internal 'clients' (other organizational units) and external ones (critical actors such as customers, distributors, partners, and so on), allowing them to log on and download marketing knowledge.[1]

One must not run the risk of forming a view of Marketing, in this new role, as simply a large supplier of market data, almost like an enormous market research office. In actual fact, becoming the heart of marketing knowledge management means, first and foremost, *to bring the relational content of marketing to the fore*. In particular, this means that Marketing must take on responsibility for four specific processes:

- *Coordination of the organizational and inter-organizational network of marketing knowledge.* Marketing has to act as a connector of knowledge and of interaction nodes both inside the organization (identifying people who possess critical marketing knowledge) and outside the organization (establishing, consolidating, and developing the relationships between actors who can contribute to the generation of relevant knowledge).[2] Marketing must enact portions of the market environment and manage the absorption of knowledge of market actors within organizational mental models and competences.

- *Dissemination of market data and information.* Marketing knowledge generation requires enactment of the market environment and generation of raw data; continuous stimulus is needed to produce these data. Marketing has to promote interaction between various organizational units so that a true market orientation is disseminated throughout the organization, and ensure that this orientation is maintained through the emersion and generation of marketing knowledge. One of Marketing's fundamental responsibilities, therefore, is to prevent the spread of an attitude of knowledge ownership which would impede the circulation of information and its use.

- *Retention of organizational marketing knowledge.* An additional task of Marketing is to retain marketing knowledge, so as to stabilize the mental models representative of the market, and utilize them for learning by various organizational units. As mentioned before, this requires the development of competences involving the management of information systems and new information technology, and the ability to provide adequate input for constructing and maintaining these systems.

- *Managing the portfolio of mental models and competences regarding the markets in which the company competes.* Marketing must also be a promoter of all activities related to interaction with the markets which, given their high experimental content, offer the organization great potential for learning. This, however, entails evaluating the adequacy of marketing knowledge available for managing current markets and for developing new ones. In this sense, a key role of Marketing becomes the management of project portfolios which centre on market interaction, with the aim of generating new marketing knowledge.

In summary, the importance of the marketing knowledge management process in truly achieving market orientation calls for the evolution of the role of

Marketing. Indeed, this department is no longer simply responsible for functional activities, but rather must become a connector of nodes of inter-functional and inter-organizational knowledge: *from the traditional view of marketing management as decision-making, to a new one of relationship building* (cf. Vargo and Lusch, 2004).

This new role calls for a re-thinking of the specific responsibilities of each member of the department. Typically, the system of individual competences of Marketing personnel, which has its beginnings in universities and business schools, is based on the ability to take decisions effectively and efficiently. The new role of Marketing requires that members of the department are capable of handling internal relations with other departments and external relations with other actors in order to guarantee the systematic emersion, generation, sharing and use of marketing knowledge.

Depending on the organizational position of the Marketing Department, each member specifically possesses particular portions of knowledge. For the sake of generalization, referring to the model of marketing knowledge described in Chapter 2, I argue that the *Department Head* (the Marketing Director or the equivalent) possesses marketing knowledge prevalently structured in mental models which describe and interpret broad market phenomena. Moreover, her/his marketing knowledge, situated in interactions, for the most part has to do with interactions with other company departments for two clear purposes: sharing knowledge on the mission, segmentation and positioning, and defining market strategies. In this sense, *the Head of the Department more properly plays the role of connector of inter-functional marketing knowledge.*

On the other hand, marketing personnel who handle daily implementation of strategies (product and brand managers, channel and key account managers, advertising managers, and so on) possess marketing knowledge localized in mental models that are more analytical than those of the Department Head. This is because their areas of responsibility are limited to a set of interactions regarding a restricted portion of the market: a single product, a single brand, a single channel. In addition, their marketing knowledge distributed in interactions is much richer both externally (since these people have stable contact with customers, service providers, distributors, and so on) and internally (as they are usually the ones who participate on project teams, inter-functional teams, and other forms of internal cooperation). In this sense, *marketing personnel more properly play a role of catalyst of knowledge connected to specific activities.*

What has been said of the evolution of the role of Marketing ties in to the initial discussion of this book. In the first chapter I argued that the theory of market orientation can be considered a theory on market information processes. Certain limitations of this theory were detailed, and from this analysis the hypothesis came forth which was debated throughout the remainder of the book: a market oriented company must be able to make marketing knowledge emerge, to generate new knowledge, to share knowledge among its organizational units, and to utilize it in making decisions and managing market relations. In order to uphold this position, I proposed a descriptive model of marketing knowledge and a normative model for managing it, broken down into three critical phases requiring different managerial methodologies and tools.

The construction of these two models helps to further qualify the theory put forth here. Having emphasized the fundamental role of action and context in the generation of marketing knowledge, I argue that *a company is market oriented if it is capable of learning in the market.*

The company, therefore, must not take up the passive stance of an entity that learns *from* the market, as traditional marketing management literature maintains, because based on the theories discussed in this book, this is not possible: the organization is a system of knowledge that continually produces its own environment.

A company is market oriented, instead, if it is capable of enacting portions of the market environment that allow it to develop new mental models and new interactions deriving from the relationships with the market. Since enactment of the market produces a co-evolution of the organization and its market, this means learning *in* the market.

This ability allows the company to renew itself, to develop and to evolve.

NOTES

1. Along the same lines, see the works by Webster (1992), Achrol and Kotler (1999) and Moorman and Rust (1999). The first two studies focus more on the relevance of the role of Marketing in different organizational configurations. The third places greater attention on content of knowledge to share.
2. Obviously, this role also necessitates an organizational reconfiguration of departments. In this regard, see Achrol (1991), Webster (1992), Piercy and Cravens (1995).

Bibliography

Abelson, R.P. (1976), 'Script Processing in Attitude Formation and Decision-Making', in J.S. Carroll and J.W. Payne (eds), *Cognition and Social Behavior*, Hillsdale: Erlbaum.

Abelson, R.P. (1981), 'Psychological Status of The Script Concept', *American Psychologist*, **36**, 715-729.

Achrol, R.S. (1991), 'Evolution of the Marketing Organization: New Forms for Turbulent Environments', *Journal of Marketing*, **55** (October), 77-93.

Achrol, R.S. and P. Kotler (1999), 'Marketing in the Network Economy', *Journal of Marketing*, **63**, Special Issue, 146-163.

Amit, R. and P.J.H. Schoemaker (1993), 'Strategic assets and organizational rent', *Strategic Management Journal*, **14**, 33-46.

Anand, V., C.C. Manz and W.H. Glick (1998), 'An Organizational Memory Approach to Information Management', *Academy of Management Review*, **23** (4), 796-809.

Anderson, J.C. and J.A. Narus (1990), 'A Model of Distributor Firm and Manufacturer Firm Working Partnerships', *Journal of Marketing*, **54** (January), 42-58.

Arcuri, L. (1985), *Conoscenza sociale e processi psicologici*, Bologna: Il Mulino.

Argyris, C. and D.A. Schön (1978), *Organizational Learning: A Theory of Action Perspective*, Reading: Addison-Wesley.

Atuahene-Gima, K. (1995), 'An Exploratory Analysis of the Impact of Market Orientation on New Product Performance: A Contingency Approach', *Journal of Product Innovation Management*, **12** (4), 275-293

Atuahene-Gima, K. (1996), 'Market Orientation and Innovation', *Journal of Business Research*, **35** (2), 93-103.

Atuahene-Gima, K. and A. Ko (2001), 'An Empirical Investigation of the Effect of Market Orientation and Entrepreneurship Orientation Alignment on Produt Innovation', *Organization Science*, **12** (January-February), 54-74.

Atuahene-Gima, K., S.F. Slater and E.M. Olson (2005), 'The Contingent Value of Responsive and Proactive Market Orientations for New Product Program Performance', *Journal of Product Innovation Management*, **22** (6), 464-482.

Axelrod, R. (ed.) (1976), *Structure of Decision. The Cognitive Maps of Political Elites*, Princeton, NJ: Princeton University Press.

Baker, W.E. and J.M. Sinkula (1999), 'The Synergistic Effect of Market Orientation and Learning Orientation on Organizational Performance', *Journal of the Academy of Marketing Science*, **27** (4), 411-427.

Baker, W.E. and J.M. Sinkula (2005), 'Market Orientation and the New Product Paradox, *Journal of Product Innovation Management*, **22** (6), 483-502.

Barnes, J.H. Jr. (1984), 'Cognitive Biases and Their Impact on Strategic Planning', *Strategic Management Journal*, **5**, 129-137.

Barney, J.B. (1986), 'Strategic Factor Markets: Expectations, Luck, and Business Strategy', *Management Science*, **32** (10), 1231-1241.

Barney, J.B. (1991), 'Firm Resources and Sustained Competitive Advantage', *Journal of Management*, **17** (1), 99-120.

Barney, J.B. (2001a) 'Is The Resource-based "View" A Useful Perspective for Strategic Management Research? Yes', *Academy of Management Review*, **26** (1), 41-56.

Barney, J.B. (2001b), 'Resource-based theories of competitive advantage: A ten-year retrospective on the resource-based view', *Journal of Management*, **27** (6), 643-650.

Barr P.S., J.L. Stimpert and A.S. Huff (1992), 'Cognitive change, strategic action, and organizational renewal', *Strategic Management Journal*, **13**, 15-36.

Bartunek, J.M. (1984), 'Changing Interpretive Schemes and Organizational Restructuring: The Example of a Religious Order', *Administrative Science Quarterly*, **29** (3), 355-372.

Bennett, R.C. and R.G. Cooper (1979), 'Beyond the Marketing Concept', *Business Horizons*, **22** (June), 76-83.

Bennett, R.C. and R.G. Cooper (1981), 'The Misuse of Marketing: An American Tragedy', *Business Horizons*, **24** (November-December), 51-61.

Berger, P.L. and T. Luckmann (1969), *The Social Construction of Reality. A Treatise in the Sociology of Knowledge*, Garden City, NY: Anchor Books.

Berthon, P., J.M. Hulbert and L. Pitt (1999), 'To serve or create? Strategic orientations toward customers and innovation', *California Management Review*, **42** (1), 37-58.

Blackler, F. (1993), 'Knowledge and the Theory of Organizations: Organizations as Activity Systems and the Reframing of Management', *Journal of Management Studies*, **30** (6), 863-884.

Bocchi, G. and M. Ceruti (eds) (1989), *La sfida della complessità*, Milano: Feltrinelli.

Boisot, M.H. (1987), *Information and Organizations. The Manager as Anthropologist*, London: Harper Collins.

Boisot, M.H. (1998), *Knowledge Assets. Securing Competitive Advantage in the Information Economy*, Oxford: Oxford University Press.

Bougon, M.G. (1983), 'Uncovering cognitive maps: The self-Q technique', in G. Morgan (ed.), *Beyond Method: Strategies for Social Research*, Beverly Hills: Sage.

Bougon, M. (1992), 'Congregate Cognitive Maps: A Unified Dynamic Theory of Organization and Strategy', *Journal of Management Studies*, **29** (3), 369-389.

Bougon, M.G. and J.M. Komocar (1990), 'Directing Strategic Change: A Dynamic Wholistic Approach', in A.S. Huff (ed.), *Mapping Strategic Thought*, Chicester: Wiley.

Bougon, M.G., K.E. Weick and D. Binkhorst (1977), 'Cognition in Organizations: An Analysis of the Utrecht Jazz Orchestra', *Administrative Science Quarterly*, **22**, 606-639.

Bougon, M.G., N. Baird, J.M. Komocar and W. Ross (1990), 'Identifying Strategic Loops: The Self-Q Interviews', in A.S. Huff (ed.), *Mapping Strategic Thought*, Chichester: Wiley.

Boulding, W., R. Staelin, M. Ehret and J. Wesley Johnston (2005), 'A Customer Relationship Management Roadmap: What Is Known, Potential Pitfalls, and Where to Go', *Journal of Marketing*, **69** (October), 155-166.

Boyce, M.E. (1995), 'Collective Centring and Collective Sense-making in the Stories and Storytelling of One Organization', *Organization Studies*, **16** (1), 107-137.

Brandenburger, A.M. and B.J. Nalebuff (1996), *Co-opetition*, New York: Doubleday.

Brown, J.S. and P. Duguid (1991), 'Organizational Learning and Communities of Practice: Toward A Unified View of Working, Learning and Innovation', *Organization Science*, **2** (1), 40-57.

Brown, J.S. and P. Duguid (1998), 'Organizing Knowledge', *California Management Review*, **40** (3), 90-111.

Brown, J.S. and P. Duguid (2000), *The Social Life of Information*, Boston: Harvard Business School Press.

Brown, S.L. (1992), 'Cognitive Mapping and Repertory Grids for Qualitative Survey Research: Some Comparative Observations', *Journal of Management Studies*, **29** (3), 287-307.

Brown, S.L. and K.M. Eisenhardt (1997), 'The Art of Continuous Change: Linking Complexity Theory and Time-paced Evolution in Relentlessly Shifting Organizations', *Administrative Science Quarterly*, **42** (March), 1-34.

Busacca, B., R. Grandinetti and G. Troilo (1999), 'Transizione del marketing e concezione sistemico-evolutiva del consumatore' in E. Rullani and S. Vicari (eds), *Sistemi ed evoluzione nel management*, Milano: Etas.

Cabrera, A. and E.F. Cabrera (2002), 'Knowledge-sharing Dilemmas', *Organization Studies*, **23** (5), 687-710.

Castaldo, S. (2002), *Fiducia e relazioni di mercato*, Bologna: il Mulino.

Cheng, Y. and A. Van de Ven (1996), 'Learning the Innovation Journey: Order out of Chaos?', *Organization Science*, **7** (6), 593-614.

Christensen, C.M. and J.L. Bower (1996), 'Customer power, strategic investment, and the failure of leading firms', *Strategic Management Journal*, **17** (1), 197-218.

Cillo, P. and G. Troilo, (2002), 'Il ruolo del senso di appartenenza nell'evoluzione dei distretti industriali: una proposta metodologica', *Finanza Marketing e Produzione*, **1**, 63-93.

Cillo P., D. Mazursky and G. Troilo, (2001), 'Retrospective and forward-looking market orientation among innovative companies: Evidence from the fashion industry', *30th EMAC Conference Proceedings*, Bergen, May.

Clark, B.H. and D.B. Montgomery (1999), 'Managerial Identification of Competitors', *Journal of Marketing*, **63** (July), 67-83.

Conner, K.R. (1991), 'A Historical Comparison of Resource-based Theory and Five Schools of Thought within Industrial Organization Economics: Do We Have a New Theory of the Firm?', *Journal of Management*, **17**, 121-154.

Conner, K.R. and C.K. Prahalad (1996), 'A Resource-based Theory of the Firm: Knowledge Versus Opportunism', *Organization Science*, **7** (5), 478-496.

Connor, T. (1999), 'Customer-led and market-oriented: A matter of balance', *Strategic Management Journal*, **20**, 1157-1163.

Cossette, P. and M. Audet (1990), 'Mapping of An Idiosyncratic Schema', *Journal of Management Studies*, **29** (3), 325-347.

Cowan, R. and D. Foray (1997), 'The Economics of Codification and the Diffusion of Knowledge', *Industrial and Corporate Change*, **6** (3), 595-622.

Crego, E.T. Jr. and P.D. Schiffrin (1995), *Customer-Centered Reengineering. Remapping for Total Customer Value*, Burr Ridge: Irwin.

Cyert, R.M. and J.G. March (1963), *A Behavioral Theory of the Firm*, Englewood Cliffs: Prentice-Hall.

Daft, R.L. and K.E. Weick (1984), 'Toward a Model of Organizations as Interpretive Systems', *Academy of Management Review*, **9** (2), 284-295.

Daneels, E. (2003), 'Tight-Loose Coupling with Customers: The Enactment of Customer Orientation', *Strategic Management Journal*, **24** (6), 559-576.

Davenport, T. (1993), *Process Innovation: Reengineering Work Through Information Technology*, Boston: Harvard Business School Press.

Davenport, T.H. and P. Klahr (1998), 'Managing Customer Support Knowledge', *California Management Review*, **40** (3), 195-208.

Davenport, T.H. and L. Prusack (1998), *Working Knowledge. How Organizations Manage What They Know*, Boston: Harvard Business School Press.

Davis, S. and C. Meyer (1998), *Blur. The Speed of Change in the Connected Economy*, Reading: Addison-Wesley.

Day, G.S. (1994a), 'The Capabilities of Market-Driven Organizations', *Journal of Marketing*, **58** (October), 37-52.

Day, G.S. (1994b), 'Continuous Learning About Markets', *California Management Review*, Summer, 9-31.

Day, G.S. and P. Nedungadi (1994), 'Managerial Representations of Competitive Advantage', *Journal of Marketing*, **58** (April), 31-44.

Day, G.S. and R. Wensley (1983), 'Marketing Theory with Strategic Orientation', *Journal of Marketing*, **47** (Autumn), 79-89.

Day, G.S. and C. Van den Bulte (2003), 'Superiority in Customer Relationship Management: Consequences for Competitive Advantage and Performance', *Marketing Science Institute Report 02-123*.

de Chernatony, L., K. Daniels and G. Johnson (1993), 'A Cognitive Perspective on Managers' Perceptions of Competition', *Journal of Marketing Management*, **9**, 373-381.

Deligönül, Z.S. and S.T. Cavuşgil (1997), 'Does the Comparative Advantage Theory of Competition Really Replace the Neoclassical Theory of Competition?', *Journal of Marketing*, **61** (October), 65-73.

Demetrio, D. (1994), 'Le biografie cognitive: laboratori di apprendimento nlle organizzazioni', in D. Demetrio, D. Fabbri and S. Gherardi, *Apprendere nelle organizzazioni. Proposte per la crescita cognitiva in età adulta*, Roma: NIS.

Deshpandé, R. (1982), 'The Organizational Context of Market Research Use', *Journal of Marketing*, **46** (Fall), 91-101.

Deshpandé, R. and J.U. Farley (1998), 'Measuring market orientation: Generalization and synthesis', *Journal of Market-Focused Management*, **2** (3), 213-232.

Deshpandé, R. and F.E. Webster Jr. (1989), 'Organizational Culture and Marketing: Defining the Research Agenda', *Journal of Marketing*, **43** (January), 3-15.

Deshpandé, R. and G. Zaltman (1982), 'Factors Affecting the Use of Market Research Information: A Path Analysis', *Journal of Marketing Research*, **19** (February), 14-31.

Deshpandé, R., J.U. Farley and F.E. Webster Jr. (1993), 'Corporate Culture, Customer Orientation, and Innovativeness in Japanese Firms: A Quadrad Analysis', *Journal of Marketing*, **57** (January), 23-37.

Dewsnap, B. and D. Jobber (2000), 'The Sales-Marketing Interface in Consumer Packaged Goods Companies: A Conceptual framework', *Journal of Personal Selling & Sales Management*, **20** (2), 109-119.

Dewsnap, B. and D. Jobber (2002), 'A social psychological model of relations between marketing and sales', *European Journal of Marketing*, **36** (7/8), 874-894.

Dickson, P.R. (1992), 'Toward a General Theory of Competitive Rationality', *Journal of Marketing*, **56** (January), 69-83.

Dickson, P.R. (1996), 'The Static and Dynamic Mechanics of Competition: A Comment on Hunt and Morgan's Comparative Advantage Theory', *Journal of Marketing*, **60** (October), 102-106.

Dickson, P.R. (1997), *Marketing Mangement*, Fort Worth: Dryden Press.

Dierickx, I. and K. Cool (1989), 'Asset Stock Accumulation and Sustainability of Competitive Advantage', *Management Science*, **35** (12), 1504-1511.

Dodgson, M. (1993), 'Organizational Learning: A Review of Some Literatures', *Organization Studies*, **14** (3), 375-394.

Dougherty, D. (1992), 'Interpretive Barriers To Successful Product Innovation in Large Firms', *Organization Science*, **3** (2), 179-202.

Douglas, M. and B. Isherwood (1979), *The World of Goods*, New York: Basic Books.

Doumas, L.A. and J.E. Hummel (2005), 'Approaches to Modeling Human Mental Representations: What Works, What Doesn't, and Why', in K.J. Holyoak and R.G. Morrison (eds), *The Cambridge Handbook of Thinking and Reasoning*, Cambridge: Cambridge University Press.

Drazin, R. and L. Sandelands (1992), 'Autogenesis: A Perspective on the Process of Organizing', *Organization Science*, **3** (2), 230-249.

Drucker, P.F. (1954), *The Practice of Management*, New York: Harper & Row.

Duncan, R. and A. Weiss (1979), 'Organizational Learning: Implications for Organizational Design', *Research in Organizational Behavior*, **1**, 75-123.

Dutton, J.E. (1992), 'The Making of Organizational Opportunities: An Interpretative Pathway to Organizational Change', *Research in Organizational Behavior*, **15**, 195-226.

Dutton, J.E. (1993), 'Interpretation on Automatic: A Different View of Strategic Issue Diagnosis', *Journal of Management Studies*, **30** (3), 339-357.

Dutton, J.E. and R.B. Duncan (1987), 'The creation of momentum for change through the process of strategic issues diagnosis', *Strategic Management Journal*, **8**, 279-295.

Dutton, J.E. and S. Jackson (1987), 'Categorizing Strategic Issues: Links to Organizational Action', *Academy of Management Review*, **12** (1), 76-90.

Dutton, J.E., L. Fahey and V.K. Narayanan (1983), 'Toward understanding strategic issue diagnosis', *Strategic Management Journal*, **4**, 307-323

Dutton, J.E., E.J. Walton and E. Abrahamson (1989), 'Important Dimensions of Strategic Issues: Separating the Wheat from the Chaff', *Journal of Management Studies*, **26** (4), 379-396.

Eccles, R.G. and N. Nohria (1992), *Beyond the Hype. Rediscovering the Essence of Management*, Boston: Harvard Business School Press.

Eden, C. (1990a), 'On The Nature of Cognitive Maps', *Journal of Management Studies*, **29** (3), 261-265.

Eden, C. (1990b), 'Strategic Thinking with Computers', *Long Range Planning*, **23** (6), 35-43.

Eden, C. and J.-C. Spender (eds) (1998), *Managerial and Organizational Cognition. Theory, Methods and Research*, London: Sage.

Eden, C., S. Jones, D. Sims and T. Smithin (1981), 'The Intersubjectivity of Issues and Issues of Intersubjectivity', *Journal of Management Studies*, **18**, 37-47.

Eisenhardt, K.M. and M.J. Zbaracki (1992), 'Strategic Decision Making', *Strategic Management Journal*, **13**, 17-37.

Ericsson, K.A. and H.A. Simon (1980), 'Verbal reports as data', *Psychological Review*, **87** (3), 215-251.

Ericsson, K.A. and H.A. Simon (1993), *Protocol Analysis: Verbal Reports as Data*, Cambridge: MIT Press.

Fahey, L. and V.K. Narayanan (1989), 'Linking Changes in Revealed Causal Maps and Environmental Change: An Empirical Study', *Journal of Management Studies*, **26** (4), 361-378.

Feldman, M.S. (1995), *Strategies for Interpreting Qualitative Data*, Thousand Oaks: Sage.

Feldman, M.S. and J.G. March (1981), 'Information in Organizations as Signal and Symbol', *Administrative Science Quarterly*, **26**, 171-186.

Felton, A.P. (1959), 'Making the Marketing Concept Work', *Harvard Business Review*, July-August, 55-65.

Fiol, C.M. and M.A. Lyles (1985), 'Organizational Learning', *Academy of Management Review*, **10** (4), 803-813.

Fisher, R.J., Maltz E. and B.J. Jaworski (1997), 'Enhancing Communication Between Marketing and Engineering: The Relative Functional Identification', *Journal of Marketing*, **61** (July), 54-70.

Ford, J.D. and W.H. Hegarty (1984), 'Decision Makers' Beliefs About the Causes and Effects of Structure: An Exploratory Study', *Academy of Management Journal*, **27** (2), 271-291.

Foss, N.J. (1996a), 'Knowledge-based Approaches to the Theory of the Firm: Some Critical Comments', *Organization Science*, **7** (5), 470-476.

Foss, N.J. (1996b), 'More Critical Comments on Knowledge-based Theories of the Firm', *Organization Science*, **7** (5), 519-523.

Frankwick, G.L., J.C. Ward, M.D. Hutt and P.H. Reingen (1994), 'Evolving Patterns of Organizational Beliefs in the Formation of Strategy', *Journal of Marketing*, **58** (April), 96-110.

Fransella, F. and D. Bannister (1977), *A Manual for Repertory Grid Technique*, London: Academic Press.

Fransman, M. (1994), 'Information, Knowledge, Vision and Theories of the Firm', *Industrial and Corporate Change*, **3** (3), 713-757.

Fritz, W. (1996), 'Market orientation and corporate success: findings from Germany', *European Journal of Marketing*, **30** (8), 59-74.

Frosch, R. (1996), 'The Customer for R&D is Always Wrong!', *Research-Technology Management*, **39** (6), 22-27.

Gatignon, H. and J. Xuereb (1997), 'Strategic Orientation of the Firm and New Product Performance', *Journal of Marketing Research*, **34** (February), 77-90.

Gavetti, G. and D. Levinthal (2000), 'Looking Forward and Looking Backward: Cognitive and Experiential Search', *Administrative Science Quarterly*, **45**, 113-137.

Gemunden, H.G., T. Ritter and P. Heydebreck (1996), 'Network Configuration and Innovation Success: An Empirical Analysis in German High-Tech Industries', *International Journal of Research in Marketing*, **13** (5), 449-462.

Ginsberg, A. (1989), 'Construing the Business Portfolio: A Cognitive Model of Diversification', *Journal of Management Studies*, **26** (4), 417-438.

Gioia, D.A. and C.C. Manz (1985), 'Linking Cognition and Behavior: A Script Processing Interpretation of Vicarious Learning', *Academy of Management Review*, **10** (3), 527-539.

Gioia, D.A. and P.P. Poole (1984), 'Scripts in Organizational Behavior', *Academy of Management Review*, **9** (3), 449-459.

Gioia, D.A. and H.P. Sims (1986), 'Introduction: Social Cognition in Organization', in Sims H.P. and D.A. Gioia (eds), *The Thinking Organization*, San Francisco: Jossey-Bass Publishers.

Glick, W.H. (1985), 'Conceptualizing and Measuring Organizational and Psychological Climate: Pitfalls in Multilevel Research', *Academy of Management Review*, **10** (3), 601-616.

Glick, W.H. (1988), 'Response: Organizations Are Not Central Tendencies: Shadowboxing in the Dark, Round Two', *Academy of Management Review*, **13** (1), 133-137.

Glynn, M.A., T.K. Lant and F.J. Milliken (1994), 'Mapping Learning Processes in Organizations: A Multi-level Framework Linking Learning and Organizing' in C.I. Stubbart, J.R. Meindl and J.F. Porac (eds),

Advances in Managerial Cognition and Organizational Information Processing, **5**, 43-83.

Gooding, R.Z. and A.J. Kinicki (1995), 'Interpreting Event Causes: The Complementary Role of Categorization and Attribution Processes', *Journal of Management Studies*, **32** (1), 1-22.

Grandori, A. and B. Kogut (2002), 'Dialogue on Organization and Knowledge', *Organization Science*, **13** (3), 224-231.

Grant, R.M. (1991), 'The Resource-Based Theory of Competitive Advantage: Implications for Strategy Formulation', *California Management Review*, **33** (Spring), 114-134.

Grant, R.M. (1996a), 'Prospering in Dynamically-competitive Environments: Organizational Capability as Knowledge Integration', *Organization Science*, **7** (4), 375-387.

Grant, R.M. (1996b), 'Towards a knowledge-based theory of the firm', *Strategic Management Journal*, **17** (Winter Special Issue), 109-122.

Greenley, G.E. (1995), 'Forms of Market Orientation in UK Companies', *Journal of Management Studies*, **32** (1), 47-66.

Griffin, A. and J.R. Hauser (1996), 'Integrating R&D and Marketing: A Review and Analysis of the Literature', *Journal of Product Innovation Management*, **13**, 191-215.

Gupta, A.K., S.P. Raj and D. Wilemon (1986), 'A Model for Studying R&D-Marketing Interface in the Product Innovation Process', *Journal of Marketing*, **50** (April), 7-17.

Gutman, J. (1982), 'A Means-End Chain Model Based on Consumer Categorization Processes', *Journal of Marketing*, **46** (Spring), 60-72.

Hagel, J. and A.G. Armstrong (1997), *Net Gain. Expanding Markets Through Virtual Communities*, Boston: Harvard Business School Press.

Hagel, J. and J.F. Rayport (1997), 'The Coming Battle for Customer Information', *Harvard Business Review*, January-February, 53-65.

Hagel, J. and M. Singer (1999), *Net Worth. Shaping Markets When Customers Make the Rules*, Boston: Harvard Business School Press.

Hall, R.I. (1984), 'The Natural Logic of Management Policy Making: Its Implications for The Survival of An Organization', *Management Science*, **30** (8), 905-927.

Hamel, G. and C.K. Prahalad (1994), *Competing for the Future*, Boston: Harvard Business School Press.

Hammer, M. and J. Champy (1993), *Reengineering the Corporation: A Manifesto for Business Revolution*, New York: Harper Collins.

Han, J.K., N. Kim and R. Srivastava (1998), 'Market Orientation and Organizational Performance: Is Innovation a Missing Link?', *Journal of Marketing*, **62** (October), 30-45.

Hansen, M. (1999), 'The Search-Transfer Problem: The Role of Weak Ties in Sharing Knowledge across Organization Subunits', *Administrative Science Quarterly*, **44**, 82-111.

Harris, L.C. and E. Ogbonna (1999), 'Developing A Market Oriented Culture: A Critical Evaluation', *Journal of Management Studies*, **36** (2), 177-196.

Harris, S. (1994), 'Organizational Culture and Individual Sensemaking: A Schema-based Perspective', *Organization Science*, **5** (3), 309-321.

Hastie, R. and R.M. Dawes (2001), *Rational Choice in an Uncertain World: The Psychology of Judgment and Decision Making*, Thousand Oaks, CA: Sage.

Hax, A.C. and N.S. Majluf (1984), *Strategic Management*, Englewood Cliffs: Prentice-Hall.

Hayes, R.H. and W.J. Abernathy (1980), 'Managing Our Way To Economic Decline', *Harvard Business Review*, **58** (July-August), 67-77.

Hedberg, B. (1981), 'How Organizations Learn and Unlearn', in P.C. Nystrom and W.H. Starbuck (eds), *Handbook of Organizational Design*, Oxford: Oxford University Press.

Hedlund, G. and I. Nonaka (1993), 'Models of Knowledge Management in the West and Japan', in P. Lorange, B. Chakravarthy, J. Roos and A. Van de Ven (eds), *Implementing Strategic Processes. Change, Learning & Co-operation*, Oxford: Basil Blackwell.

Henderson, R. and I. Cockburn (1994), 'Measuring Competence? Exploring Firm Effects in Pharamceutical Research', *Strategic Management Journal*, **15**, 63-84.

Henderson, R. and W. Mitchell (1997), 'The Interactions of Organizational and Competitive Influences on Strategy and Performance', *Strategic Management Journal*, **18** (Summer Special Issue), 5-14.

Hitt, M.A. and B.B. Tyler (1991), 'Strategic decision models: Integrating different Perspectives', *Strategic Management Journal*, **12**, 327-351.

Hodgkinson, G.P. and G. Johnson (1994), 'Exploring the Mental Models of Competitive Strategists: The Case for a Processual Approach', *Journal of Management Studies*, **31** (4), 525-551.

Hofer, C.W. and D. Schendel (1978), *Strategy Formulation, Analytical Concepts*, St. Paul: West Publishing Company.

Hogarth, R.M. and S. Makridakis (1981), 'Forecasting and Planning: An Evaluation', *Management Science*, **27** (2), 115-138.

Holyoak, K.J. and R.G. Morrison (2005), 'Thinking and reasoning: A Reader's Guide', in K.J. Holyoak and R.G. Morrison (eds), *The Cambridge Handbook of Thinking and Reasoning*, Cambridge: Cambridge University Press.

Homburg, C. and C. Pflesser (2000), 'A Multiple-Layer Model of Market-Oriented Organizational Culture: Measurement Issues and Performance Outcomes', *Journal of Marketing Research*, **37** (November), 449-462.

Hooley, G.J., G.E. Greenley, J.W. Cadogan and J. Fahy (2005), 'The performance impact of marketing resources', *Journal of Business Research*, **58**, 18-27.

Houston, F.S. (1986), 'The Marketing Concept: What It Is and What It Is Not', *Journal of Marketing*, **50** (April), 81-87.

Huber, G.P. (1991), 'Organizational Learning: The Contributing Processes and the Literatures', *Organization Science*, **2** (1), 88-115.

Huff, A.S. (ed.) (1990), *Mapping Strategic Thought*, Chicester: Wiley.

Hult, G.T.M. and D.J. Ketchen Jr. (2001), 'Does market orientation matter? A test of the relationship between positional advantage and performance', *Strategic Management Journal*, **22** (9), 899-906.

Hunt, S.D. and R.M. Morgan (1995), 'The Comparative Advantage Theory of Competition', *Journal of Marketing*, **59** (April), 1-15.

Hunt, S.D. and R.M. Morgan (1997), 'Resource-Advantage Theory: A Snake Swallowing Its Tail or a General Theory of Competition?', *Journal of Marketing*, **61** (October), 74-82.

Hurley, R.F. and G.T.M. Hult (1998), 'Innovation, Market Orientation, and Organizational Learning: An Integration and Empirical Examination', *Journal of Marketing*, **62** (July), 42-54.

Im, S. and J.P. Workman Jr. (2004), 'Market Orientation, creativity, and New Product Performance in High-Technology Firms', *Journal of Marketing*, **68** (April) 114-132.

Isabella, L. (1990), 'Evolving Interpretation as Change Unfolds: How Managers Construct Key Organizational Events', *Academy of Management Journal*, **33** (1), 7-41.

Itami, H. (1987), *Mobilizing Invisible Assets*, Boston: Harvard Business School Press.

Jackson, S. and J.E. Dutton (1988), 'Discerning Threats and Opportunities', *Administrative Science Quarterly*, **33**, 370-387.

James, L.M., W.F. Joice and J.W. Slocum (1988), 'Comment: Organizations Do Not Cognize', *Academy of Management Review*, **13** (1), 129-132.

Jaworski, B.J. and A.K. Kohli (1993), 'Market Orientation: Antecedents and Consequences', *Journal of Marketing*, **57** (July), 53-70.

Jayachandran, S., S. Sharma, P. Kaufman and P. Raman (2005), 'The Role of Relational Information Processes and Technology Use in Customer Relationship Management', *Journal of Marketing*, **69** (October), 177-192.

Jelinek, M. and J.A. Litterer (1994), 'Toward a Cognitive Theory of Organizations', in C. Stubbart, J.R. Meindl and J.F. Porac (eds), *Advances* in *Managerial Cognition and Organizational Information Processing*, **5**, 3-41.

Johansson, J. and I. Nonaka (1996), *Relentless. The Japanese Way of Marketing*, New York: Harper Business.

Johnson, P., K. Daniels and R. Asch (1998), 'Mental Models of Competition', in C. Eden, and J.-C. Spender (eds), *Managerial and Organizational Cognition. Theory, Methods and Research*, London: Sage.

Jorgensen, D.L. (1989), *Participant Observation. A Methodology for Human Studies*, Newbury Park: Sage.

Journal of Management Studies (1989), **26** (4).

Journal of Management Studies (1992), **29** (3).

Kahn, K.B. (1996), 'Interdepartmental Integration: A Definition with Implications for Product Development Performance', *Journal of Product Innovation Management*, **13**, 137-151.

Kahn, K.B. (2001), 'Market orientation, interdepartmental integration, and product development performance', *Journal of Product Innovation Management*, **18**, 314-323.

Kahn, K.B. and J.T. Mentzer (1998), 'Marketing's Integration with Other Departments', *Journal of Business Research*, **42**, 53-62.

Keith, R.J. (1960), 'The Marketing Revolution', *Journal of Marketing*, **24** (January), 35-38.

Kelly, G.A. (1955), *The Psychology of Personal Constructs*, New York: Norton.

Kickert, W.J.M. (1993), 'Autopoiesis and the Science of (Public) Administration: Essence, Sense and Nonsense', *Organization Studies*, **14** (2), 261-278.

Kim, W.C. and R. Mauborgne (1997), 'Fair Process: Managing in the Knowledge Economy', *Harvard Business Review*, July-August, 65-75.

Kim, W.C. and R. Mauborgne (1998), 'Procedural justice, strategic decision making, and the knowledge economy', *Strategic Management Journal*, **19**, 323-338.

Kirca, A.H., S. Jayachandran and W.O. Bearden (2005), 'Market Orientation : A Meta-Analytic Review and Assessment of Its Antecedents and Impact on Performance', *Journal of Marketing*, **69** (April), 24-41.

Kogut, B. and U. Zander (1992), 'Knowledge of the Firm, Combinative Capabilities, and the Replication of Technology', *Organization Science*, **3** (3), 383-397.

Kogut, B. and U. Zander (1995), 'Knowledge and the Speed of the Transfer of Organizational Capabilities: An Empirical Test', *Organization Science*, **6** (1), 76-92.

Kogut B. and U. Zander (1996), 'What Firms Do? Coordination, Identity, and Learning', *Organization Science*, **7** (5), 502-518.

Kohli, A.K. and B.J. Jaworski (1990), 'Market Orientation: the Construct, Research Proposition, and Managerial Implications', *Journal of Marketing*, **54** (April), 1-18.

Kolb, D.A. (1976), 'Management and the Learning Process', *California Management Review*, **18** (3), 21-31.

Kolb, D.A. (1984), *Experiential Learning*, San Francisco: Jossey-Bass.

Kotler, P. (1967), *Marketing Management. Analysis, Planning and Control*, Englewood Cliffs: Prentice-Hall.

Kotler, P. (2000), *Marketing Management*, Upper Saddle River, NY: Prentice Hall.

Kotler, P. and M. Sawhney (1999), *Marketing in the Age of Information Democracy*, working paper, Northwestern University.

Krohmer, H., C. Homburg and J.P. Workman (2002), 'Should marketing be cross-functional? Conceptual development and international empirical evidence', *Journal of Business Research*, **55**, 451-465.

Langfield-Smith, K. (1992), 'Exploring the Need for a Shared Cognitive Map', *Journal of Management Studies*, **29** (3), 349-368.

Laukkanen, M. (1989), *Understanding the Formation of Managers' Cognitive Maps: A Comparative Study of Context Traces in Two Business Firm Clusters*, Helsinki: Helsinki School of Economics Publications.

Lee, G.K. and R.E. Cole (2003), 'From A Firm-Based to a Community-Based Model of Knowledge Creation: The Case of the Linux Kernel Development', *Organization Science*, **14** (6), 633-649.

Leenders, M.A. and B. Wierenga (2002), 'The effectiveness of different mechanisms for integrating marketing and R&D', *Journal of Product Innovation Management*, **19**, 305-317.

Leonard-Barton, D. (1992), 'Core capabilities and core rigidities: A paradox in managing new product development', *Strategic Management Journal*, **13**, 111-125.

Leonard-Barton, D. (1995), *Wellspring of Knowledge. Building and Sustaining the Sources of Innovation*, Boston: Harvard Business School Press.

Leonard, D. and J.F. Rayport (1997), 'Spark Innovation Through Empathic Design', *Harvard Business Review*, November-December, 102-113.

Levitt, M.B. and J.G. March (1988), 'Organizational Learning', *Annual Review of Sociology*, **14**, 319-340.

Levitt, T. (1960), 'Marketing Myopia', *Harvard Business Review*, July-August, 45-56.

Li, T. and R.J. Calantone (1998), 'The Impact of Market Knowledge Competence on New Product Advantage: Conceptualization and Empirical Examination', *Journal of Marketing*, **62** (October), 13-29.

Lichtenthal, J.D. and D.T. Wilson (1992), 'Becoming Market Oriented', *Journal of Business Research*, **24**, 191-207.

Lippman, S. and R. Rumelt (1992), 'Uncertain Imitability: An Analysis of Interfirm Differences in Efficiency under Competition', *Bell Journal of Economics*, **13** (2), 418-438.

Liu, H. (1995), 'Market orientation and firm size: an empirical examination in UK firms', *European Journal of Marketing*, **29** (1), 57-71.

Lord, R.G. and R.J. Foti (1986), 'Schema Theories, Information Processing, and Organizational Behavior', in H.P. Sims and D.A. Gioia (eds), *The Thinking Organization*, San Francisco: Jossey-Bass.

Low, G.S. (2000), 'Correlates of Integrated Marketing Communications', *Journal of Advertising Research*, **40** (3).

Lukas, B.A. and O.C. Ferrell (2000), 'The Effect of Market Orientation on Product Innovation', *Journal of the Academy of Marketing Science*, **28** (2), 239-247.

Lyles, M. and I. Mitroff (1980), 'Organizational Problem Formulation: An Empirical Study', *Administrative Science Quarterly*, **25**, 102-119.

Lyles, M.A. and C.R. Schwenk (1992), 'Top Management, Strategy and Organizational Knowledge Structures', *Journal of Management Studies*, **29** (2), 155-174.

Lynch, J.E. (1994), 'Only Connect: The Role of Marketing and Strategic Management in the Modern Organization', *Journal of Marketing Management*, **10**, 527-542.

Macdonald, S. (1995), 'Too Close for Comfort?: The Strategic Implications of Getting Close to the Customer', *California Management Review*, **37** (4), 8-27.

Maltz, E. and A.K. Kohli (1996), 'Market Intelligence Dissemination Across Functional Boundaries', *Journal of Marketing Research*, **33** (February), 47-61.

Maltz E. and A.K. Kohli (2000), 'Reducing Marketing's Conflict With Other Functions: The Differential Effects of Integrating Mechanisms', *Journal of the Academy of Marketing Science*, **28** (4), 479-492.

March, J.G. and J.P. Olsen (1975), 'The Uncertainty of the Past: Organizational Learning under Ambiguity', *European Journal of Political Research*, **3**, 147-171.

March, J.G. and H.A. Simon (1958), *Organizations*, New York: Wiley.

March, J.G., L.S. Sproull and M. Tamuz (1991), 'Learning from Samples of One or Fewer', *Organization Science*, **2** (1), 1-13.

Maturana, H.R. and F.J. Varela (1980), *Autopoiesis and Cognition: the Realization of the Living*, Dordrecht: Reidel.

Maturana, H.R. and F.J. Varela (1987), *The Tree of Knowledge: the Biological Roots of Human Understanding*, Boston: Shambhala.

Matsuno, K., Mentzer, J.T. and A. Ozsomer (2002), 'The Effects of Entrepreneurial Proclivity and Market Orientation on Business Performance', *Journal of Marketing*, **66** (July), 18-32.

McArthur, D.N. and T. Griffin (1997), 'A Marketing Management Views of Integrated Marketing Communication', *Journal of Advertising Research*, **37** (5), 19-26.

McDermott, R. (1999), 'Why Information Technology Inspired But Cannot Deliver Knowledge Management', *California Management Review*, **41** (4), 103-117.

McGrath, R.G., I.C. MacMillan and S. Venkataraman (1995), 'Defining and Developing Competence: A Strategic Process Paradigm', *Strategic Management Journal*, **16**, 251-275.

McKeown, B. and D. Thomas (1988), *Q Methodology*, Newbury Park: Sage.

McNamara, C.P. (1972), 'The Present Status of the Marketing Concept', *Journal of Marketing*, **36** (January), 50-57.

Menon, A. and P.R. Varadarajan (1992), 'A Model of Marketing Knowledge Use Within Firms', *Journal of Marketing*, **56** (October), 53-71.

Miles, R.E., C.C. Snow, J.A. Mathews, G. Miles and H.J. Coleman (1997), 'Organizing in the Knowlege Age: Anticipating the Cellular Form', *Academy of Management Executive*, **11** (4), 7-20.

Milliken, F. (1990), 'Perceiving and Interpreting Environmental Change: An Examination of College Administrators' Interpretations of Changing Demographics', *Academy of Management Journal*, **33** (1), 42-63.

Mir, R. and A. Watson (2000), 'Strategic management and the philosophy of science: The case for a constructivist methodology', *Strategic Management Journal*, **21**, 941-953.

Moorman, C. (1995), 'Organizational Market Information Processes: Cultural Antecedents and New Product Outcomes', *Journal of Marketing Research*, **32** (August), 318-335.

Moorman, C. and R.T. Rust (1999), 'The Role of Marketing', *Journal of Marketing*, **63** (Special Issue), 180-197.

Moorman, C., R. Deshpandé and G. Zaltman (1993), 'Factors Affecting Trust in Market Research Relationships', *Journal of Marketing*, **57** (January), 81-101.

Moorman, C., G. Zaltman and R. Deshpandé (1992), 'Relationships Between Providers and Users of Market Research: The Dynamic of Trust Within and Between Organizations', *Journal of Marketing Research*, **29** (August), 314-328.

Morgan, N.A., E.W. Anderson and V. Mittal (2005), 'Understanding Firms' Customer Satisfaction Information Usage', *Journal of Marketing*, **69** (July), 131-151.

Morgan, R.E., C.S. Katsikeas and K. Appiah-Adu (1998), 'Market Orientation and Organizational Learning Capabilities', *Journal of Marketing Management*, **14**, 353-381.

Morris, M.H. and L.F. Ritt (1994), 'The Organization of the Future: Unity of Marketing and Strategy', *Journal of Marketing Management*, **10**, 553-560.

Myers, J.G., W.F. Massy and S.A. Greyser (1980), *Marketing Research and Knowledge Development. An Assessment for Marketing Management*, Englewood Cliffs: Prentice-Hall.

Nakata, C. and K. Sivakumar (2001), 'Instituting the Marketing Concept in a Multinational Setting: The Role of National Culture', *Journal of the Academy of Marketing Science*, **29** (3), 255-275.

Narver, J.C. and S.F. Slater (1990), 'The Effect of Market Orientation on Business Profitability', *Journal of Marketing*, **54** (October), 20-35.

Narver, J.C., S.F. Slater and D.L. MacLachlan (2004), 'Responsive and Proactive Market Orientation and New Product Success', *Journal of Product Innovation Management*, **21**, 334-347.

Neisser, U. (1976), *Cognition and Reality*, San Francisco: Freeman.

Nelson, R.R. and S.G. Winter (1982), *An Evolutionary Theory of Economic Change*, Cambridge: The Belknap Press.

Nemiro, J.E. (2000), 'The Glue that Binds Creative Virtual Teams', in Y. Malhotra (ed.), *Knowledge Management and Virtual Organizations*, Hershey: Idea Group Publishing.

Newell, A. and H.A. Simon (1972), *Human Problem Solving*, Englewood Cliffs: Prentice-Hall.

Nickerson, J.A. and T.R. Zenger (2004), 'A Knowledge-Based Theory of the Firm–The Problem Solving Perspective', *Organization Science*, **15** (6), 617-632.

Noble, C.H., R.K. Sinha and A. Kumar (2002), 'Market Orientation and Alternative Strategic Orientations: A Longitudinal Assessment of Performance Impmications, *Journal of Marketing*, **66** (4), 25-39.

Nonaka, I. (1988), 'Toward Middle-Up-Down Management: Accelerating Information Creation', *Sloan Management Review*, **3**, 9-18.

Nonaka, I. (1990), 'Redundant, Overlapping Organization: A Japanese Approach to Managing the Innovation Process', *California Management Review*, **32** (3), 27-37.

Nonaka, I. (1991), 'The Knowledge-Creating Company', *Harvard Business Review*, November-December, 96-104.

Nonaka, I. (1994), 'A Dynamic Theory of Organizational Knowledge Creation', *Organization Science*, **5** (1), 14-37.

Nonaka, I. and N. Konno (1998), 'The Concept of "Ba": Building a Foundation for Knowledge creation', *California Management Review*, **40** (3), 40-54.

Nonaka, I. and H. Takeuchi (1995), *The Knowledge-Creating Company. How Japanese Companies Create the Dynamics of Innovation*, New York: Oxford University Press.

Nonaka, I., P. Reinmoeller and D. Senoo (2000a), 'Integrated IT Systems to Capitalize on Market Knowledge', in G. von Krog, I. Nonaka and T. Nishiguchi (eds), *Knowledge Creation. A Source of Value*, London: Macmillan.

Nonaka, I., R. Toyama and A. Nagata (2000b), 'A Firm as a Knowledge-creating Entity: A New Perspective on the Theory of the Firm', *Industrial and Corporate Change*, **9** (1), 1-20.

Norman Kennedy, K., J.R. Goolsby and E.J. Arnould (2003), 'Implementing a Customer Orientation: Extension of theory and Application', *Journal of Marketing*, **67** (October), 67-81.

O'Dell, C. and C.J. Grayson (1998), 'If Only We Knew What We Know: Identification and Transfer of Internal Best Practices', *California Management Review*, **40** (3), 154-174.

Ocasio, W. (1997), 'Towards an attention-based view of the firm', *Strategic Management Journal*, Summer Special Issue, 187-206.

Orr, J. (1990), 'Sharing knowledge, celebrating identities. War stories and community memories in a serivce culture', in D.S. Middleton and D. Edwards (eds), *Collective Remembering: Memory in Society*, Beverly Hills, CA: Sage Publications.

Ostillio, M.C. and G. Troilo (2001), 'La progettazione del sistema informativo di marketing: un approccio marketing-driven', *Economia & Management*, **2**, 65-77.

Payne, A.F. (1988), 'Developing Marketing-Oriented Organizations', *Business Horizons*, **31** (May-June), 46-53.

Payne, A. and P. Frow (2005), 'A Strategic Framework for Customer Relationship Management', *Journal of Marketing*, **69** (October), 167-176.

Pentland, B.T. and H.H. Rueter (1994), 'Organizational Routines as Grammars of Action', *Administrative Science Quarterly*, **39**, 484-510.

Perrone, V. and C. Chiacchierini (1999), 'Fiducia e comportamenti di cittadinanza organizzativa', *Economia & Management*, **4**, 87-100.

Peteraf, M.A. (1993), 'The cornerstones of competitive advantage: A resource-based view', *Strategic Management Journal*, **14**, 179-191.

Piaget, J. (1953), *The Origin of Intelligence in the Child*, London: Routledge & Kegan Paul.

Piercy, N.F. and D.W. Cravens (1995), 'The Network Paradigm and the Marketing Organization: Developing a New Marketing Agenda', *European Journal of Marketing*, **29** (3), 7-34.

Podsakoff, P.M., S.B. MacKenzie, J.B. Paine and D.G. Bachrach (2000), 'Organizational Citizenship Behaviors: A Critical Review of the

Theoretical and Empirical Literature and Suggestions for Future Research', *Journal of Management*, **26** (3), 513-563.

Polanyi, M. (1958), *Personal Knowledge. Toward a Post-Critical Philosophy*, London: Routledge & Kegan Paul.

Polanyi, M. (1967), *The Tacit Dimension*, London: Routledge & Kegan Paul.

Porac, J.F. and H. Thomas (1990), 'Taxonomic Mental Models in Competitor Definition', *Academy of Management Review*, **15** (2), 224-240.

Porac, J.F., H. Thomas and C. Baden-Fuller (1989), 'Competitive Groups as Cognitive Communities: The Case of Scottish Knitwear Manufacturers', *Journal of Management Studies*, **26** (4), 397-416.

Porter, M. (1980), *Competitive Strategy. Techniques for Analyzing Industries and Competitors*, New York: The Free Press.

Prahalad, C.K. and R.A. Bettis (1986), 'The dominant logic: A new linkage between diversity and performance', *Strategic Management Journal*, **7**, 485-501.

Prahalad, C.K. and G. Hamel (1990), 'The Core Competence of the Corporation', *Harvard Business Review*, May-June, 79-91.

Prahalad, C.K. and V. Ramaswamy (2000), 'Co-opting Customer Competence', *Harvard Business Review*, January-February, 79-87.

Priem, R.L. and J.E. Butler (2001), 'Is The Resource-based "View" a Useful Perspective for Strategic Management Research?', *Academy of Management Review*, **26** (1), 22-40.

Probst, G., B. Büche and S. Raub (1998), 'Knowledge as a Strategic Resource', in G. von Krogh, J. Roos and D. Kleine (eds), *Knowing in Firms. Understanding, Managing and Measuring Knowledge*, London: Sage.

Provasi, G. (1995), 'Oltre il modello di "razionalità limitata". Il contributo del cognitivismo', *Rassegna italiana di sociologia*, **36** (2), 249-278.

Reger, R.K. (1990a), 'Managerial Thought Structures and Competitive Positioning', in A.S. Huff (ed.), *Mapping Strategic Thought*, Chicester: Wiley.

Reger, R.K. (1990b), 'The Repertory Grid Technique for Eliciting Content and Structure of Cognitive Constructive Systems', in A.S. Huff (ed.), *Mapping Strategic Thought*, Chicester: Wiley.

Reger, R.K. and A.S. Huff (1993), 'Strategic groups: A cognitive perspective', *Strategic Management Journal*, **14**, 103-124.

Reger, R.K. and T.B. Palmer (1996), 'Managerial Categorization of Competitors: Using Old Maps to Navigate New Environments', *Organization Science*, **7** (1), 22-39.

Rice, R., A. Majchrazak, N. King, S. Ba and A. Malhotra (2000), 'Computer Mediated Interorganizational Knowledge Sharing: Insights from a Virtual Team Innovating, Using a Collaborative Tool', in Y. Malhotra, (ed.),

Knowledge Management and Virtual Organizations, Hershey: Idea Group Publishing.

Rodriguez Cano, C., F.A. Carrillat and F. Jaramillo (2004), 'A meta-analysis of the relationship between market orientation and business performance: evidence from five continents', *International Journal of Research in Marketing*, **21** (2), 179-200.

Rosa, J.A. and J. Spanjol (2005), 'Micro-Level Product-Market Dynamics: Shared Knowledge and Its Relationship to Market Development', *Journal of the Academy of Marketing Science*, **33** (2), 197-216.

Rosa, J.A., J.F. Porac, J. Runser-Spanjol and M.S. Saxon (1999), 'Sociocognitive Dynamics in a Product Market', *Journal of Marketing*, **63** (Special Issue), 64-77.

Rosch, E. (1975), 'Cognitive Representations of Semantic Categories', *Journal of Experimental Psychology: General*, **104**, 192-233.

Rosch, E. (1978), 'Principles of Categorization', in E. Rosch and B.B. Lloyd (eds), *Cognition and Categorization*, Hillsdale: Erlbaum.

Rossiter, J.R. (2001), 'What is marketing knowledge?', *Marketing Theory*, **1** (1), 9-26.

Rouziès, D., E. Anderson, A.K. Kohli, R.E. Michaels, B.A. Weitz and A.A. Zoltners (2005), 'Sales and Marketing Integration : A Proposed Framework', *Journal of Personal Selling & Sales Management*, **25** (2), 113-122.

Ruekert, R.W. (1992), 'Developing A Market Orientation: An Organizational Strategy Perspective', *International Journal of Reaserch in Marketing*, **9**, 225-245.

Ruekert, R.W. and O.C. Walker (1987), 'Marketing's Interaction with Other Functional Units: A Conceptual framework and Empirical Evidence', *Journal of Marketing*, **51** (January), 1-19.

Ruggles, R. (1998), 'The State of the Notion: Knowledge Management in Practice', *California Management Review*, **40** (3), 80-89.

Rullani, E. (1987), 'L'impresa come sistema artificiale: linguaggi e apprendimento nell'approccio evolutivo alla complessità', *Economia e politica industriale*, **56**, 215-243.

Rullani, E. (1994), 'Il valore della conoscenza', *Economia e politica industriale*, **82**, 47-73.

Rumelhart, D.E. and J.L. McClelland (1986), *Parallel Distributed Processing: Explorations in the Microstructure of Cognition*, Cambridge, MA: MIT Press.

Rumelt, R. (1984), 'Towards a Strategic Theory of the Firm', in R.B. Lamb (ed.), *Competitive Strategic Management*, Englewood Cliffs: Prentice-Hall.

Ryals, L. (2005), 'Making Customer Relationship Management Work: The Measurement and Profitable Management of Customer Relationships', *Journal of Marketing*, **69** (October), 252-261.

Sackmann, S.A. (1991), *Cultural Knowledge in Organizations. Exploring the Collective Mind*, Newbury Park: Sage.

Sawhney, M. and E. Prandelli (2000a), 'Beyond Customer Knowledge Management: Customers as Knowledge Co-Creators', in Y. Malhotra (ed.), *Knowledge Management and Virtual Organizations*, Hershey: Idea Group Publishing.

Sawhney, M. and E. Prandelli (2000b), 'Communities of Creation: Managing Distributed Innovation in Turbulent Markets', *California Mangement Review*, **42** (4), 24-54.

Schank, R.C. and R.P. Abelson (1977), *Scripts, Plans, Goals and Understanding*, Hillsdale: Erlbaum.

Schneider, S.C. (1994), 'Interpreting Strategic Issues: Making Sense of "1992"', in C.I. Stubbart, J.R. Meindl and J.F. Porac (eds), *Advances in Managerial Cognition and Organizational Information Processing*, **5**, 243-274.

Schneider, S.C. and R. Angelmar (1993), 'Cognition in Organizational Analysis: Who's Minding the Store?', *Organization Studies*, **14** (3), 347-374.

Schön, D.A. (1983), *The Reflexive Practitioner*, New York: Basic Books.

Schulze, W.S. (1994), 'The Two Schools of Thought in Resource-Based Theory: Definitions and Implications for Research', *Advances in Strategic Management*, **10**, 127-151.

Schwenk, C.R. (1984), 'Cognitive simplification processes in strategic decison-making', *Strategic Management Journal*, **5**, 111-128.

Scribner, S. (1984), 'Studying working intelligence', in B. Rogoff and J. Lave (eds), *Everyday Cognition. Its Development in Social Context*, Cambridge, MA: Harvard University Press.

Senge, P.M. (1990), *The Fifth Discipline. The Art & Practice of The Learning Organization*, New York: Doubleday Currency.

Shapiro, C. and H.R. Varian (1999), *Information Rules. A Strategic Guide to the Network Economy*, Boston: Harvard Business School Press.

Shapiro, B.P. (1989), 'What the Hell Is "Market Oriented"?', *Harvard Business Review*, November-December, 119-125.

Shrivastava, P. (1983), 'A Typology of Organizational Learning Systems', *Journal of Management Studies*, **20** (1), 7-28.

Siguaw, J.A., G. Brown and R.E. Widing (1994), 'The Influence of the Market Orientation of the Firm on Salesforce Behavior and Attitudes', *Journal of Marketing Research*, **31** (February).

Simon, H.A. (1947), *Administrative Behavior*, New York: Macmillan.

Simon, H.A. (1955), 'A Behavioral Model of Rational Choice', *Quarterly Journal of Economics*, **69** (1), 99-118.

Simon, H.A. (1973), *Le scienze dell'artificiale*, Isedi, Milano (original edition (1969), *The Sciences of the Artificial*, Cambridge, MA: The MIT Press).

Simon, H.A. (1991), 'Bounded Rationality and Organizational Learning', *Organizational Science*, **2** (1), 125-134.

Sinkula, J.M. (1990), 'Perceived Characteristics, Organizational Factors, and the Utilization of External Market Research Suppliers', *Journal of Business Research*, **21**, 1-17.

Sinkula, J.M. (1994), 'Market Information Processing and Organizational Learning', *Journal of Marketing*, **58** (January), 35-45.

Slater, S.F. and J.C. Narver (1994), 'Does Competitive Environment Moderate the Market Orientation-Performance Relationship?', *Journal of Marketing*, **58** (January), 46-55.

Slater, S.F. and J.C. Narver (1995), 'Market Orientation and the Learning Organization', *Journal of Marketing*, **59** (July), 63-74.

Slater, S.F. and J.C. Narver (1998), 'Customer-Led and Market-Oriented: Let's not Confuse the Two', *Strategic Management Journal*, **19**, 1001-1006.

Slater, S.F. and J.C. Narver (1999), 'Market-Oriented Is More Than Being Customer-Led', *Strategic Management Journal*, **20**, 1165-1168.

Slater, S.F. and J.C. Narver (2000), 'Intelligence Generation and Superior Customer Value', *Journal of the Academy of Marketing Science*, **28** (1), 120-127.

Smircich, L. and C.I. Stubbart (1985), 'Strategic Management in an Enacted World', *Academy of Management Review*, **10** (4), 724-736.

Smith, K.G., C.J. Collins and K.D. Clark (2005), 'Existing Knowledge, Knowledge Creation Capability, and The Rate of New Product Introduction in High-Technology Firms', *Academy of Management Journal*, **48** (2), 346-357.

Song, X.M. and M.E. Parry (1997), 'Teamwork Barriers in Japanese High-Technology Firms: The Sociocultural Differences Between R&D and Marketing Managers', *Journal of Product Innovation Management*, **14**, 356-367.

Sparrow, J. (1998), *Knowledge in Organizations. Access to Thinking at Work*, London: Sage.

Spender, J.-C. (1992), 'Strategy Theorizing: Expanding the Agenda', *Advances in Strategic Management*, **8**, 3-32.

Spender, J.-C. (1996), 'Making knowledge the basis of a dynamic theory of the firm', *Strategic Management Journal*, **17** (Winter Special Issue), 45-62.

Spender, J.-C. (1998), 'The Dynamics of Individual and Organizational Knowledge', in C. Eden and J.-C. Spender (eds), *Managerial and Organizational Cognition. Theory, Methods and Research*, London: Sage.

Stacey, R.D. (1995), 'The science of complexity: An alternative perspective for strategic change processes', *Strategic Management Journal*, **16**, 477-495.

Stacey, R.D. (1996), *Complexity and Creativity in Organizations*, San Francisco: Berrett-Koehler Publishers.

Stalk, G., P. Evans and L.E. Shulman (1992), 'Competing on Capabilities: The New Rules of Corporate Strategy', *Harvard Business Review*, March-April, 57-69.

Stephenson, W. (1935), 'Technique of Factor Analysis', *Nature*, **136**, 297.

Stubbart, C.I. (1988), 'Managerial Cognition: A Missing Link in Strategic Management Research', *Journal of Management Studies*, **26** (4), 325-347.

Stubbart, C.I., J.R. Meindl and J.F. Porac (1994), 'Introduction', in C.I. Stubbart, J.R. Meindl and J.F. Porac (eds), *Advances in Managerial Cognition and Organizational Information Processing*, **5**, xi-xv.

Szulanski, G. (1996), 'Exploring internal stickiness: Impediments to the transfer of best practice within the firm', *Strategic Mangement Journal*, **17** (Winter Special Issue), 27-43.

Takeuchi, H. and I. Nonaka (1986), 'The New New Product Development Game', *Harvard Business Review*, January-February, 137-146.

Taylor, S.E. and J. Crocker (1981), 'Schematic Bases of Social Information Processing', in E.I. Higgins, C.H. Harman and M.P. Zanna (eds), *Social Cognition: The Ontario Symposium on Personality and Social Psychology*, Hillsdale: Erlbaum.

Taylor, S.E., L.A. Paplau and D.O. Sears (2006), *Social Psychology*, 12th edition, Upper Sadler River, NJ: Pearson Education.

Teece, D.J., G. Pisano and A. Shuen (1997), 'Dynamic capabilities and strategic management', *Strategic Management Journal*, **18** (7), 509-533.

Thomas, J.B. and R.R. McDaniel Jr. (1990), 'Interpreting Strategic Issues: Effects of Strategy and The Information-Processing Structure of Top Management Teams', *Academy of Management Journal*, **33** (2), 286-306.

Thomke, S. and E. von Hippel (2002), 'Customers as Innovators: A New Way to Create Value', *Harvard Business Review*, April, 74-81.

Tolman, E.C. (1948), 'Cognitive Maps in Rats and Men', *Psychological Review*, **55**, 189-208.

Troilo, G. (1993), 'L'evoluzione del concetto di marketing mix: una proposta interpretativa', *Finanza, Marketing e Produzione*, **2**, 41-74.

Tsoukas, H. (1996), 'The firm as a distributed knowledge system: A constructionist approach', *Strategic Management Journal*, **17** (Winter Special Issue), 11-25.

Tversky, A. and D. Kahneman (1974), 'Judgement Under Uncertainty: Heuristics and Biases', *Science*, **185**, 1124-1131.

Tversky, A. and D. Kahneman (1982), *Judgement Under Uncertainty: Heuristics and Biases*, New York: Cambridge University Press.

Urban, G.L. and J.R. Hauser (2004), '"Listening In" to Find and Explore New Combinations of Customer Needs', *Journal of Marketing*, **68** (April), 72-87.

Valdani, E. (1994), 'Le capacità market driving', *Micro & Macro Marketing*, **2**, 201-219.

Valdani, E., B. Busacca and M. Costabile (1994), *La soddisfazione del cliente: un'indagine empirica sulle imprese italiane*, Milano: Egea.

Van de Ven, A.H. and D. Polley (1992), 'Learning While Innovating', *Organization Science*, **3** (1), 92-116.

Varela, F.J., E. Thompson and E. Rosch (1991), *Embodied Mind: Cognitive Science and Human Experience*, Cambridge, MA: The MIT Press.

Vargo, S.L. and R.F. Lusch (2004), 'Evolving to a New Dominant Logic for Marketing', *Journal of Marketing*, **68** (January), 1-17.

Venzin, M., G. von Krogh and J. Roos (1998), 'Future Research into Knowledge Management', in G. von Krogh, J. Roos and D. Kleine (eds), *Knowing in Firms. Understanding, Managing and Measuring Knowledge*, London: Sage.

Verhoef, P.C. (2003), 'Understanding the Effect of Customer Relationship Management Efforts on Customer Retention and Customer Share Development', *Journal of Marketing*, **67** (October), 30-45.

Verona, G. (2000), *Innovazione continua. Risorse e competenze per sostenere il vantaggio competitivo*, Milano: Egea.

Vicari, S. (1989), 'Invisible assets e comportamento incrementale', *Finanza Marketing e Prodiuzione*, **1**, 63-86.

Vicari, S. (1991), *L'impresa vivente. Itinerario in una diversa concezione*, Milano: Etaslibri.

Vicari, S. and G. Troilo (1997), 'Affrontare il Possibile: le mappe cognitive', *Economia & Management*, **1**, 93-109.

Vicari, S. and G. Troilo (1998), 'Errors and Learning in Organizations', in G. von Krogh, J. Roos and D. Kleine (eds), *Knowing in Firms. Understanding, Managing and Measuring Knowledge*, London: Sage.

Vicari, S. and G. Troilo (2000), 'Organizational Creativity: A New Perspective from Cognitive Systems Theory', in G. von Krog, I. Nonaka and T. Nishiguchi (eds), *Knowledge Creation. A Source of Value*, London: Macmillan.

von Foerster, H. (1984), 'On constructing a reality', in P. Watzlawick (ed.), *The Invented Reality. How do we Know what we Believe we Know? Contributions to Constructivism*, New York: Norton.

von Glasersfeld, E. (1984), 'An introduction to radical constructivism', in P. Watzlawick (ed.), *The Invented Reality. How do we Know what we Believe we Know? Contributions to Constructivism*, New York: Norton.

von Hippel, E. (1986), 'Lead Users: A Source of Novel Product Concepts', *Management Science*, **32** (7), 791-805.

von Hippel, E. (1988), *The Sources of Innovation*, New York: Oxford University Press.

von Hippel, E., S. Thomke and M. Sonnack (1999), 'Creating Breakthroughs at 3M', *Harvard Business Review*, September-October, 47-57.

von Krogh, G. (1998); 'Care in Knowledge Creation', *California Management Review*, **40** (3), 133-153.

von Krogh, G. and J. Roos (1995), *Organizational Epistemology*, London, Macmillan.

von Krogh, G. and J. Roos (1996a), 'Arguments on Knowledge and Competence', in G. von Krogh and J. Roos (eds), *Managing Knowledge. Perspectives on cooperation and competition*, London: Sage.

von Krogh, G. and J. Roos (eds) (1996b), *Managing Knowledge. Perspectives on cooperation and competition*, London: Sage.

von Krogh, G. and S. Vicari (1993), 'An Autopoietic Approach to Experimental Strategic Learning', in P. Lorange, B. Chakravarthy, J. Roos and A. Van de Ven (eds), *Implementing Strategic Processes. Change, Learning & Co-operation*, Oxford: Basil Blackwell.

von Krogh, G., I. Nonaka and K. Ichijo (1997), 'Develop Knowledge Activists!', *European Management Journal*, **15** (5), 475-483.

von Krogh, G., J. Roos and K. Slocum (1994), 'An Essay on Corporate Epistemology', *Strategic Management Journal*, **15**, 53-71.

Vorhies, D.W., M. Harker, and CP Rao (1999), 'The capabilities and performance advantages of market-driven firms', *European Journal of Marketing*, **33** (11/12), 1171-1202.

Voss, G.B. and Z.G. Voss (2000), 'Strategic Orientation and Firm Performance in an Artistic Environment', *Journal of Marketing*, **64** (July), 67-83.

Walldrop, M.M. (1992), *Complexity. The Emerging Science of Order and Chaos*, New York: Simon & Schuster.

Walsh, J.P. (1995), 'Managerial and Organizational Cognition: Notes from a Trip Down Memory Lane', *Organization Science*, **6** (3), 280-321.

Walsh, J.P. and G.R. Ungson (1991), 'Organizational Memory', *Academy of Management Review*, **16** (1), 57-91.

Watzlawick, P. (ed.) (1984), *The Invented Reality. How do we Know what we Believe we Know? Contributions to Constructivism*, New York: Norton.

Webster, F.E. Jr. (1988), 'The Rediscovering of the Marketing Concept', *Business Horizons*, **31** (May), 2-39.

Webster, F.E. Jr. (1992), 'The Changing Role of Marketing in the Corporation', *Journal of Marketing*, **56** (October), 1-17.

Webster, F.E. Jr., A.J. Malter and S. Ganesan (2005), 'The Decline and Dispersion of Marketing Competence', *MIT Sloan Management Review*, **46** (4), 35-43.

Weerawardena, J. (2003), 'Exploring the role of market learning capability in competitive strategy', *European Journal of Marketing*, **37** (3/4), 407-429.

Weick, K.E. (1969), *The Social Psychology of Organizing*, Reading, MA: Addison-Wesley.

Weick, K.E. (1977), 'Enactment Processes in Organizations', in B.M. Staw and G. Salancik (eds), *New Directions in Organizational Behavior*, Chicago: St. Clair.

Weick, K.E. (1979), 'Cognitive Processes in Organizations', *Research in Organizational Behavior*, **1**, 41-74.

Weick, K.E. (1993), 'The Collapse of Sensemaking in Organizations: The Mann Gulch Disaster', *Administrative Science Quarterly*, **38**, 628-652.

Weick, K.E. (1995), *Sensemaking in Organizations*, Thousand Oaks: Sage.

Weick, K.E. and K.H. Roberts (1993), 'Collective Mind in Organizations: Heedful Interrelating on Flight Decks', *Administrative Science Quarterly*, **38**, 357-381.

White, J.C., P.R. Varadarajan and P.A. Dacin (2003), 'Market Situation Interpretation and Response: The Role of Cognitive Style, Organizational Culture, and Information Use', *Journal of Marketing*, **67** (July), 63-79.

Wind, Y. and T. Robertson (1983), 'Marketing Strategies: New Directions for Theory and Research', *Journal of Marketing*, **47** (Spring), 12-25.

Winter, S.G. (1987), 'Knowledge and Competence as Strategic Assets', in D.J. Teece (ed.), *The Competitive Challenge. Strategies for Industrial Innovation and Renewal*, Cambridge: Ballinger.

Workman, J.P. (1993), 'Marketing's Limited Role in New Product Development in One Computer Systems Firm', *Journal of Marketing Research*, **30** (November), 405-421.

Workman, J.P., C. Homburg and K. Gruner (1998), 'Marketing Organization: An Integrative Framework of Dimensions and Determinants', *Journal of Marketing*, **62** (July), 21-41.

Zollo, M. and S.G. Winter (2002), 'Deliberate Learning and the Evolution of Dynamic Capabilities', *Organization Science*, **13** (3), 339-351.

Index